IMAGES
of America

PEACE DALE

IMAGES
of America

PEACE DALE

Betty J. Cotter

ARCADIA
PUBLISHING

ISBN 978-0-7385-9023-3

Published by Arcadia Publishing
Charleston, South Carolina

Printed in the United States of America

Library of Congress Catalog Card Number: 98-87322

For all general information contact Arcadia Publishing at:
Telephone 843-853-2070
Fax 843-853-0044
E-mail sales@arcadiapublishing.com
For customer service and orders:
Toll-Free 1-888-313-2665

Visit us on the Internet at www.arcadiapublishing.com

Contents

ACKNOWLEDGMENTS

This book would not have been possible without the unfailing support of the organizations and individuals who came forward with photographs.

I wish to thank The Pettaquamscutt Historical Society, the Peace Dale Library, the Peace Dale Fire Department, Anthony Guarriello Jr., David Gates, Gary Dinonsie, Grace Pesta, Betty Tucker, Everett Hopkins, Clara W. Smith, Donald and Shirley Southwick, Fred Lyons, Janice Lyons Staruch, Daniel G. Dunn, and Robert Ryan.

For historical materials, I am indebted to Diane Smith, Rick Wilson, Connie Lachowicz and the staff at the Peace Dale Library, and Christine MacManus. For proofreading assistance, I wish to thank Diane Smith, Gary Dinonsie, Grace Pesta, and David Gates.

Also, to my colleagues at the *South County Independent*, I am grateful for their patience while I completed this project.

Finally, and most important, I wish to dedicate this work to my husband, Timothy, and my three children, Perry, Colby, and Mary, whose love, patience, and understanding helped me do two jobs at once.

INTRODUCTION

Perhaps it would be more fitting to title this work "The Hazards of Peace Dale." For in every photograph one can find the influence of the mill owners and philanthropists who gave the village its name, identity, and livelihood.

While any author would be hard pressed not to acknowledge the influence of the Hazards, this book is also a showcase of the hard-working men and women who made the Hazard business and lifestyle possible. Coming first after the Irish potato famine of 1848 and then in a second wave of immigration from Italy after the turn of the century, these people brought with them perseverance, enterprise, and community spirit. Although many toiled in the mills, making the woolen garments that would receive awards the world over, they also made Peace Dale Flats into a thriving commercial center of its own.

The reminders of the Hazards are everywhere, in the granite buildings and bridges they left behind as monuments to themselves and gifts to the community. We think the Hazards themselves would want it known that these buildings are also monuments to the stone masons who built them, to the workers who labored inside them, and to the sewing teachers, weavers, craft makers, fire volunteers, and others who helped weave the thread of Peace Dale's community life.

This is a tribute to the Hazards, yes, but it is also a tribute to all the men and women of Peace Dale who today continue to make this picturesque village unique.

Betty J. Cotter
Peace Dale, Rhode Island
1998

One

The Hazards and Their Legacy

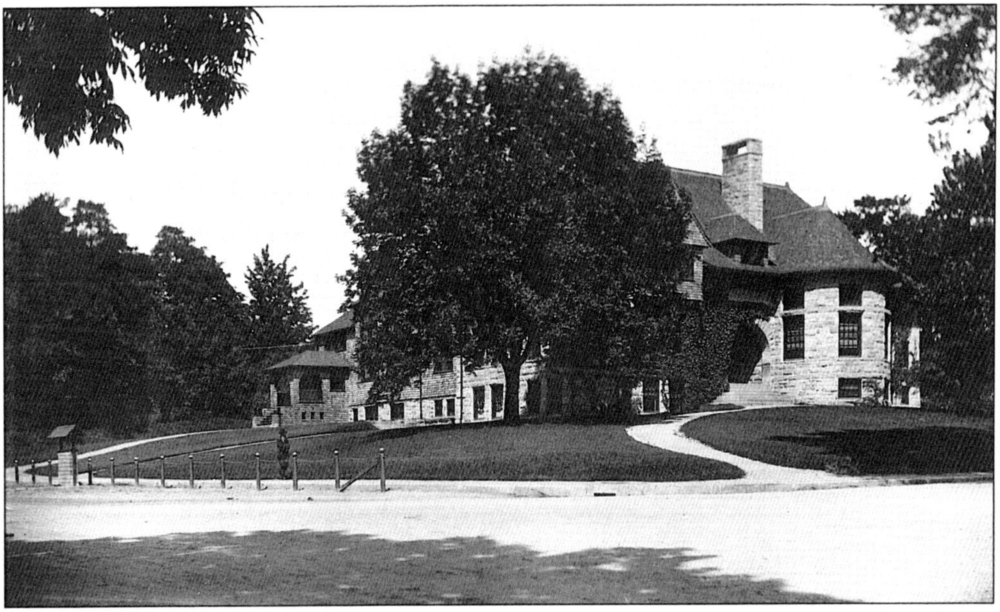

Hazard Memorial Hall, now the Peace Dale branch of the South Kingstown Public Library, is one of the more visible public buildings left behind by the Hazard family. Mill owners, intellectuals, and philanthropists, this remarkable family was the driving force behind virtually every community program and building in Peace Dale. Rowland Hazard—who founded the first mill in Peace Dale around 1800—named the village for his wife, Mary Peace. (Courtesy of Pettaquamscutt Historical Society.)

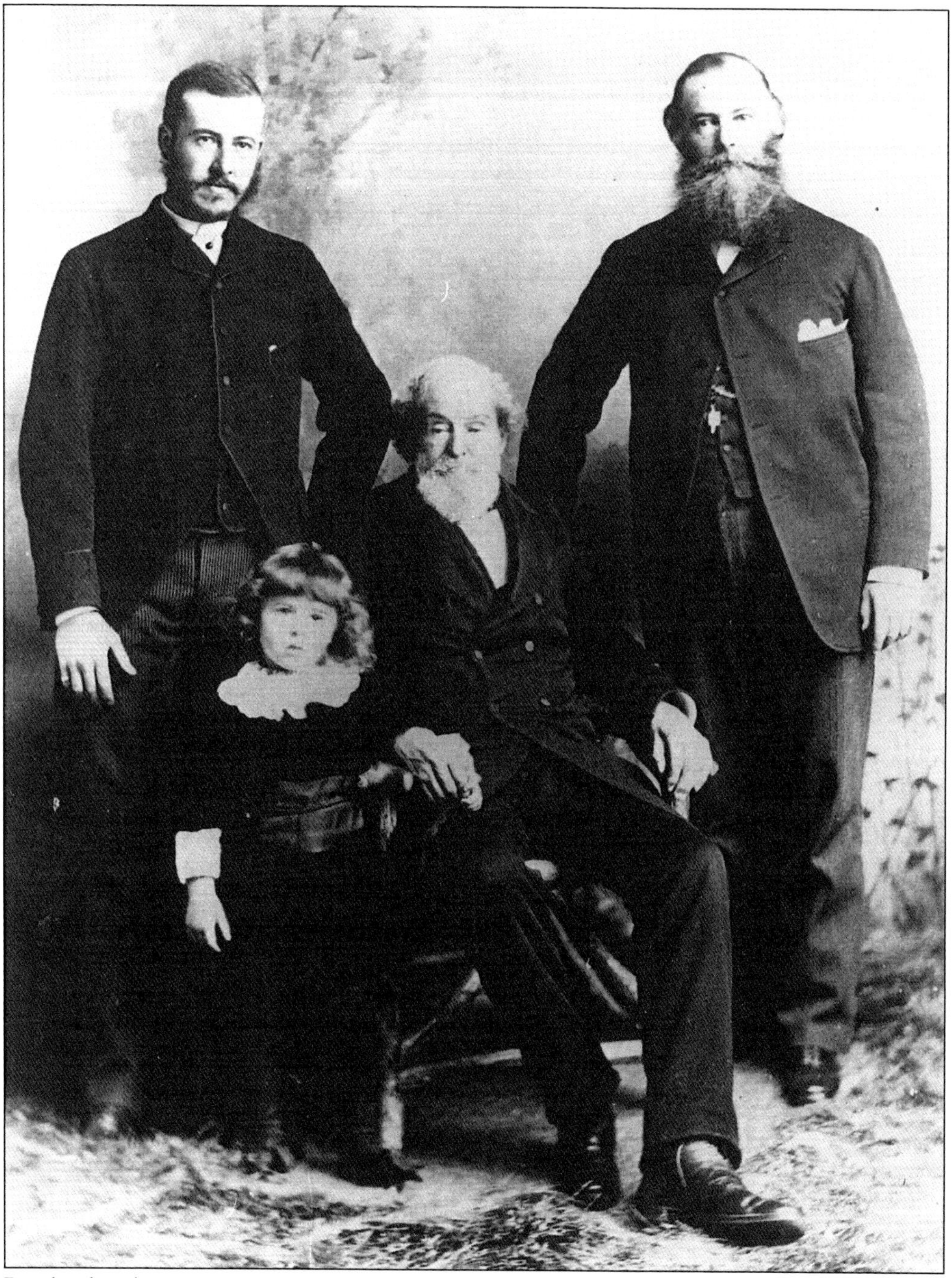

Rowland Gibson Hazard sits here surrounded by his progeny. Shown with him are his son, Rowland Hazard (1829–1898), to the right; his grandson, Rowland Gibson Hazard (1855–1918), to the left; and his great-grandson, Rowland Hazard (1881–1945). (Courtesy of Peace Dale Library.)

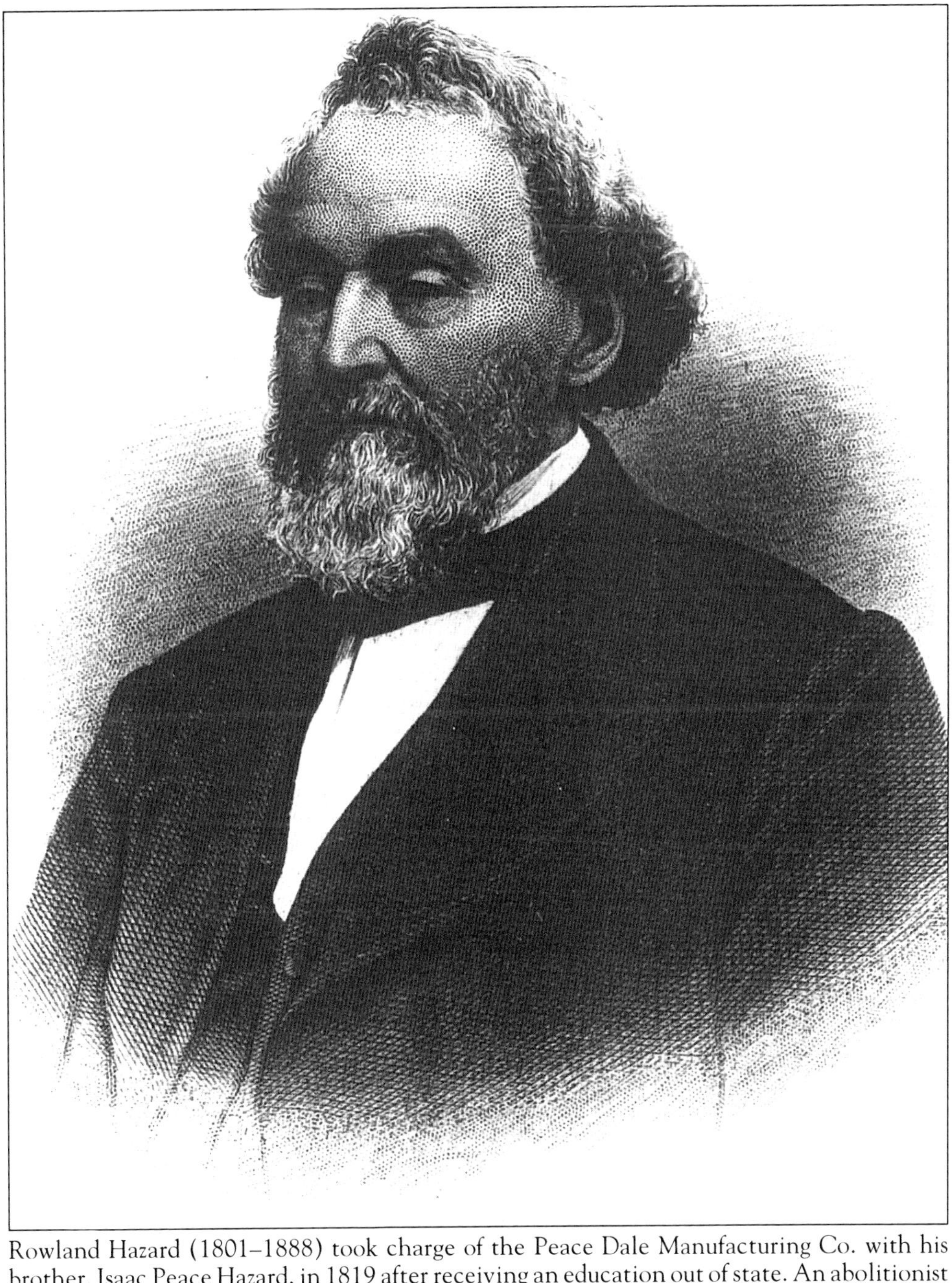

Rowland Hazard (1801–1888) took charge of the Peace Dale Manufacturing Co. with his brother, Isaac Peace Hazard, in 1819 after receiving an education out of state. An abolitionist who was active politically, he served as a delegate to the Philadelphia convention in 1856 that nominated Abraham Lincoln. An author of such works as "Essay on Language," Hazard was friends with John Stuart Mill and traveled to Europe three times. (Courtesy of Peace Dale Library.)

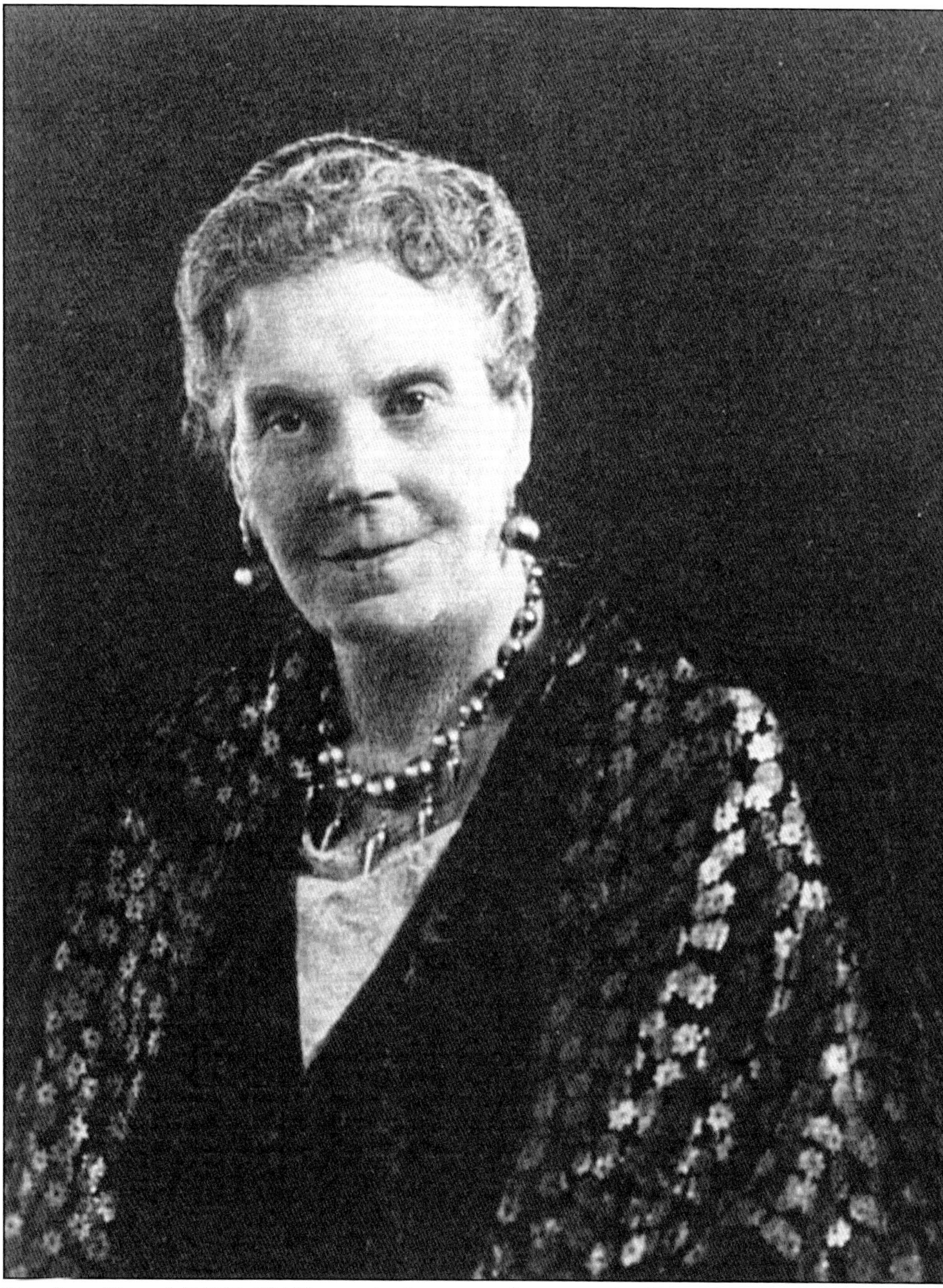

Caroline Hazard (1856–1945) was the last great figure in the Hazard family. After serving as president of Wellesley College for 11 years, she returned to Peace Dale in 1910 to build the Scallop Shell mansion and settle into community affairs. She helped carry on the Stepping Stone Kindergarten founded by her mother, Margaret Rood Hazard, and was the driving force behind the founding of South County Hospital in 1920. The author of numerous books of poetry, including *A Scallop Shell of Quiet* and *The Yosemite*, Miss Caroline often wrote of the lands she saw in her travels. She died on March 18, 1945, at her summer home in Santa Barbara, California. (Courtesy of Pettaquamscutt Historical Society.)

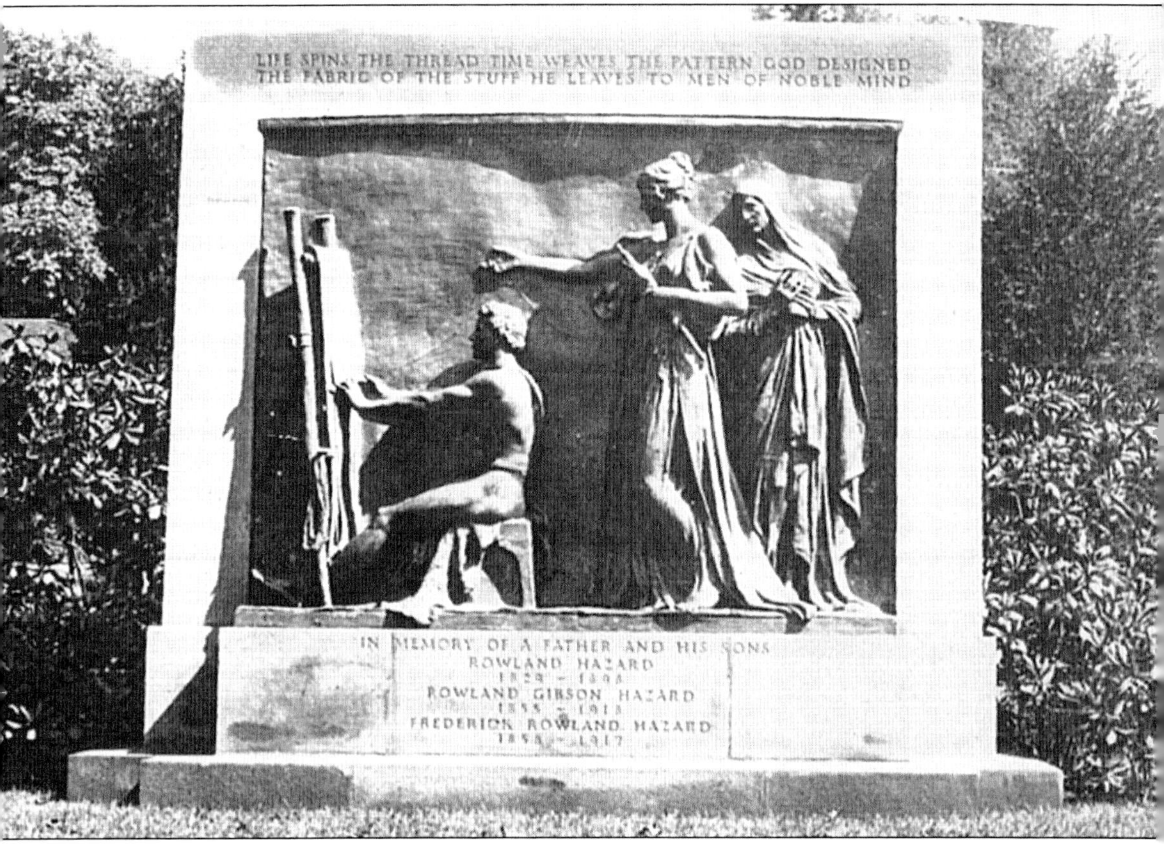

This monument, by Daniel Chester French, was Caroline Hazard's tribute to her father, Rowland Hazard, and her brothers, Rowland Gibson Hazard and Frederick Rowland Hazard. The inscription was her own—"Life spins the thread Time weaves the pattern God designed the fabric of the stuff he leaves to men of noble mind." The monument, in front of Hazard Memorial Hall, was dedicated in October 1920. (Courtesy of Peace Dale Library.)

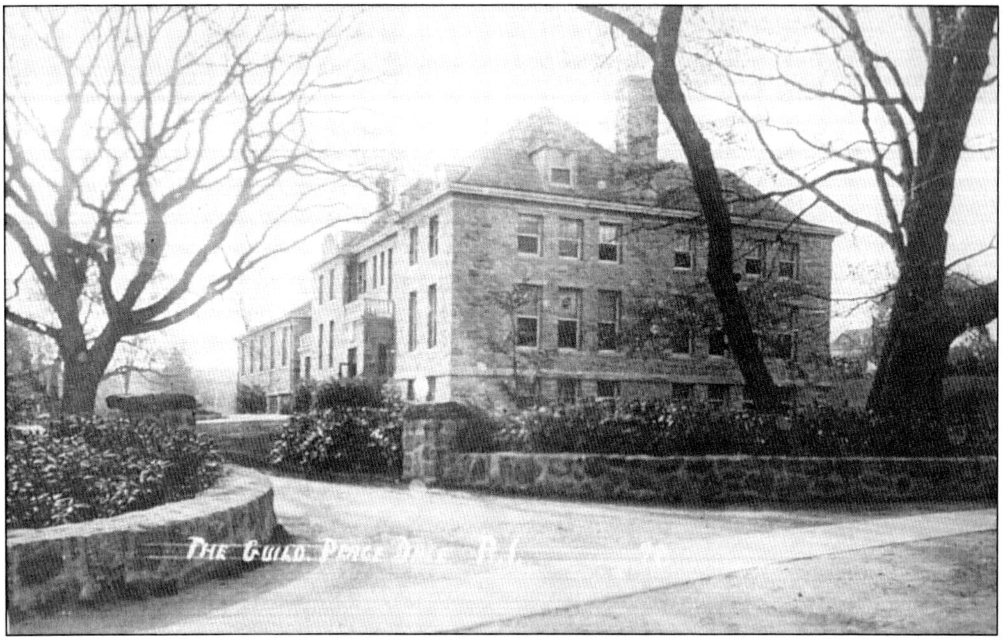

The Neighborhood Guild was built in 1908 at the behest of Augusta (Mrs. John N.) Hazard to accommodate the growing number of domestic science classes the Hazards were offering in the Peace Dale Office Building. The grand building, which also included a gymnasium, is today the center of the town's recreation program. (Courtesy of Pettaquamscutt Historical Society.)

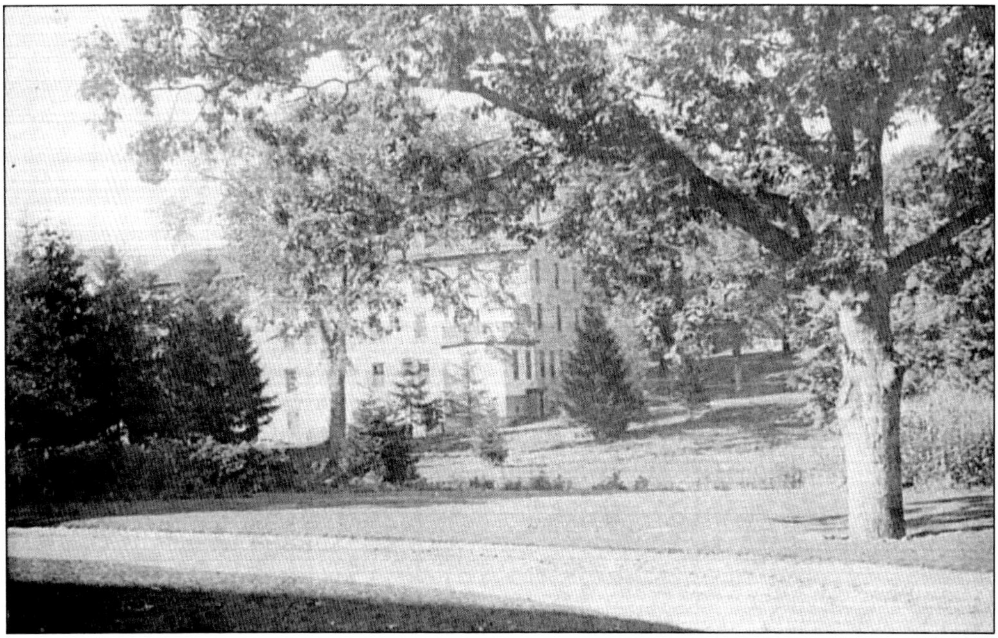

This view of the Peace Dale Office Building—also called the Peace Dale House—is from the Neighborhood Guild. The office building, constructed by the Hazards, housed a number of ventures over the years, including the Peace Dale Cooperative Stores, W.G. Gould's grocery store, mill housing, a third-floor hall, a telegraph office, a cloth store, and a post office. (Courtesy of Pettaquamscutt Historical Society.)

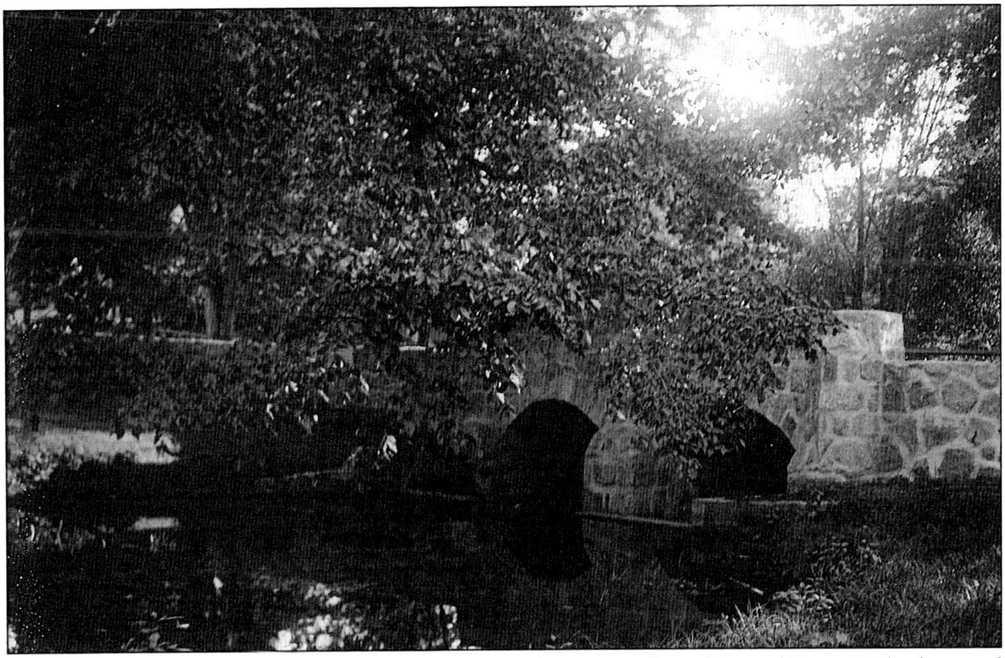

This arched bridge over Columbia Street is one of seven in the village of Peace Dale designed and paid for by Rowland Hazard and built by masons working for Kneeland Partelow and George H. Bullock. (Courtesy of Pettaquamscutt Historical Society.)

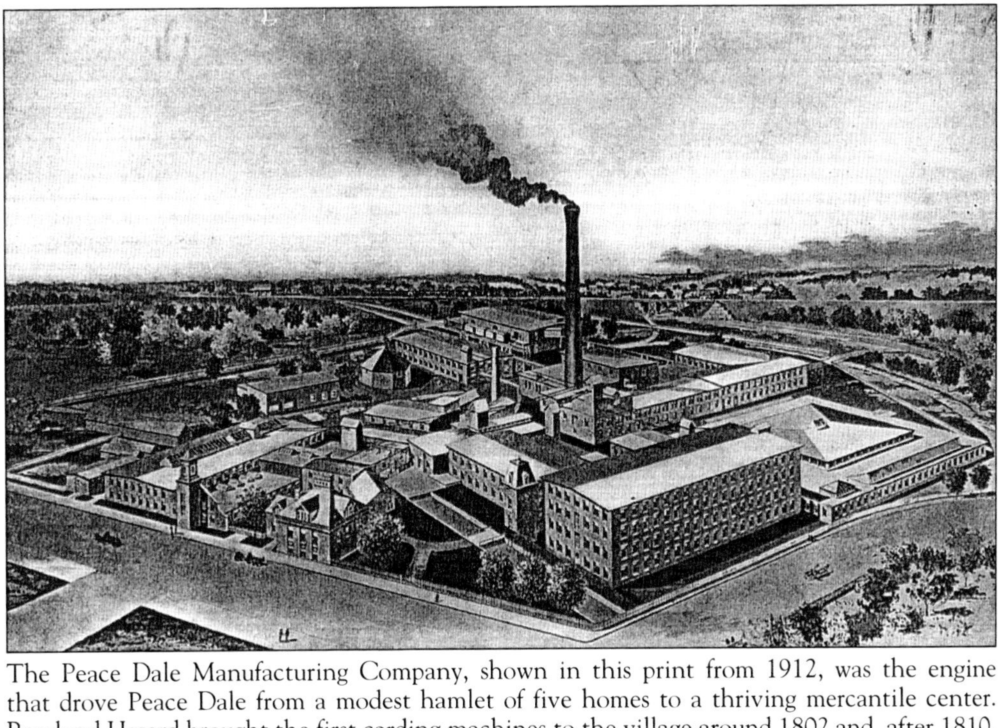

The Peace Dale Manufacturing Company, shown in this print from 1912, was the engine that drove Peace Dale from a modest hamlet of five homes to a thriving mercantile center. Rowland Hazard brought the first carding machines to the village around 1802 and, after 1810, had installed looms and begun the manufacture of woolen cloth that would gain a worldwide reputation for quality. (Courtesy of Pettaquamscutt Historical Society.)

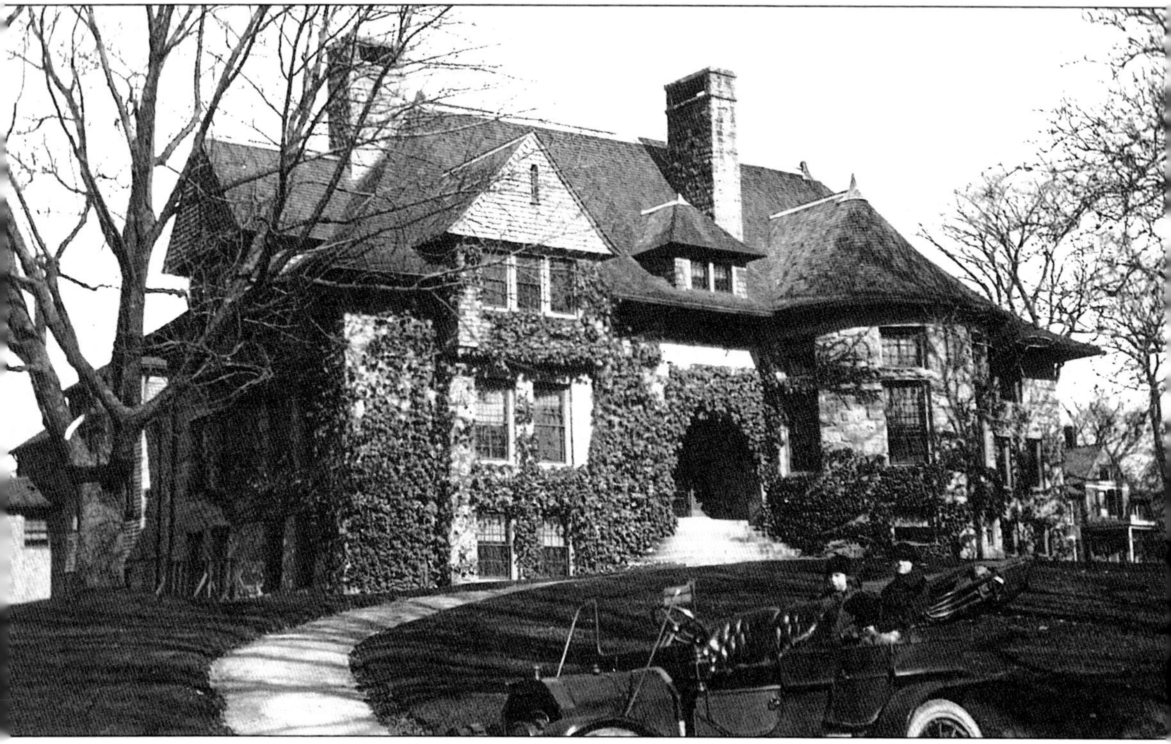

Hazard Memorial Hall was dedicated October 9, 1891, on the 90th anniversary of Rowland Gibson Hazard's birth. The festive occasion included music and a lyric invocation written by Caroline Hazard and Dr. Jules Jordan. (Courtesy of Peace Dale Library.)

Two

THE MILLS

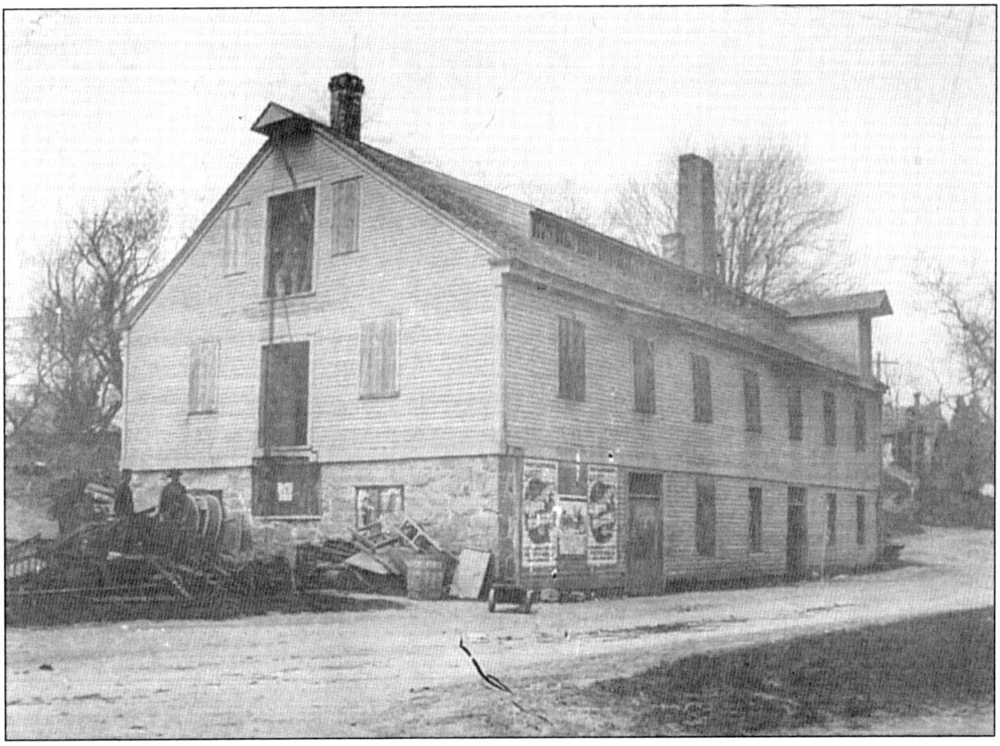

This building, the Old Fisk Mill at Peace Dale Flats, was built by Joseph Peace Hazard as an ax factory in 1835 and eventually was used by Stephen C. Fisk of Voluntown, Connecticut, to manufacture a lightweight wool known as kersey. A number of mills sprang up along the Saugatucket River and its tributaries in the 19th century, but none would attain the prominence of the Peace Dale Manufacturing Company. (Courtesy of Peace Dale Library.)

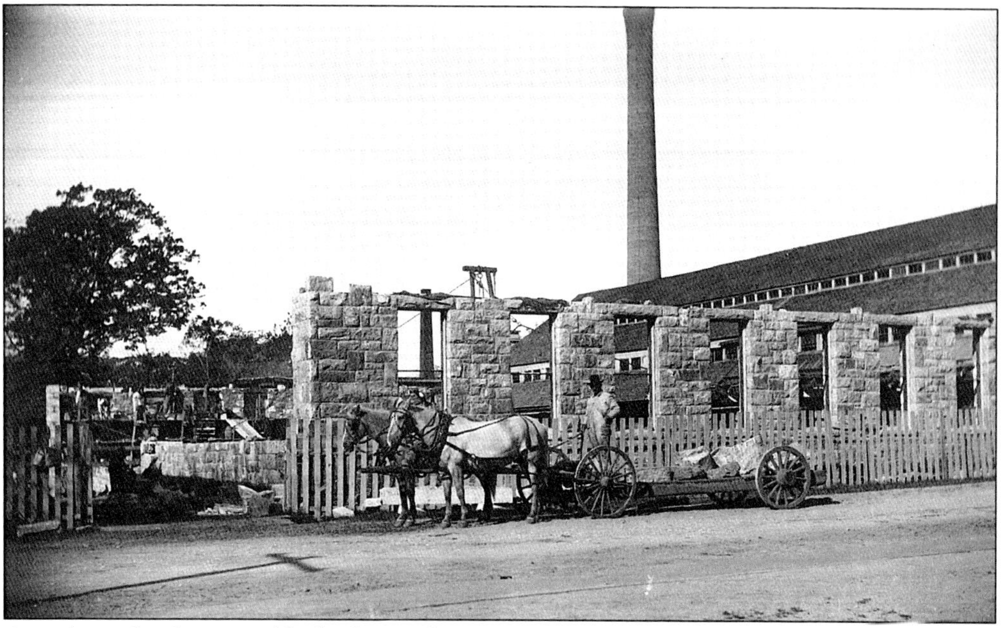

A workman hauls granite blocks during the reconstruction of a building in the Peace Dale mill complex. In 1844, Rowland Hazard's original mill burned and was replaced by one-story stone building with a bell tower. (Courtesy of Pettaquamscutt Historical Society.)

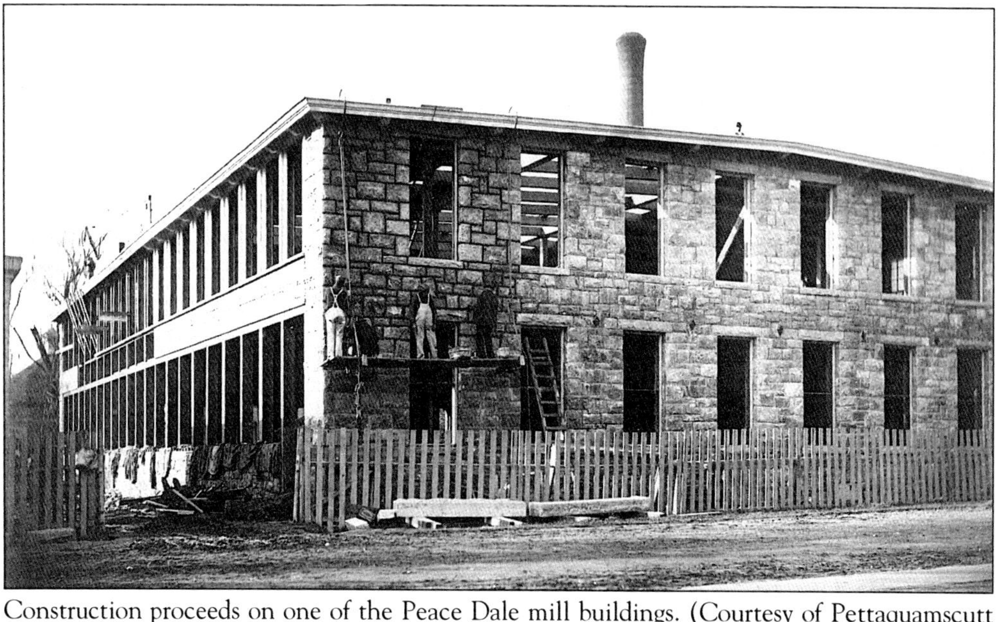

Construction proceeds on one of the Peace Dale mill buildings. (Courtesy of Pettaquamscutt Historical Society.)

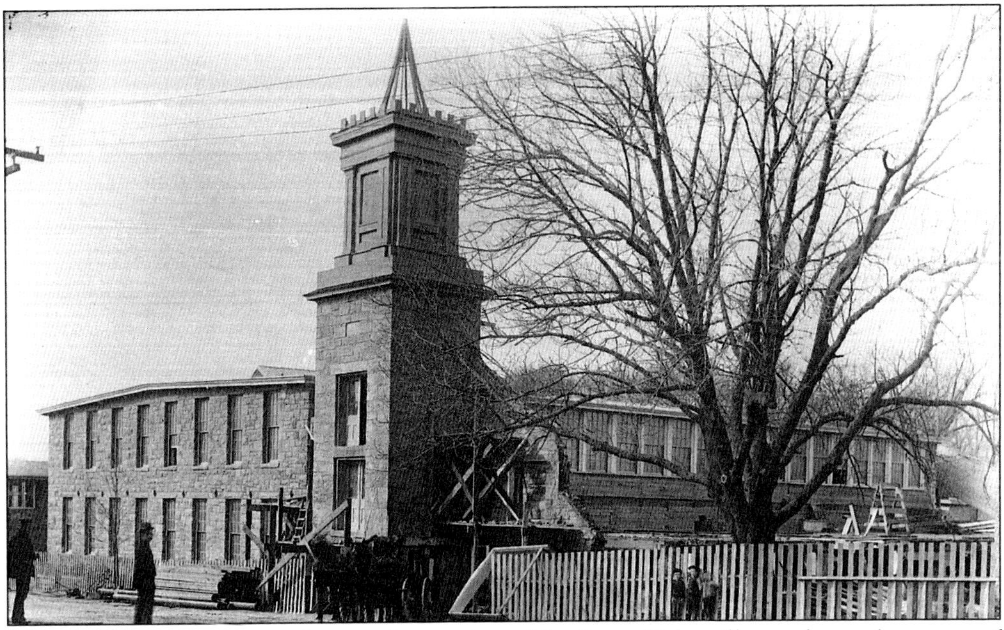

Construction is nearly complete on this portion of the Peace Dale mill complex at the corner of Kingstown Road and Columbia Street. Note the three lads up against the fence who must have been fascinated by the experience. (Courtesy of Pettaquamscutt Historical Society.)

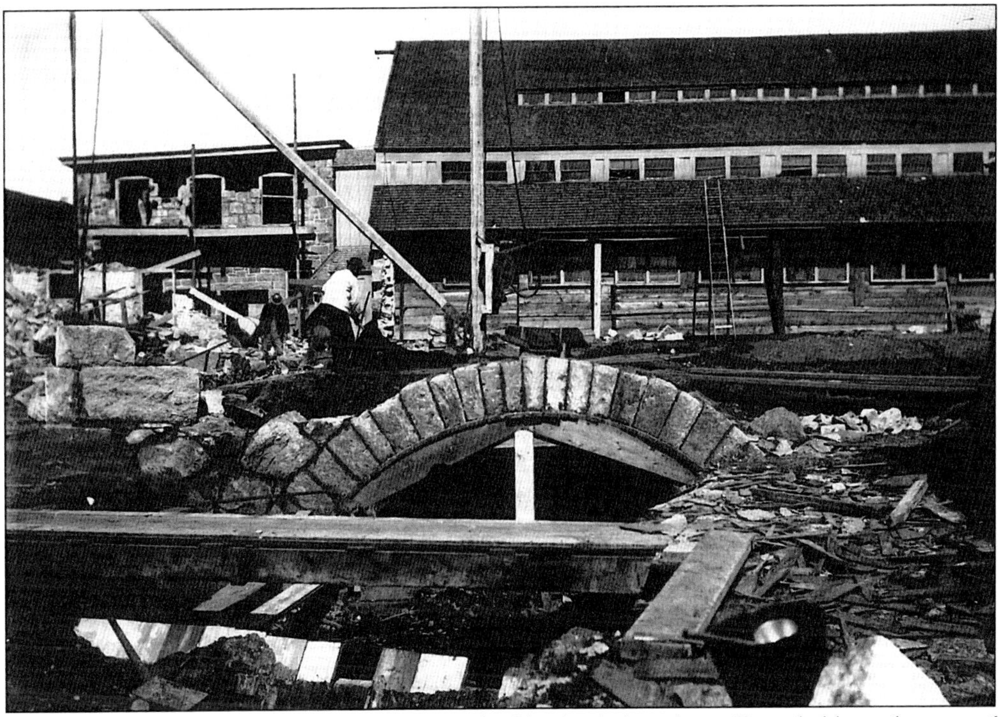

This picture shows the construction of an arched bridge below the mill, probably at the turn of the century. (Courtesy of Pettaquamscutt Historical Society.)

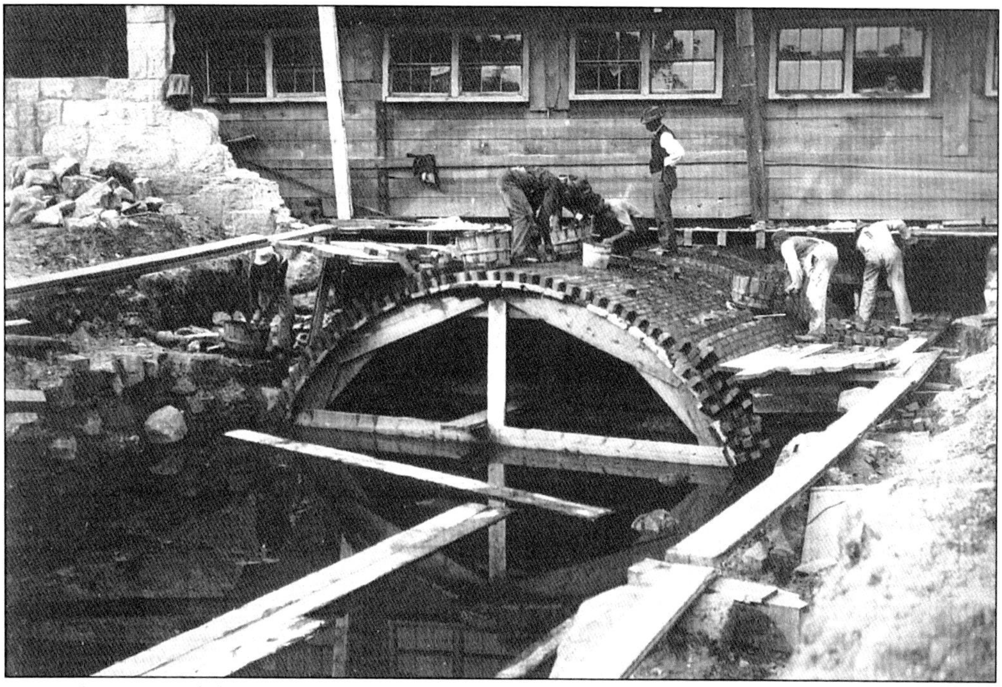

An earlier view of the arched construction gives insight into how it was done. (Courtesy of Pettaquamscutt Historical Society.)

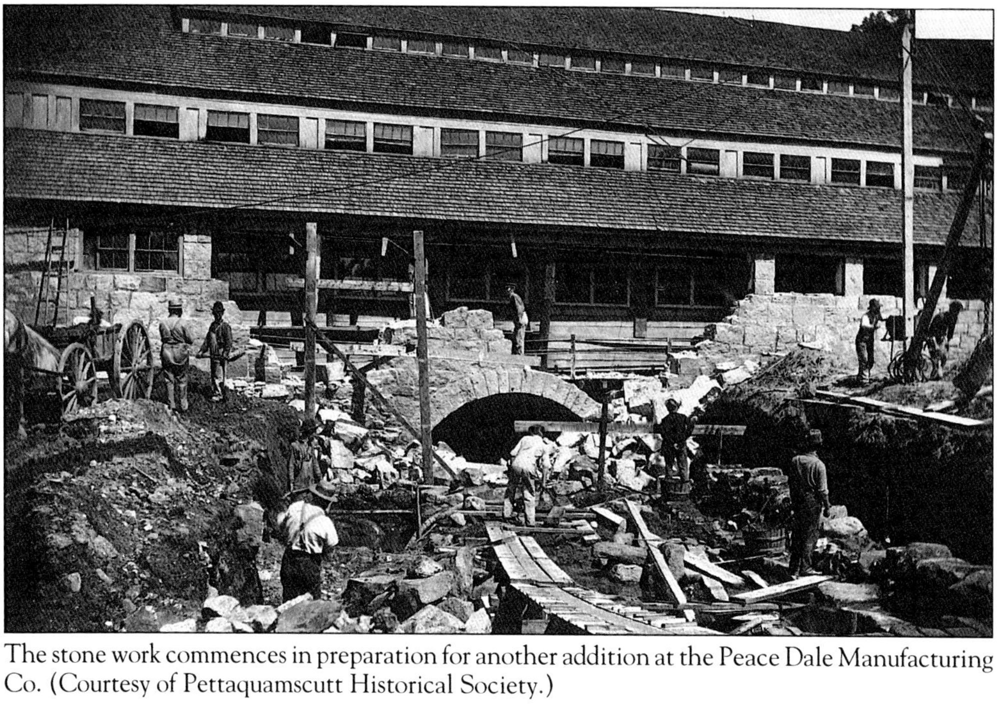

The stone work commences in preparation for another addition at the Peace Dale Manufacturing Co. (Courtesy of Pettaquamscutt Historical Society.)

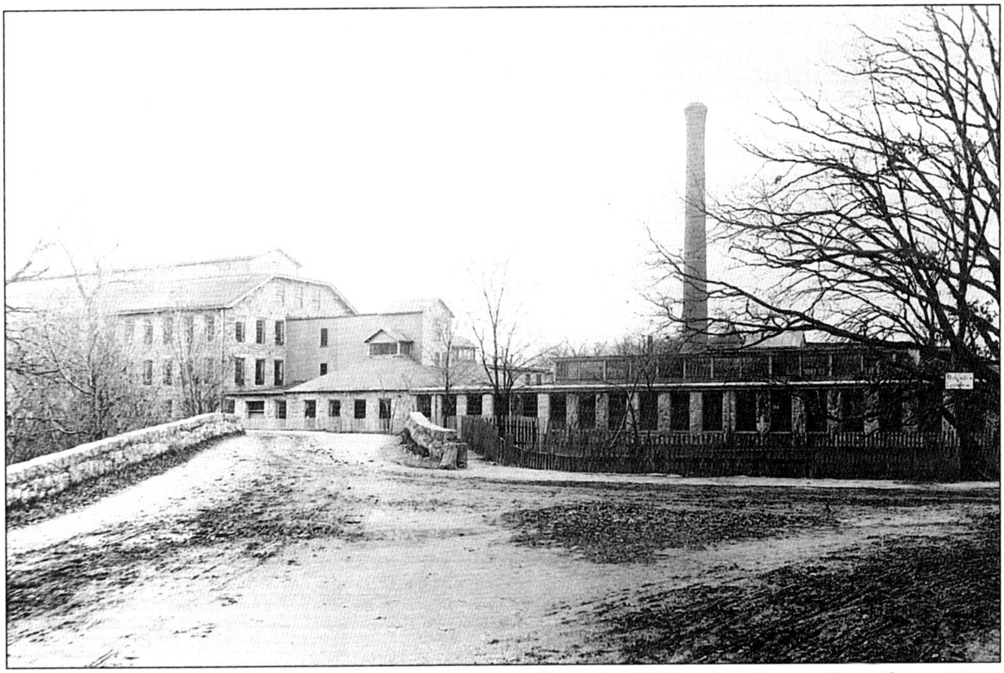

This view of the Peace Dale Manufacturing Co. is from North Road and was taken about 1900. (Courtesy of Pettaquamscutt Historical Society.)

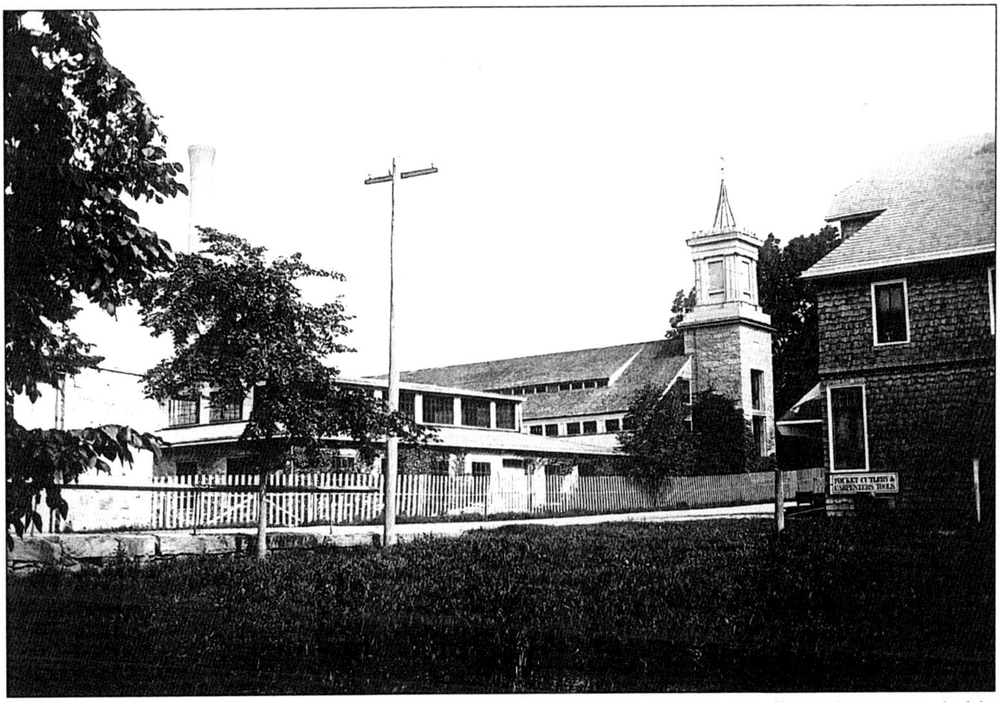

This is a view of the mill, from Columbia Street and what is now the Village Green, probably taken around the same time as the photograph at the top of the page. (Courtesy of Pettaquamscutt Historical Society.)

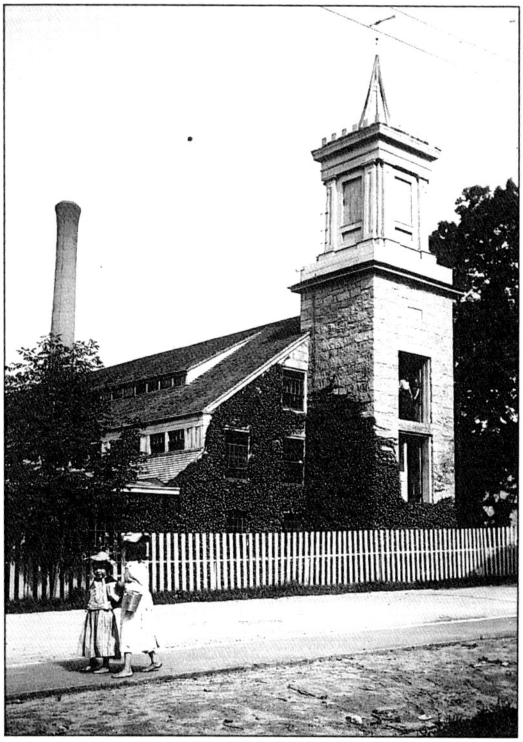

A child carries a lunch pail—to a father working in the mill, perhaps?—in this turn-of-the-century view of the mill from Kingstown Road. (Courtesy of Pettaquamscutt Historical Society.)

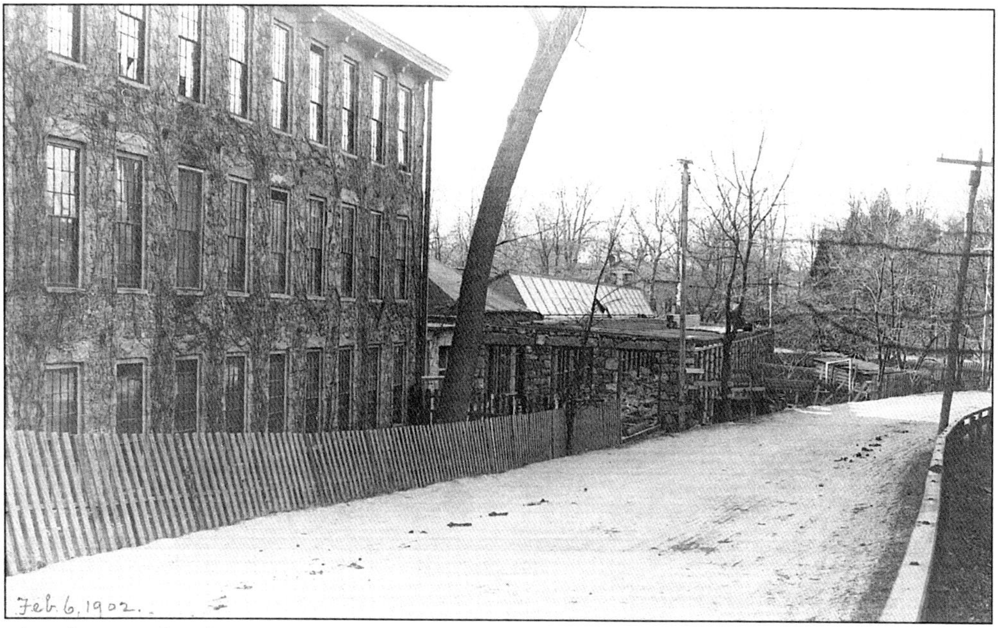

This photograph, taken February 6, 1902, shows the addition to the mill's weave shed. The space allowed the mill to expand by 50 looms. At the same time, the Hazards were building an addition to the worsted mill that would be four stories high and a new finishing room of three stories. In March 1902, the *Narragansett Times* reported that the company expected to add 150 people to its workforce, which already numbered more than 600. (Courtesy of Anthony Guarriello Jr.)

On April 28, 1908, an accident at the Peace Dale Manufacturing Co. took the life of forty-year-old Benjamin Frank Taylor. Taylor was oiling the superstructure above the engine room when a drum wheel that carried the rope drive from the powerhouse to the spinning department burst. Killed instantly, Taylor was carried with the twisted wreckage of cables and pulley 25 feet to the ground below. The *Narragansett Times* reported that his watched stopped at two minutes before one o'clock. (Courtesy of Anthony Guarriello Jr.)

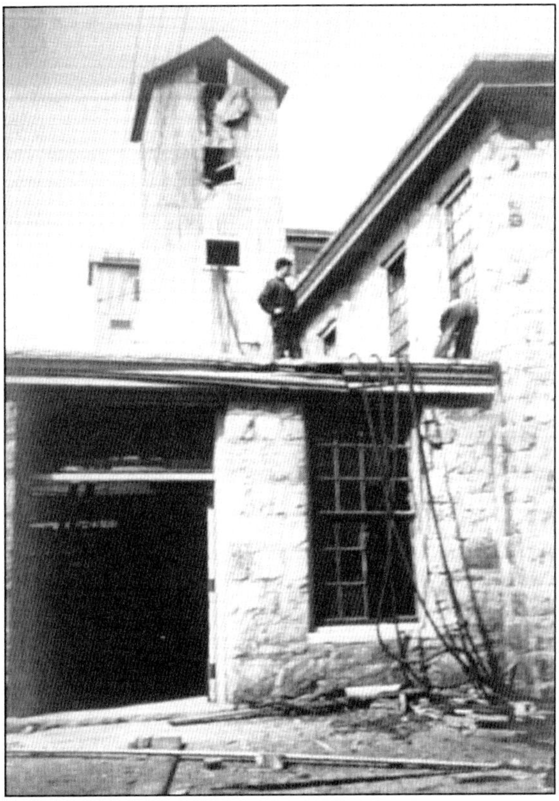

Debris from the 1908 accident can be seen in this picture. Although the road was filled with employees returning after the lunch hour, no one was injured. The only victim was Benjamin Frank Taylor, who left a widow and seven children. (Courtesy of Anthony Guarriello Jr.)

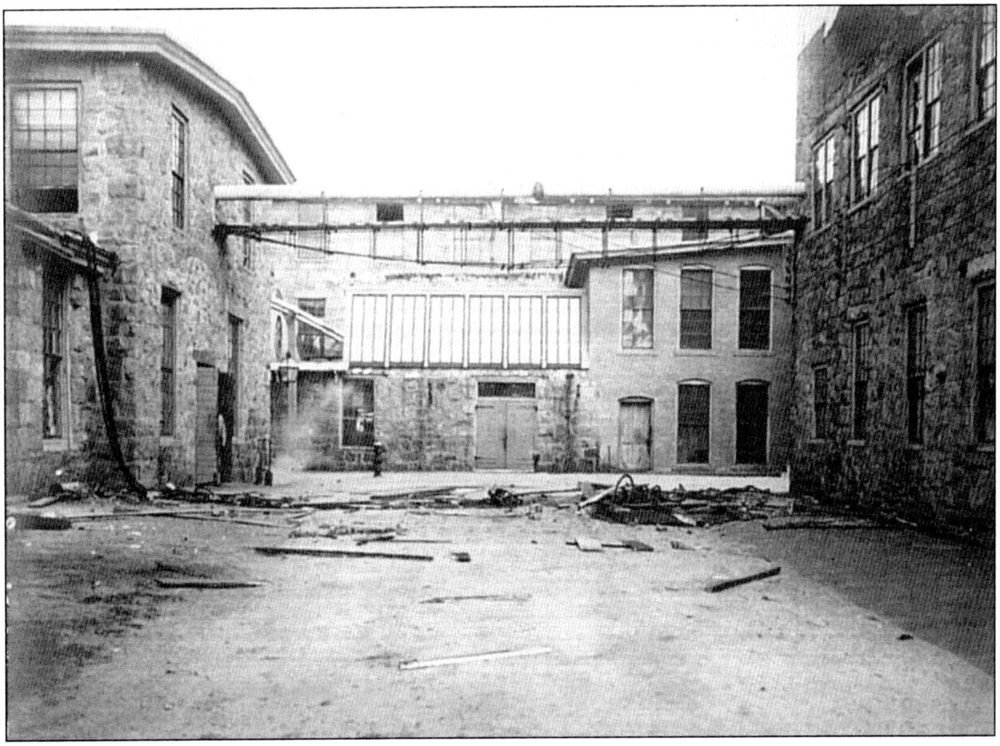

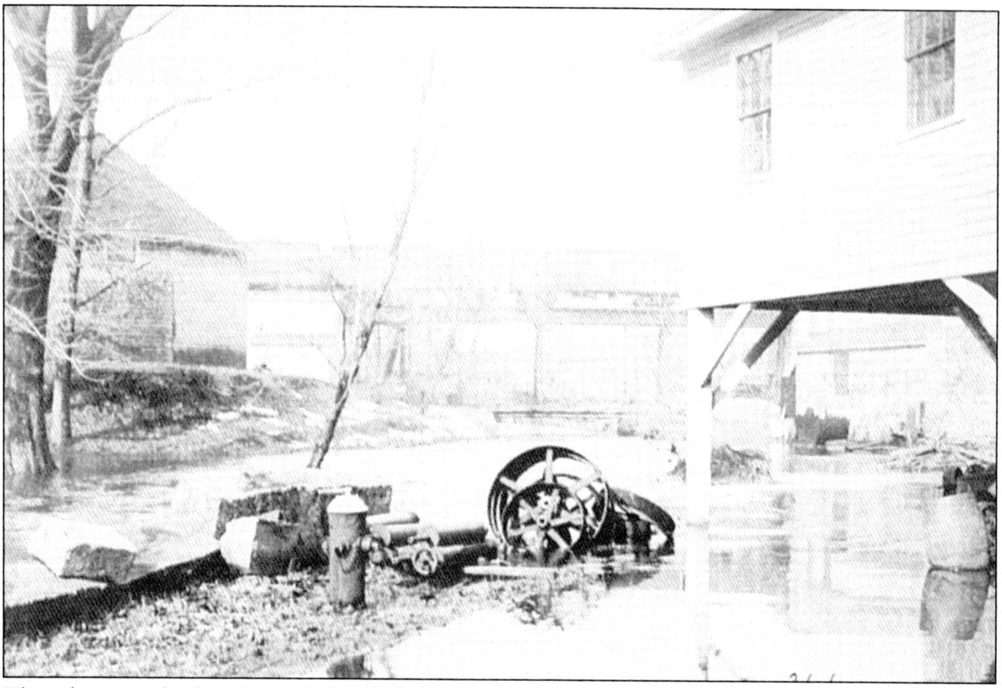

This photograph, dated March 1, 1902, appears to be of a flood near the mill. The Saugatucket River has crested its banks many times over the years, most recently on February 18, 1998, when the dam at California Jim's Pond burst and sent flood waters rushing through Peace Dale Flats. (Courtesy of Anthony Guarriello Jr.)

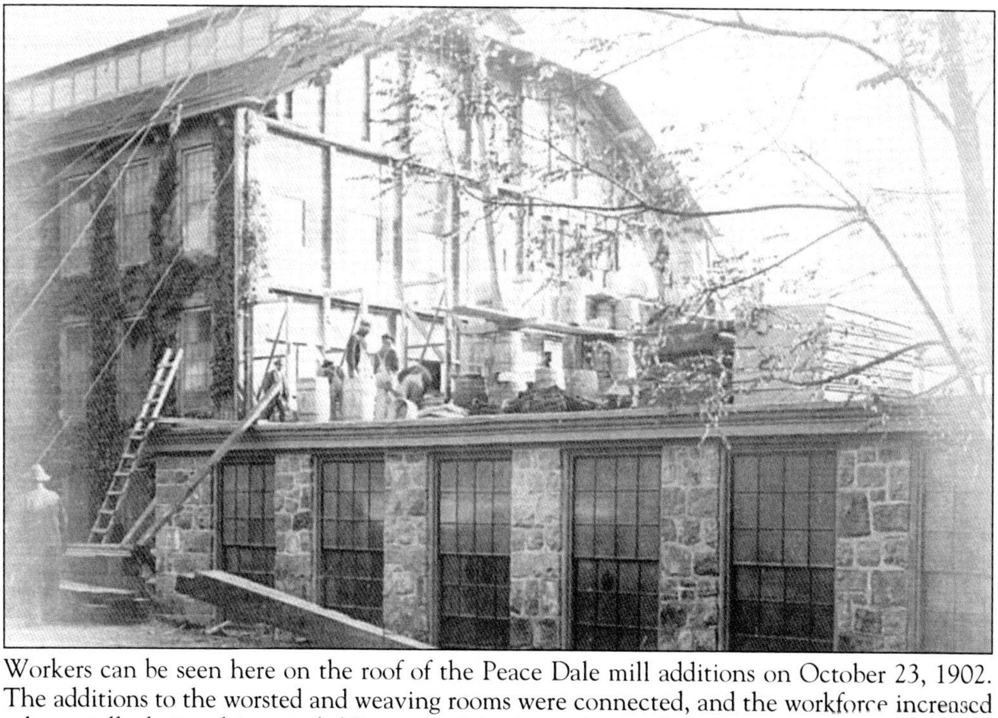

Workers can be seen here on the roof of the Peace Dale mill additions on October 23, 1902. The additions to the worsted and weaving rooms were connected, and the workforce increased substantially during this period. (Courtesy of Anthony Guarriello Jr.)

Three

Mill Workers

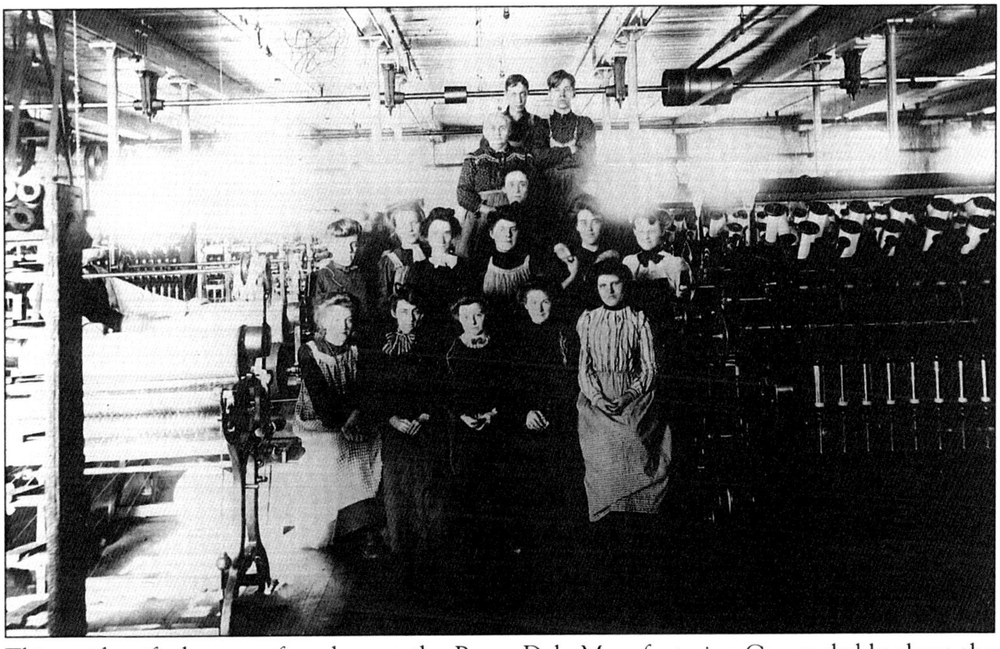

This unidentified group of workers at the Peace Dale Manufacturing Co., probably about the turn of the century, can be seen to represent all the men, women, and children who toiled in the textile mill in the 19th and 20th centuries. Coming first from Ireland and later Italy, these mill workers were the backbone of Peace Dale's economy. (Courtesy of Pettaquamscutt Historical Society.)

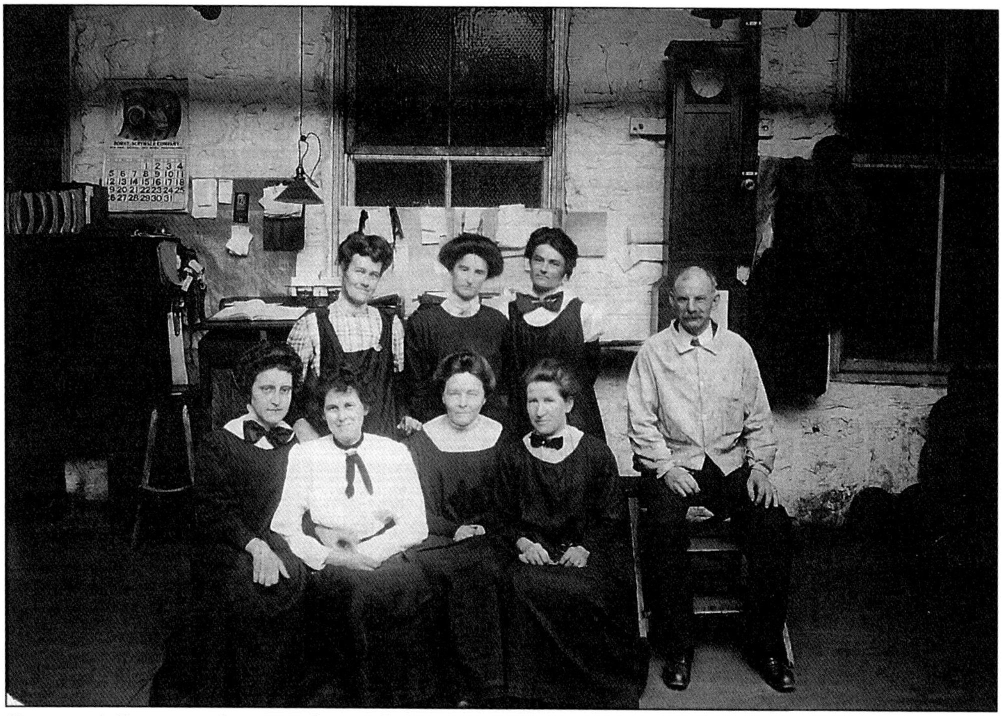

Sources differ as to these workers' identities. Taken in March 1911, the photograph is said to show workers in the weave shed, but they also appear to be office workers of some type. It was the weavers whose strike in 1906 was the most bitter and divisive in the company's history. The workers, upset at having to work two looms at different speeds, walked out in late February that year in a work stoppage that would not be settled until June. (Courtesy of Pettaquamscutt Historical Society.)

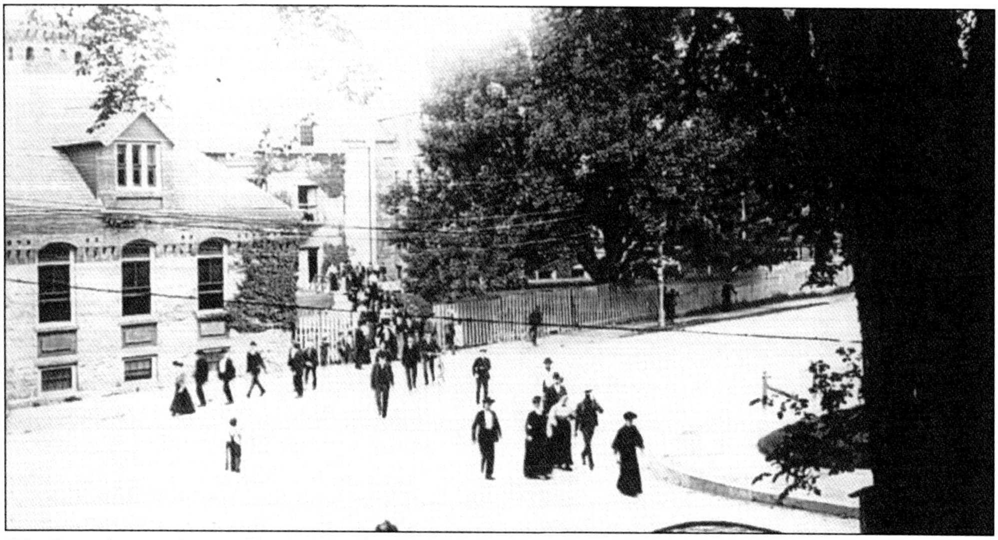

Workers leave the mill near Columbia Street and Kingstown Road. The women may be heading to the Neighborhood Guild, where a dining room was set aside for "use of girls in the mill during the noon hour," according to the *Narragansett Times* of July 10, 1908. (Courtesy of Pettaquamscutt Historical Society.)

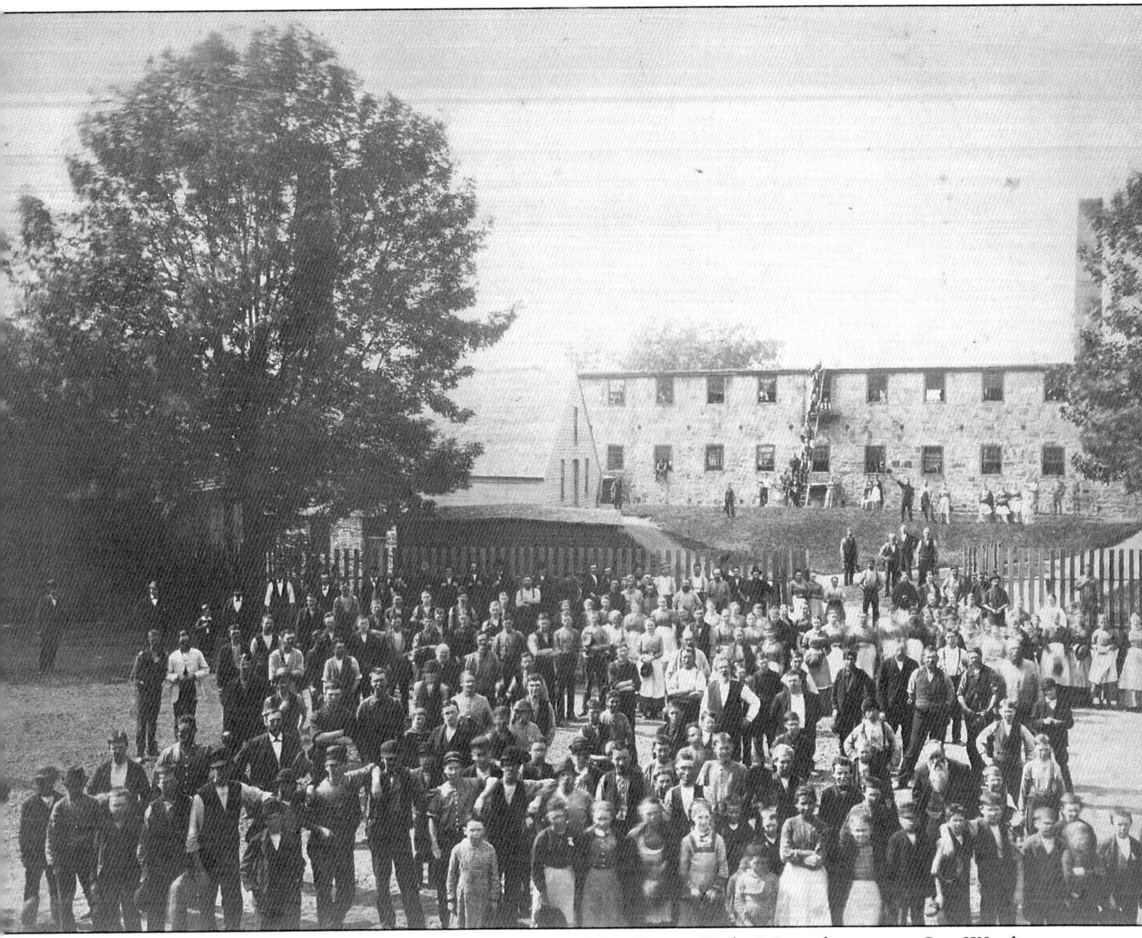

In this photograph, workers leave the east gate of the Peace Dale Manufacturing Co. Workers in the Peace Dale mills were considerably better off than in some textile concerns, but the "operatives," as they were called, still toiled for much less money than the supervisors and lived a life that was tightly controlled by the company, which owned their housing and deducted store bills from their pay. At the time of the 1906 strike, the *Narragansett Times* reported the weekly payroll to be about $6,500, or an average pay of $9 a week. The disparity in pay was noted by Peter Crawford Stewart in his 1962 master's thesis, "A History of the Peace Dale Manufacturing Co." In the 1880s, he noted, the average mill worker made between $1 and $1.50 a day while overseers made $2 to $5 a day and supervisors were paid between $4,000 and $10,000 a year. (Courtesy of Pettaquamscutt Historical Society.)

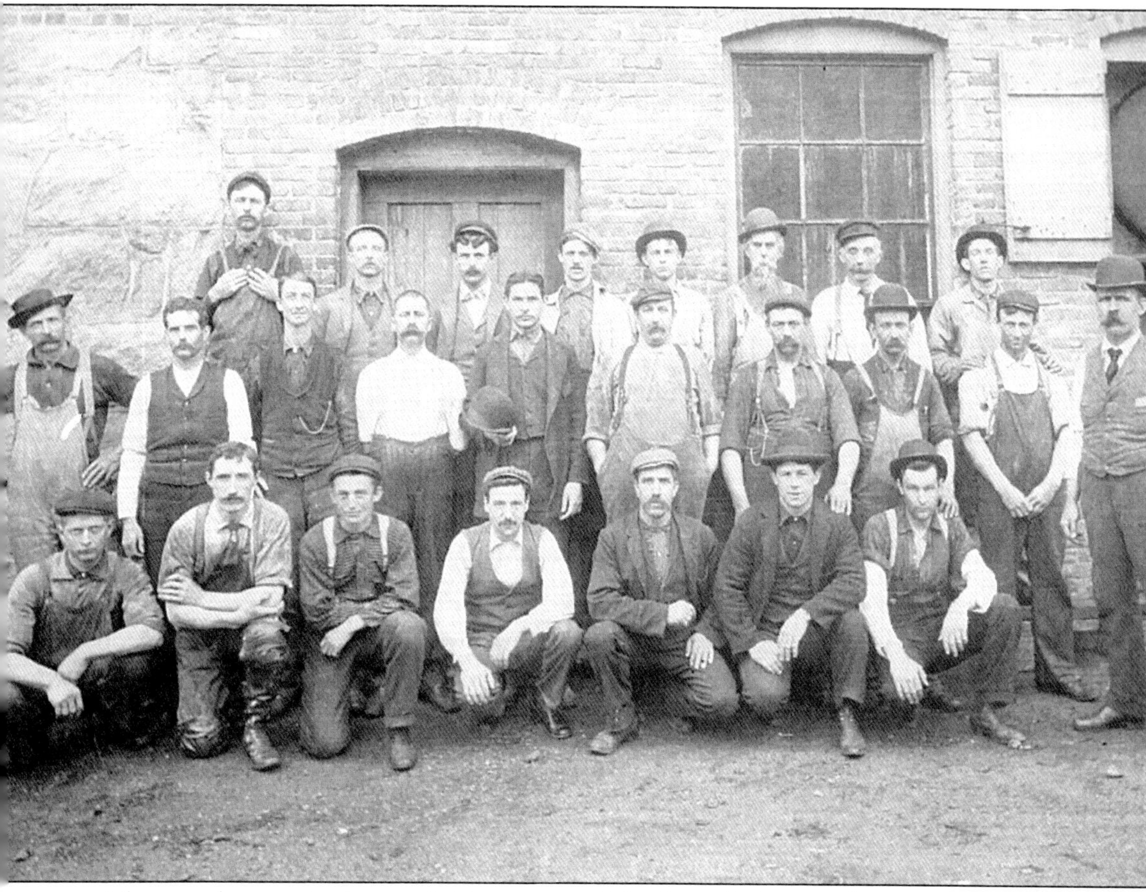

These workers are in the wet finishing room of the Peace Dale Manufacturing Co. They are, from left to right, as follows: (front row) Wilbert Saunders, Pete Corcoran, Ed Davis, Jonas Hoyle, Charles Lewis, Walter Potter, and Stephen Holland; (middle row) Bill Holland, Ralph Northup, Ike Holland, Henry Gardiner, Percy Hathaway, Elisha Rodman, Henry Oatley, Perry Arnold, Bill Tingley, and Henry Curtis; (back row) Stanton Clarke, Jim Firth, Amos Champlin, Gus Allen, Henry Lamphere, Henry Moore, Bill Lloyd, and ? Mason. On April 27, 1906, during the weavers' strike, the *Narragansett Times* reported that James Firth had sought work in the mills of Lawrence, Massachusetts, like many who left as the strike wore on. (Courtesy of Pettaquamscutt Historical Society.)

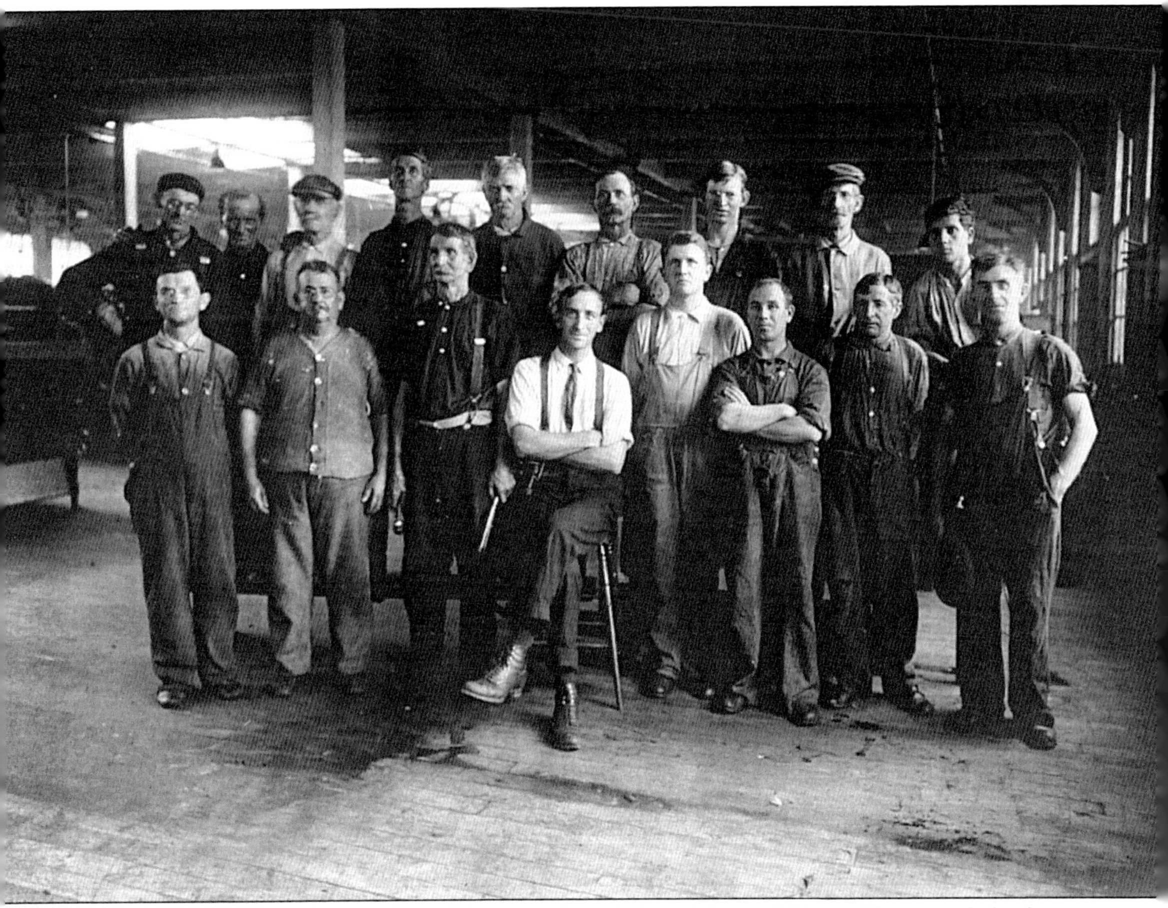

More mill workers can be seen here. They are, from left to right, as follows: (front row) the first three are unidentified, Ralph Week, Rowland Albro, Tommy O'Donnell, Howard Tourgee, and unidentified; (back row) Ralph Holland, Joe Baton, Gus Allen, Isaac Holland, Jerry Holland, unidentified, James Baton, unidentified, and ? Mattera. (Courtesy of Pettaquamscutt Historical Society.)

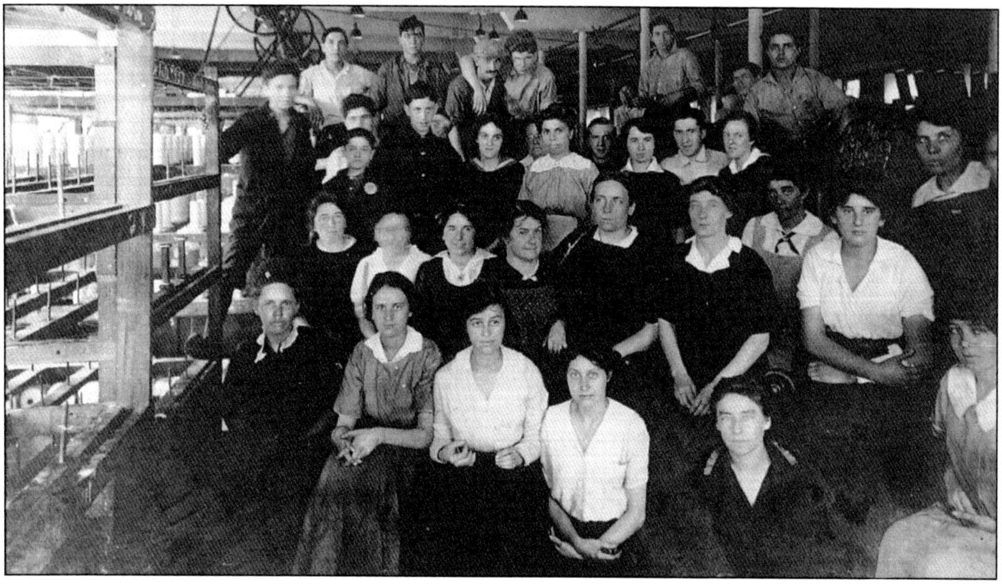

Turn-of-the-century mill workers pose next to spools in the Peace Dale mill. It is hard for many of us today to imagine the demands of mill work in the late 19th and early 20th centuries. Although the Peace Dale mill was probably as safe as any other, accidents were not uncommon. A typical issue of the *Narragansett Times*, on November 20, 1908, reported that Julius Desino was bruised in a fall from some staging, and Henry L. Curtis, in charge of the wet finishing room, had caught his hand between a pair of rollers while cleaning the machine and was badly lacerated. (Courtesy of Anthony Guarriello Jr.)

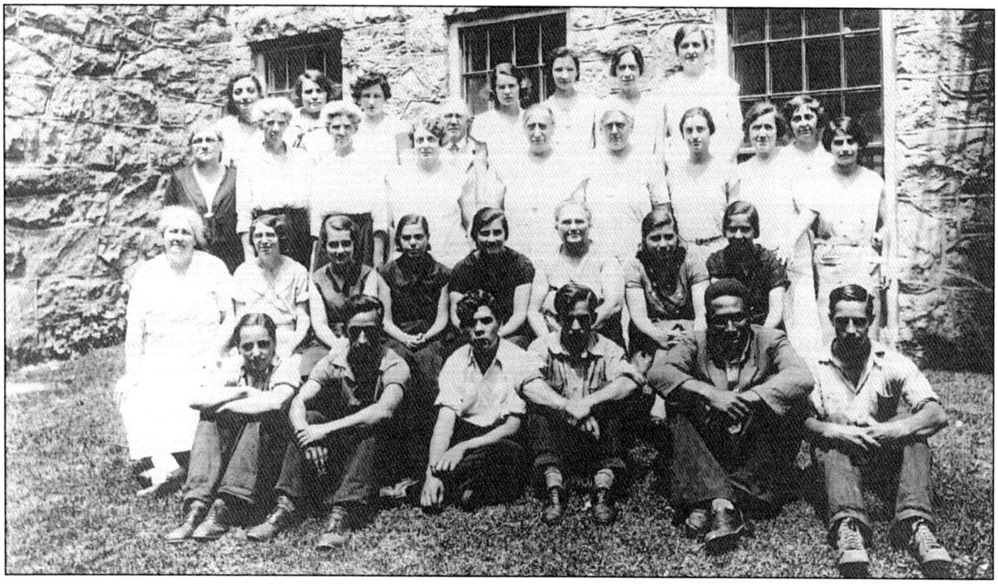

Workers pose outside the Peace Dale mill. Note the men's practical apparel versus the women's long dresses. Although the strike of 1906 was resolved, another briefer one ensued in 1913 when about 155 mill workers walked out in a dispute over the radical group Industrial Workers of the World. The strike fizzled out after a week of picketing when the community failed to rally around the strikers. In 1906, community support—both moral and financial—had been key to helping the workers hang on as long as they did. (Courtesy of Anthony Guarriello Jr.)

Tom O'Brien was a mill employee until an accident took three of his fingers. To compensate, the Hazards set him up in his own variety store on Columbia Street. The building, which is no longer standing, was located across from what is now the Gates Insurance Agency. (Courtesy of Everett Hopkins.)

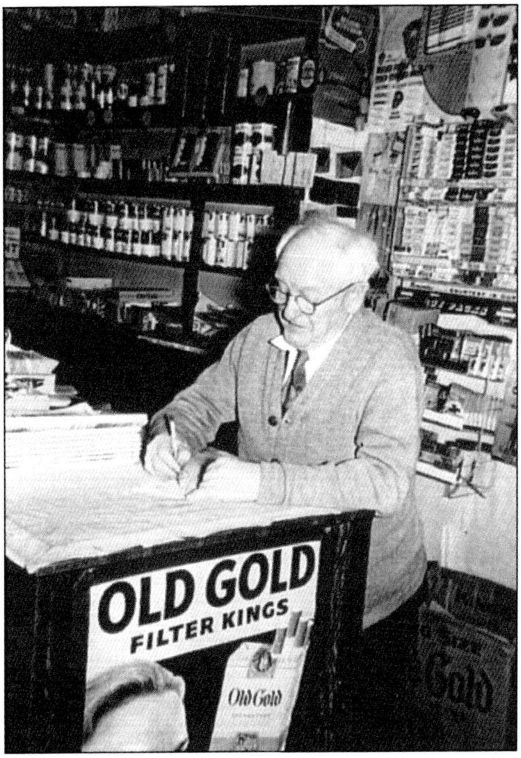

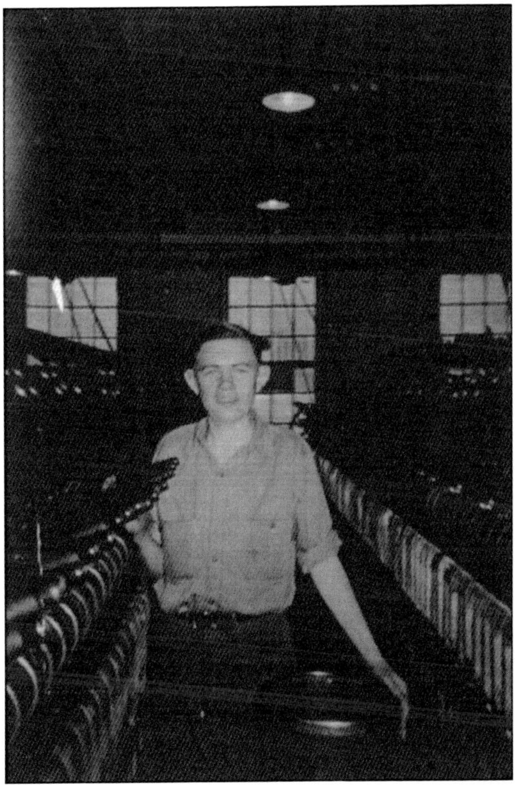

Frank M. Hopkins was just 16 when this photograph was taken of him in the spinning room on the third floor of the Peace Dale mill, working as a bobbin boy in 1942. It was not uncommon for young men and women to leave school at an early age to work in the mill. (Courtesy of Everett Hopkins.)

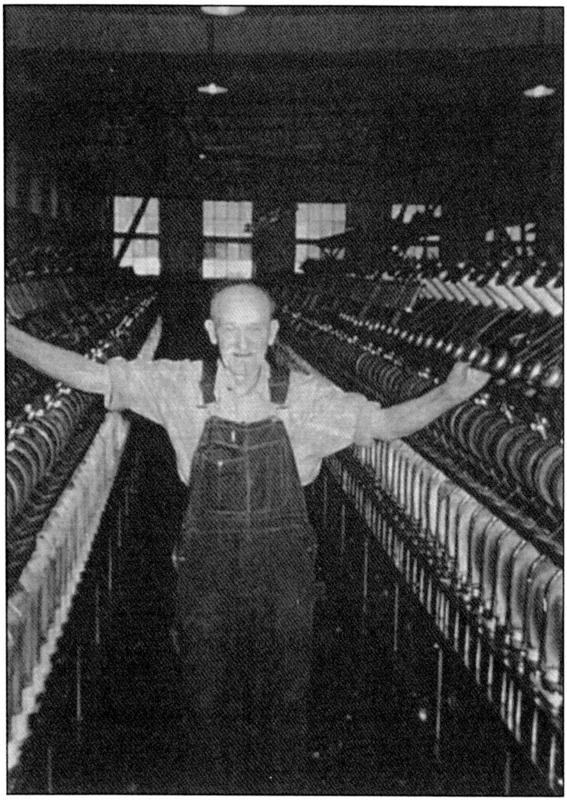

Mill workers ranged from the young to the old, especially during World War II, when labor shortages were so acute. This unidentified man worked in the spinning room of the Peace Dale mill in 1942. (Courtesy of Everett Hopkins.)

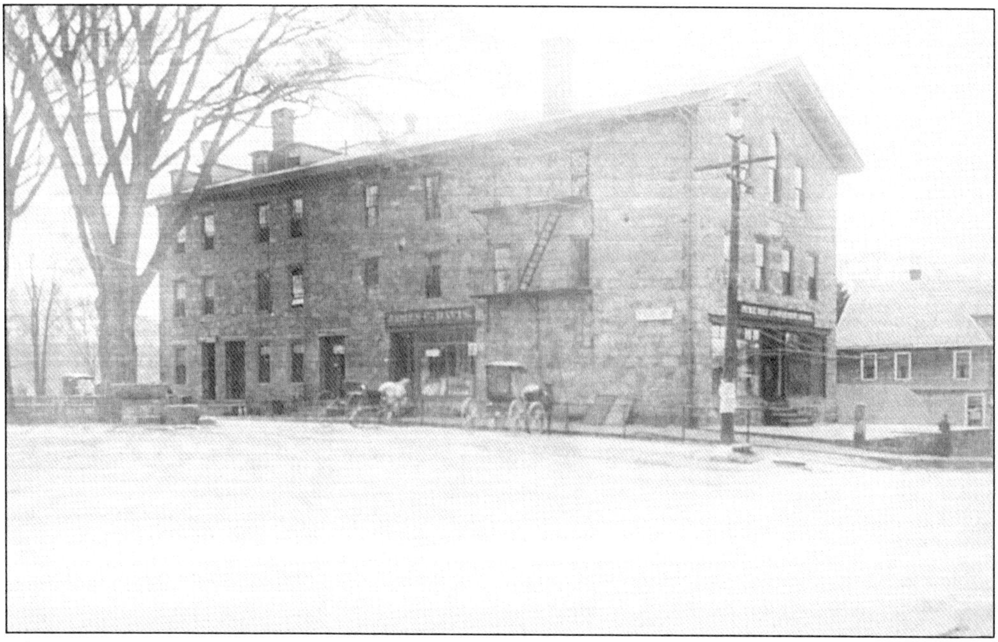

This picture shows the Peace Dale Cooperative Stores. (Courtesy of Peace Dale Library.)

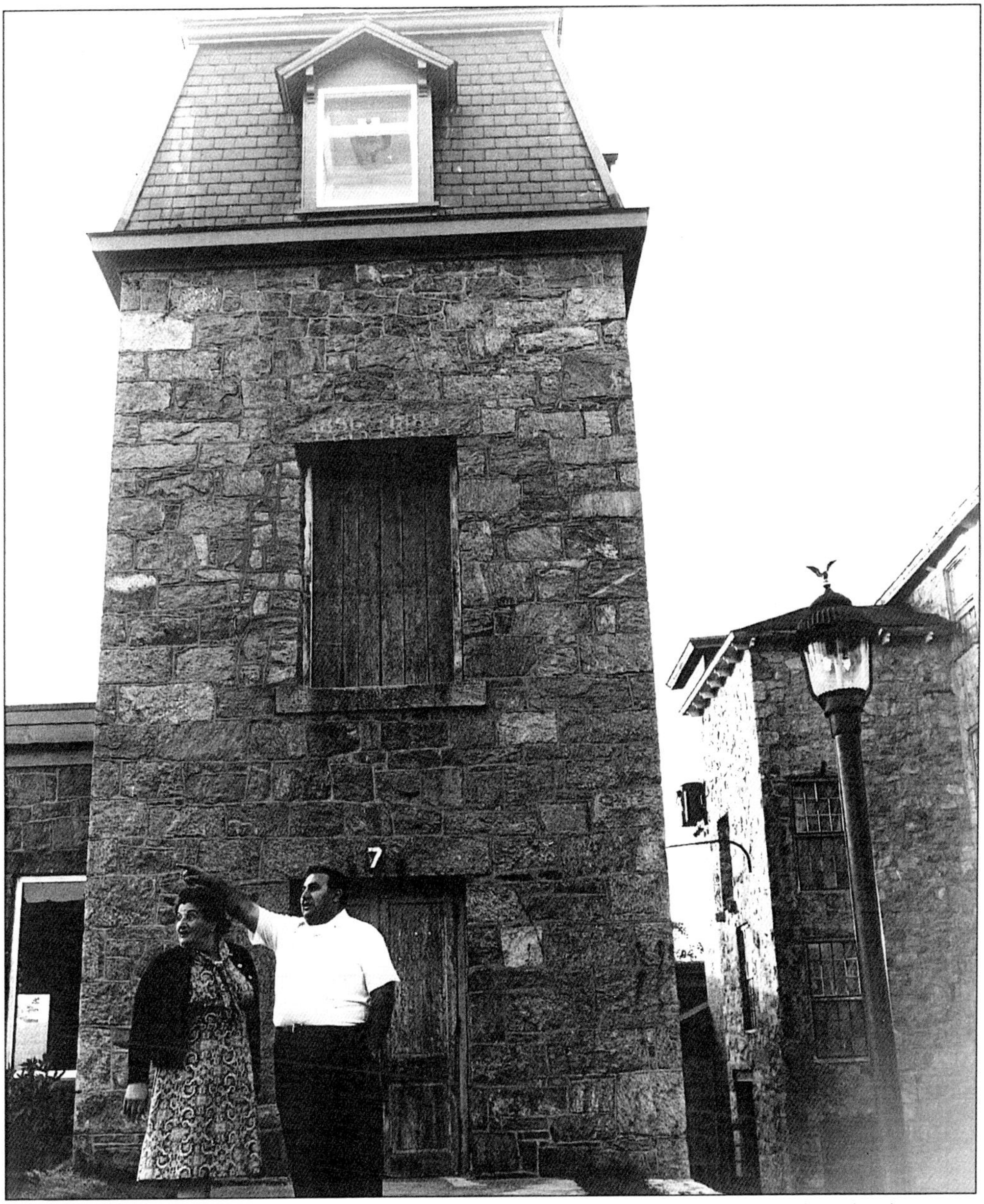

Anthony Guarriello Jr. came to Peace Dale from New Jersey in the 1960s. He bought the Peace Dale mills and, in 1972, the Homestead, the ancestral Hazard home. Mr. Guarriello, pictured here with Mrs. Josephine Vergas, established Palisades Industries in the mills and conducted extensive renovations of the buildings. Mr. Guarriello resurrected the philanthropy of the Hazards with his keen interest in improving the village. He was a founder of the South County Housing Improvement Foundation, and he served on the South Kingstown Town Council. But he long felt that the Hazards' Narragansett Pier Railroad had walled in the village and he wasted no time in ripping up the tracks and tearing out the overpasses when he acquired the railroad in the early 1980s. Today, mill space is occupied by Palisades, which has a modest workforce of about 20 people, as well as South County Community Action, a lawyer's office, and a technology company. (Courtesy of Anthony Guarriello Jr.)

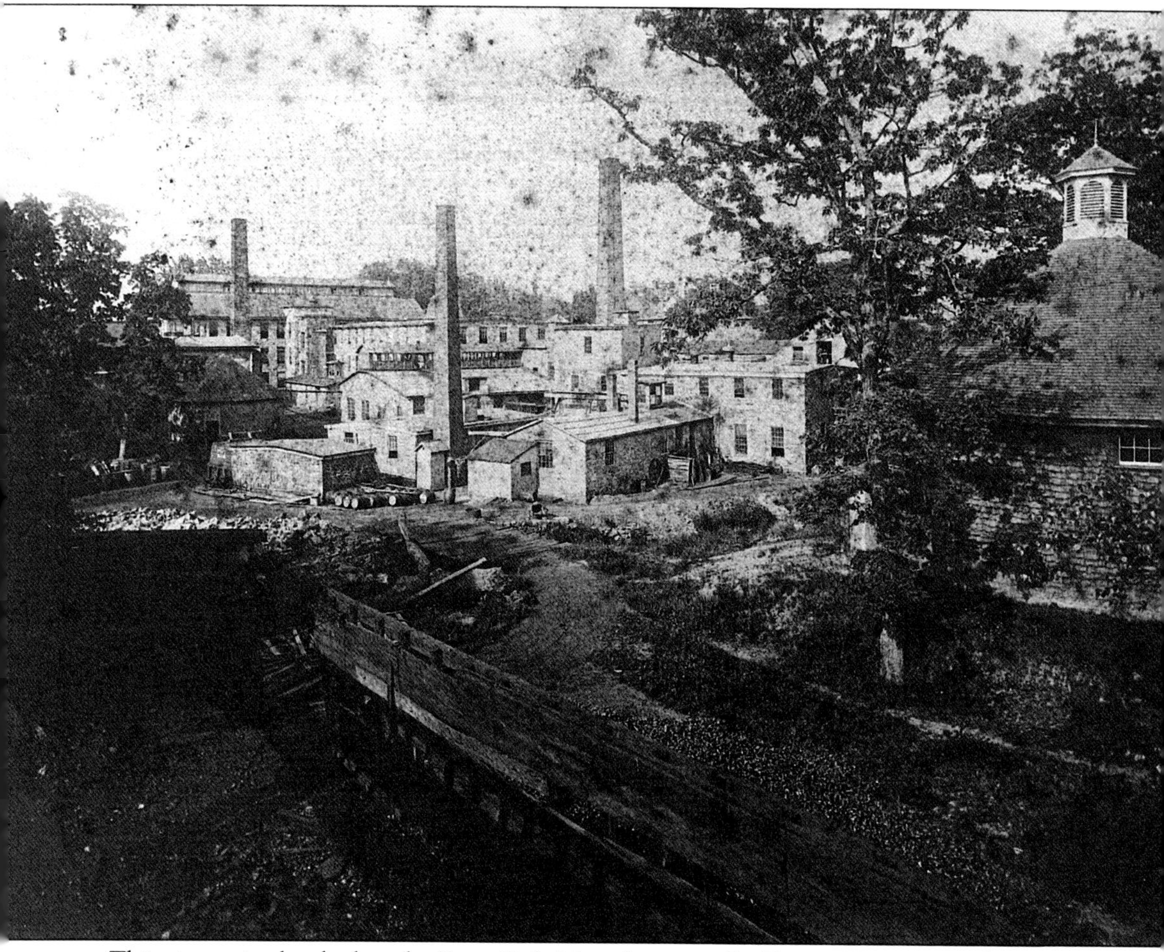

This picture is a last look at the Peace Dale Manufacturing Co. From 1802 to 1918, the Hazards' mill was the dominant force in the village of Peace Dale. But a series of factors, from labor unrest after the turn of the century to cheaper wages in the South, served to make the factory less and less profitable. In 1918, the family decided to sell the business because there was no heir apparent to take it over; Rowland Hazard was busy with the Solvay Process Co. in Syracuse, New York, another family business, and his father and brother had recently passed away. The Stevens Company of North Andover, Massachusetts, bought the Peace Dale mills for $905,920 cash and $600,000 in Stevens stock. The company closed the mills in 1948.

Four

Mill Houses

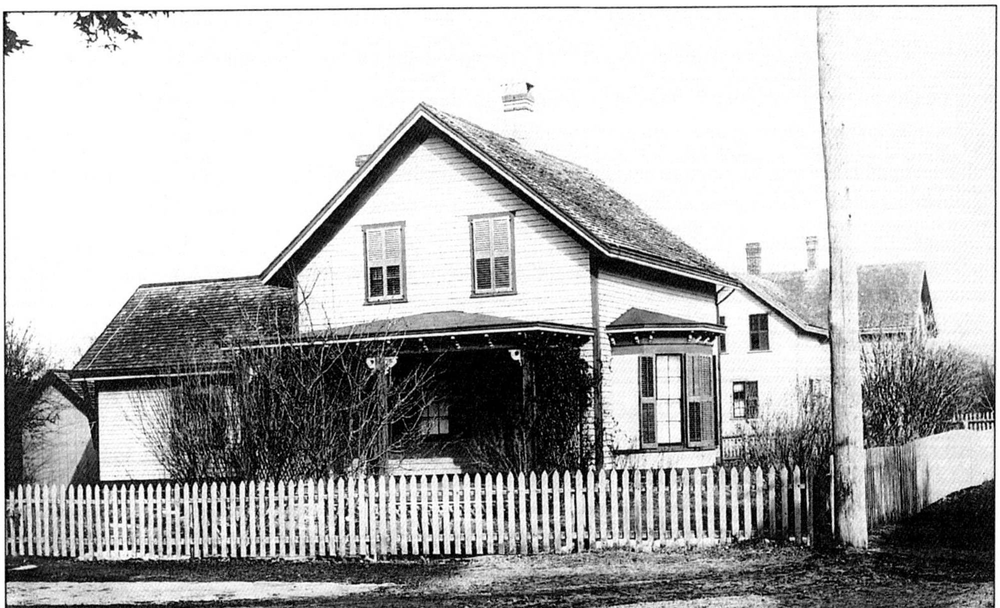

This house at the corner of Spring and Church Streets was moved from Columbia Street. Four rooms in the cottage rented for $7.50 per month. (Courtesy of Anthony Guarriello Jr.)

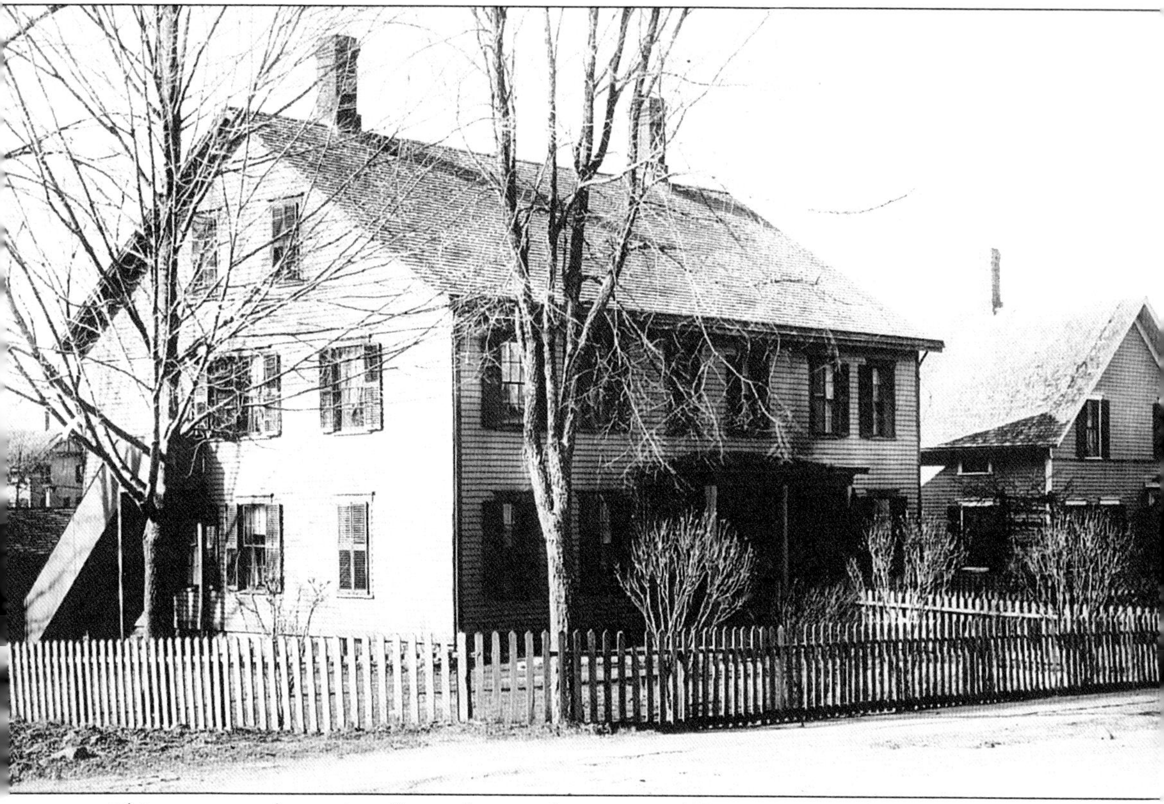

This tenement house is still standing at the corner of Kingstown Road and Spring Street. It contained three tenements that rented for between $3.45 and $6.92 per month, as well as a cottage on the property with eight rooms and a barn that rented for $8.50 per month. Housing for mill workers was tightly controlled by the Peace Dale Manufacturing Co., which built and retained ownership of the tenements. During the bitter strike of 1906, the company gave the striking weavers a week to vacate their tenements and quickly contracted Louis F. Bell to build a tenement house for single men who were being brought in from elsewhere to take the strikers' places. Families of replacement operatives were to be housed in the company's regular tenements. (Courtesy of Anthony Guarriello Jr.)

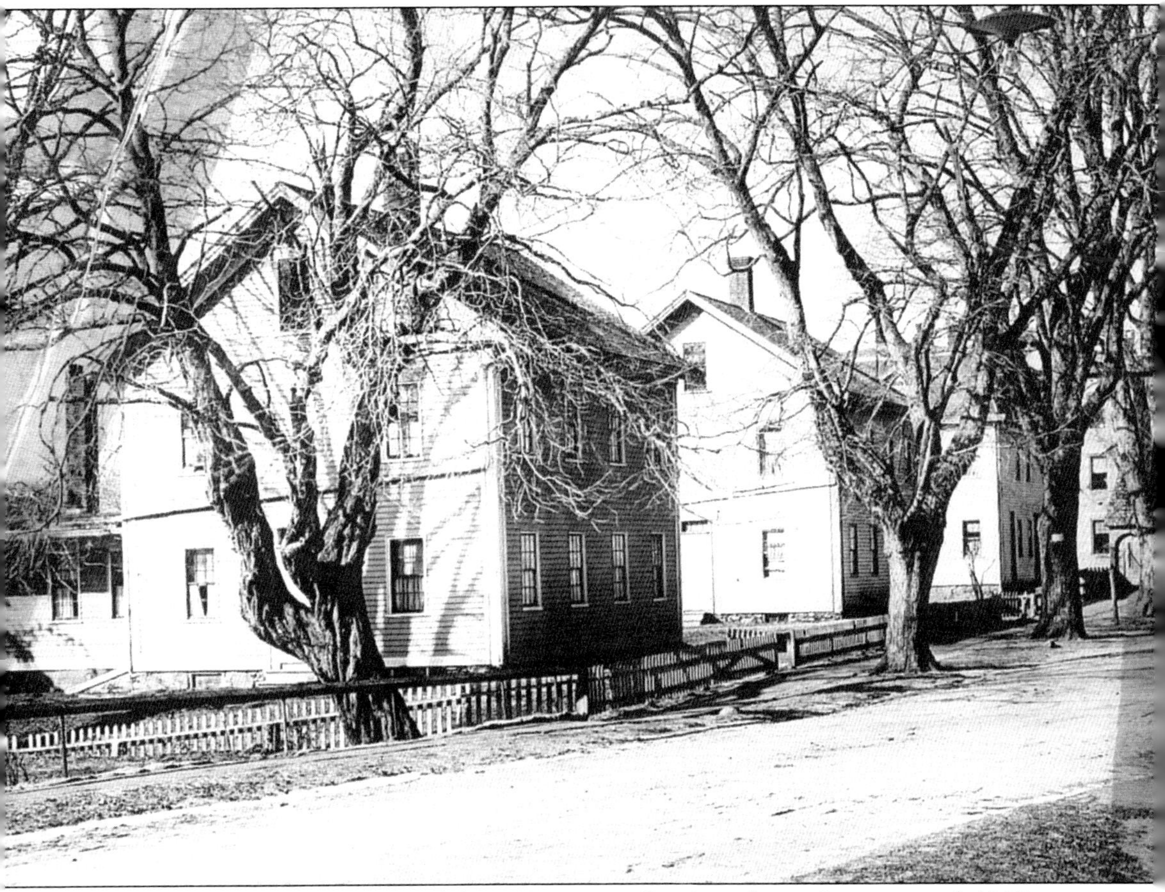

These mill tenements were moved from Kingstown Road to Amos Street around 1907 to make way for the Village Green. Seven rooms in these houses rented for $4.42 per month. Mrs. Augusta Hazard, who gave the money to build the Neighborhood Guild, envisioned the green as a graceful lawn set off by an English elm tree already on the site. The tenements were seen as an impediment to her plan. Almost immediately, the Village Green was embraced for community activities; in July 1908, the Citizens' Band "gave a very pleasing open air concert on the Village Green," reported the *Narragansett Times*. "There was a large audience present and a number of encores." (Courtesy of Anthony Guarriello Jr.)

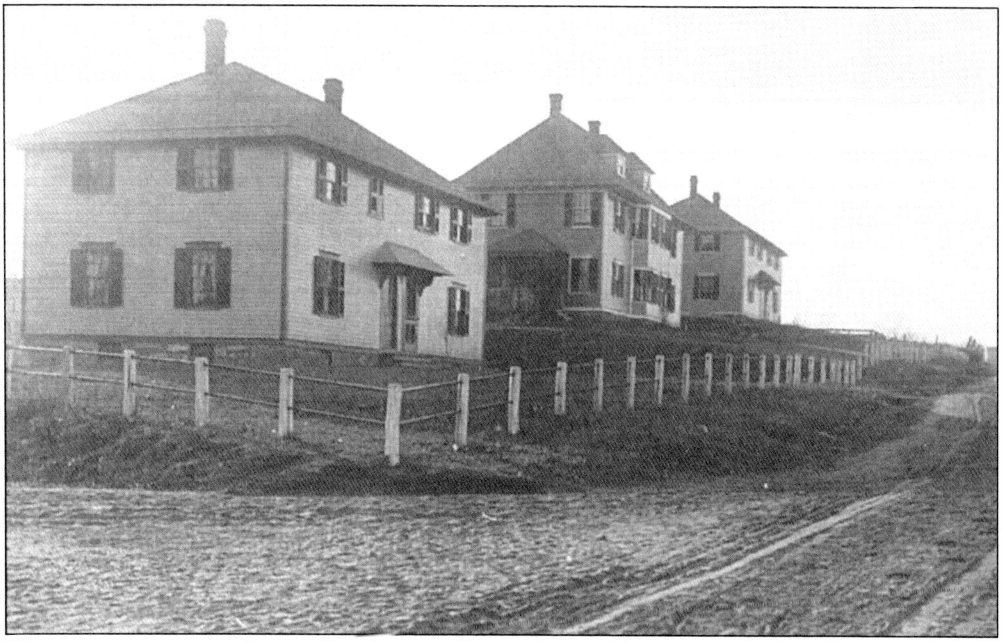

These tenements on Kersey Road are still standing, although the landscape has changed considerably since this photograph was taken. Kersey Road does not appear to be paved in this picture, and there isn't a tree in sight. Renamed for the type of wool for which Peace Dale manufacturers were famous, Kersey Road was originally called Mount Pleasant Avenue. (Courtesy of Anthony Guarriello Jr.)

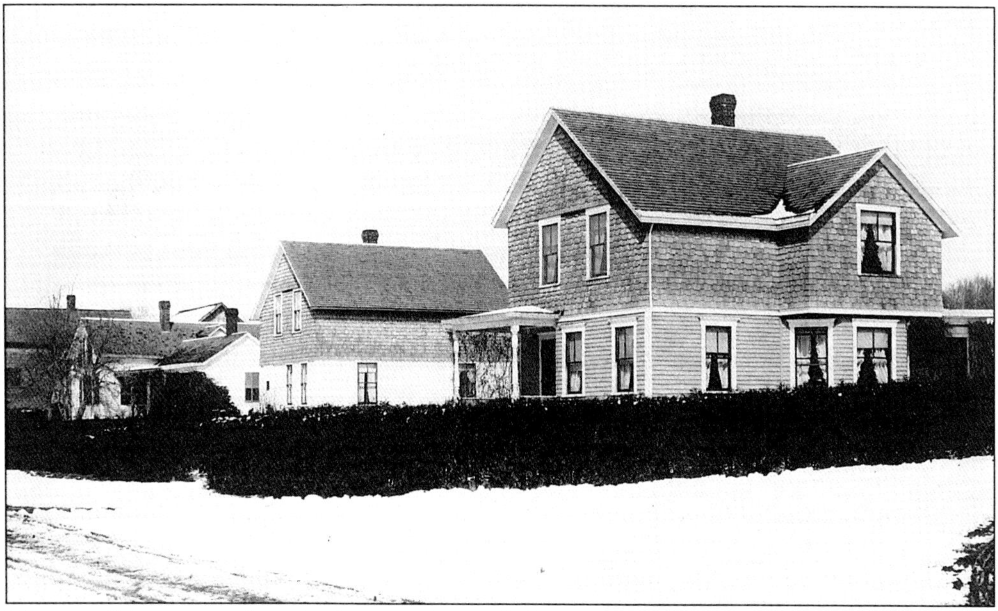

These mill houses on Branch Street in Peace Dale were apparently built and owned by mill workers. (Courtesy of Anthony Guarriello Jr.)

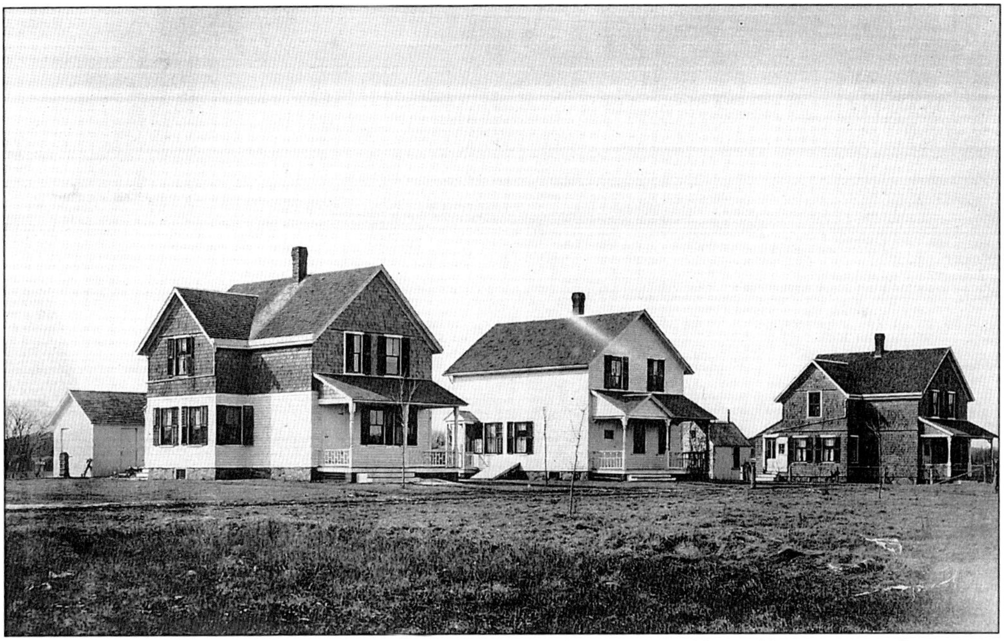

These houses on Branch Street in Peace Dale were built and owned by mill operatives. (Courtesy Anthony Guarriello Jr.)

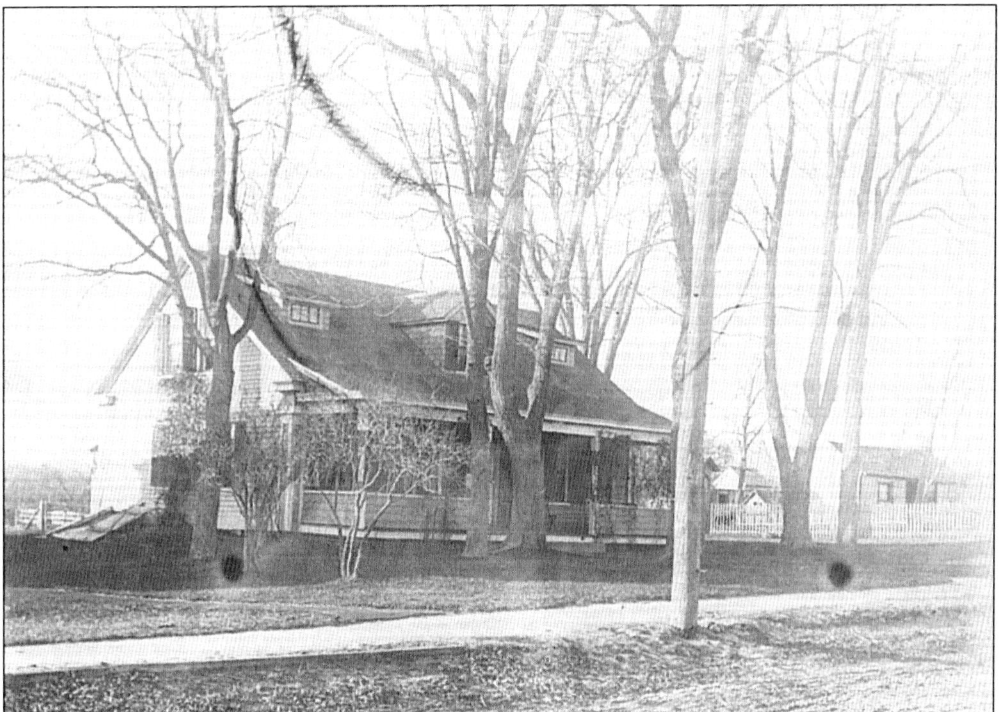

This house on North Road was owned by George Booth. North Road, often called simply "the north road," was coated with macadam in 1908. (Courtesy of Anthony Guarriello Jr.)

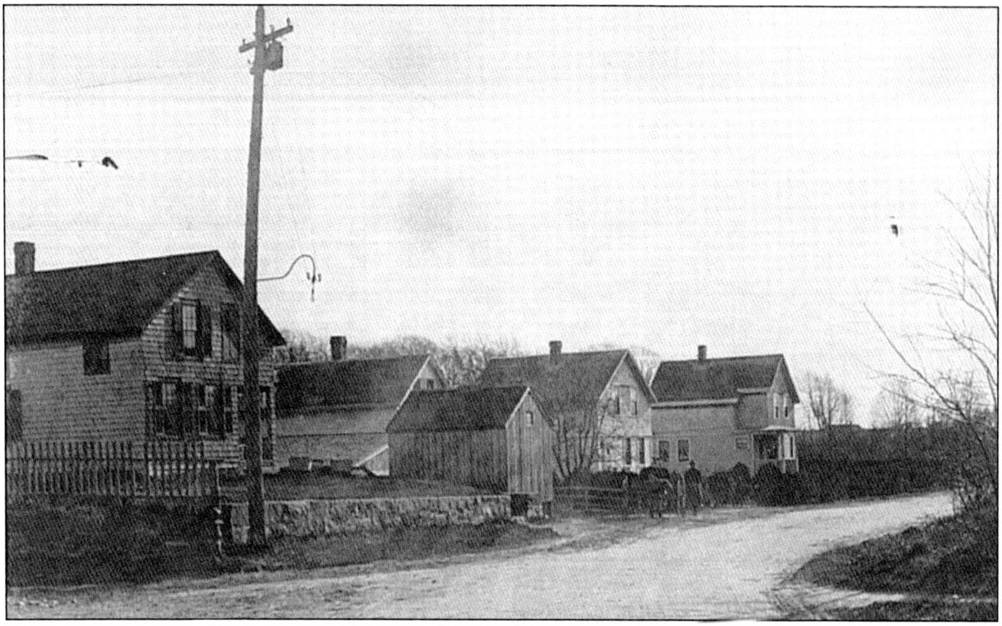

The intersection of Kingstown Road and Broad Rock Road (at extreme left) has changed a great deal since this photograph was taken, although, with the exception of the shed or barn near the road, the houses are still standing. (Courtesy of Anthony Guarriello Jr.)

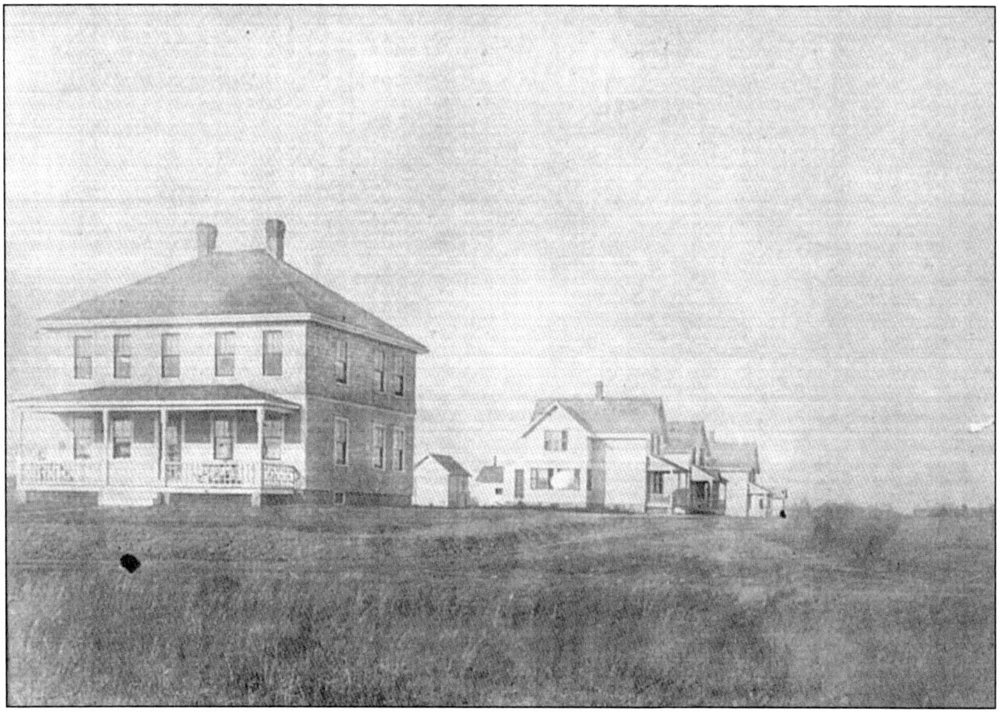

This photograph shows the intersection of School Street (foreground) and Branch Street. Although this house at the corner is still standing, it is barely visible today behind a buffer of vegetation. When many of Peace Dale's streets were first laid out the landscape was bare of trees. (Courtesy of Anthony Guarriello Jr.)

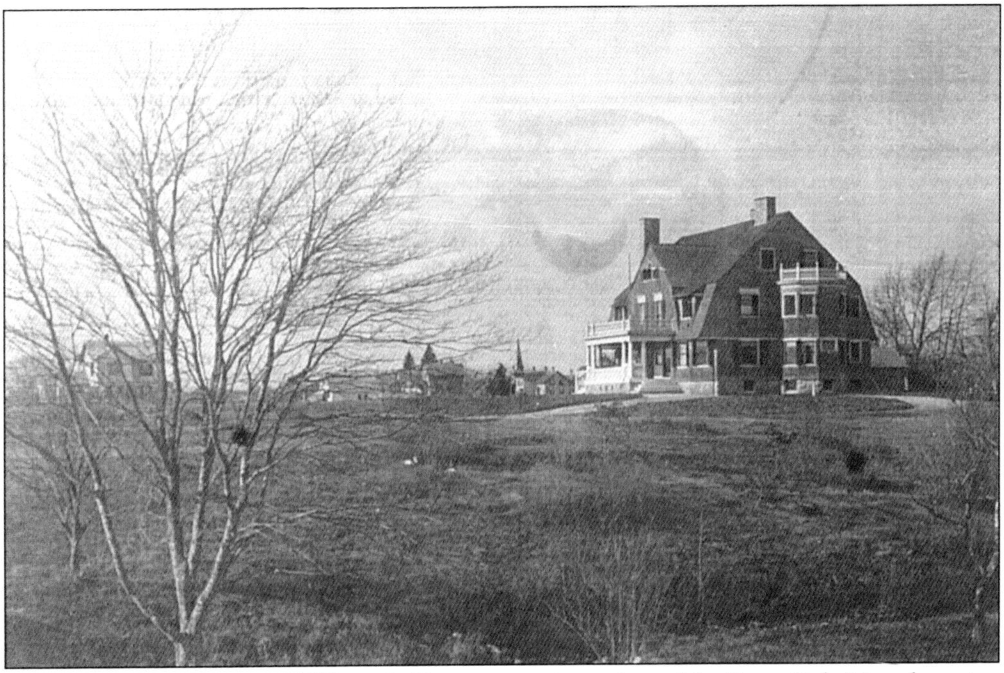

This was the grand home of William C. Greene, superintendent of the Peace Dale Manufacturing Company. This view is from Kingstown Road, and the house was located about where Rose Circle is now. Note the spire of the Peace Dale Congregational Church in the distance. Mill officials lived quite differently than the operatives. (Courtesy of Anthony Guarriello Jr.)

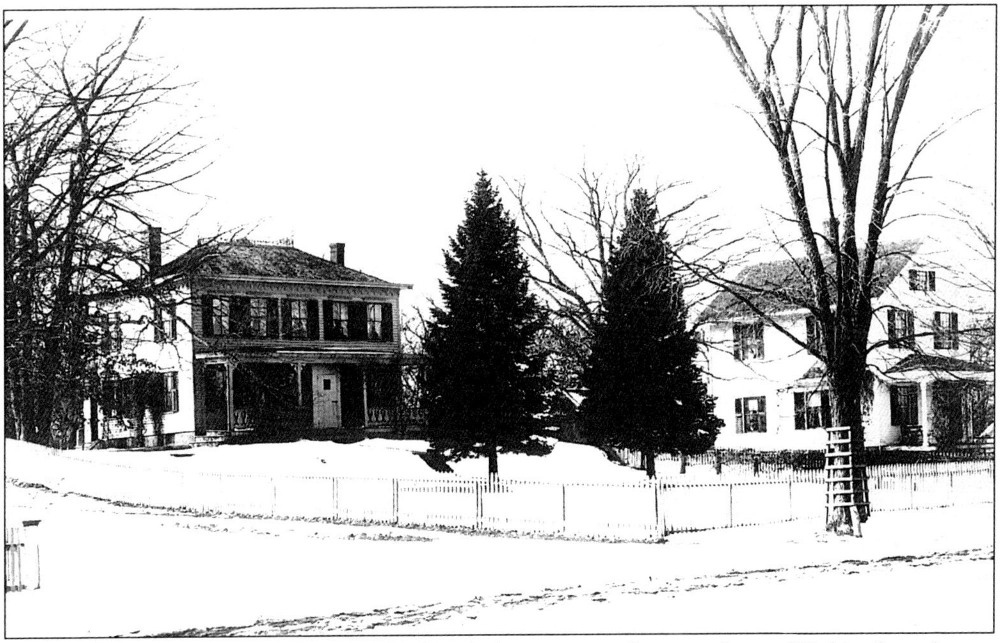

A mill superintendent's house on Railroad Avenue can be seen here. Within less than a block, mill operatives led a much simpler lifestyle in company housing. (Courtesy of Anthony Guarriello Jr.)

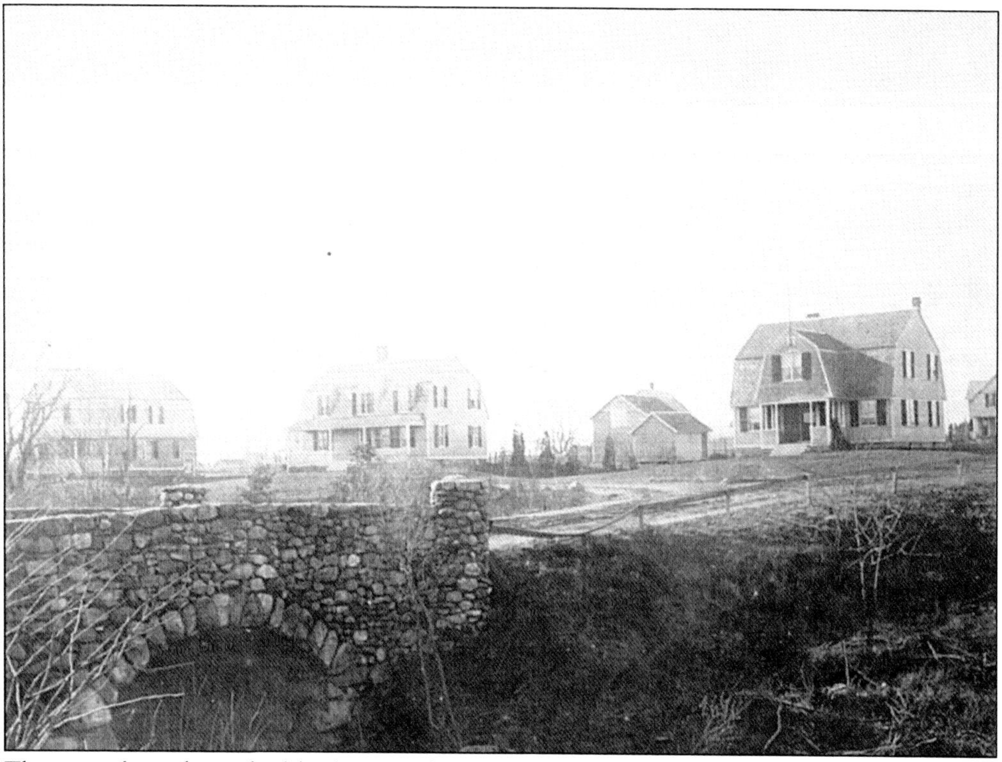

This view from the arched bridge on Church Street shows houses on Indian Run. Few trees obstructed the view. (Courtesy of Anthony Guarriello Jr.)

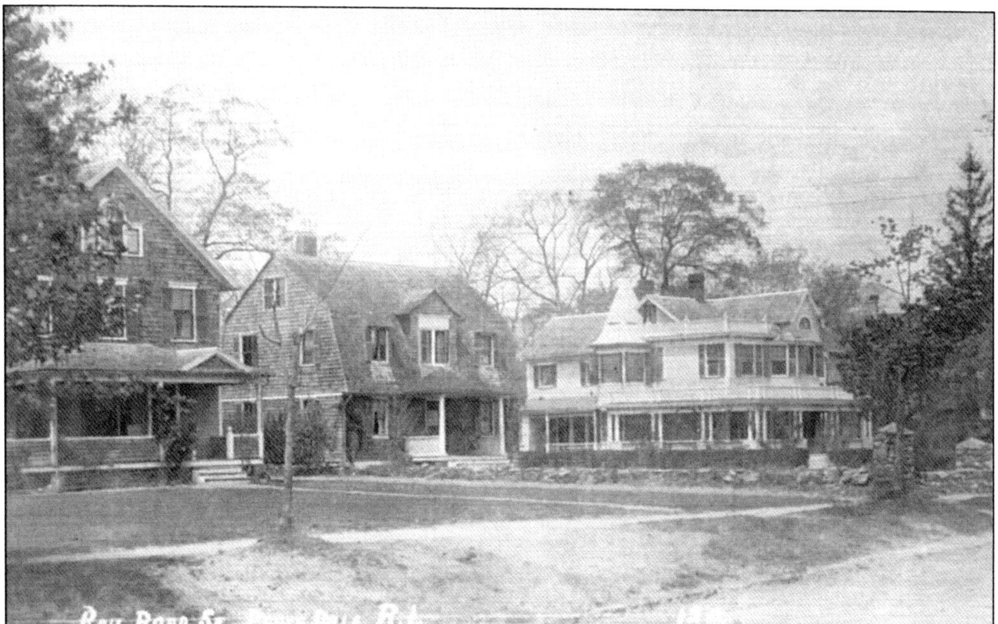

This is another view of Railroad Avenue. Set back from the road, these houses had the size and style that were appealing to more prominent members of the community. (Courtesy of Everett Hopkins.)

Five

Peace Dale Flats

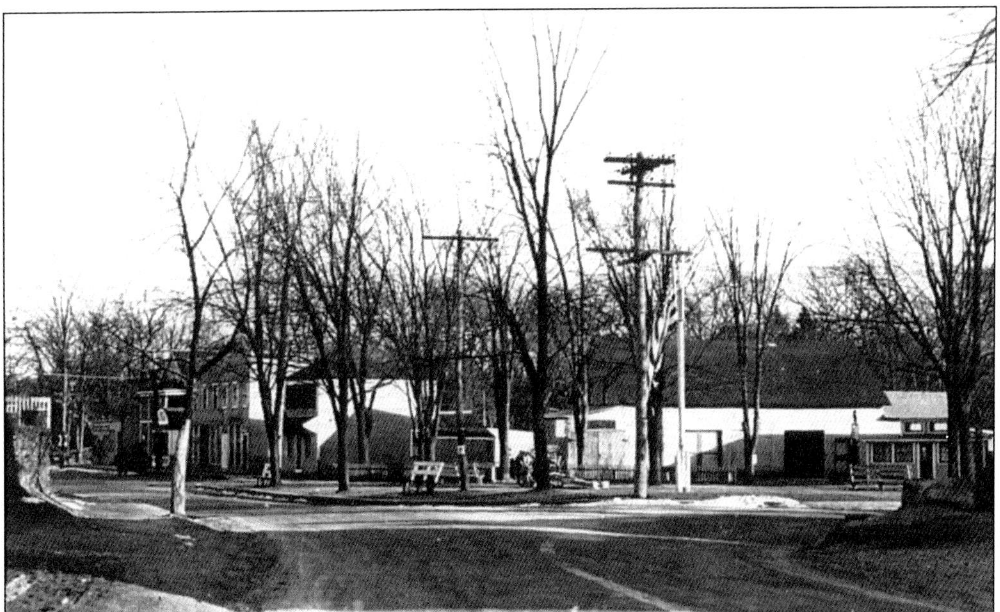

This early view—probably from about 1908—of Peace Dale Flats, or Fisk's Flat, shows a treeless landscape. A thriving commercial center that rivaled Wakefield, the Flats, at one time, featured an opera house where dances were held and movies shown; stores selling furniture, dry goods, and groceries; and restaurants. (Courtesy of Donald and Shirley Southwick.)

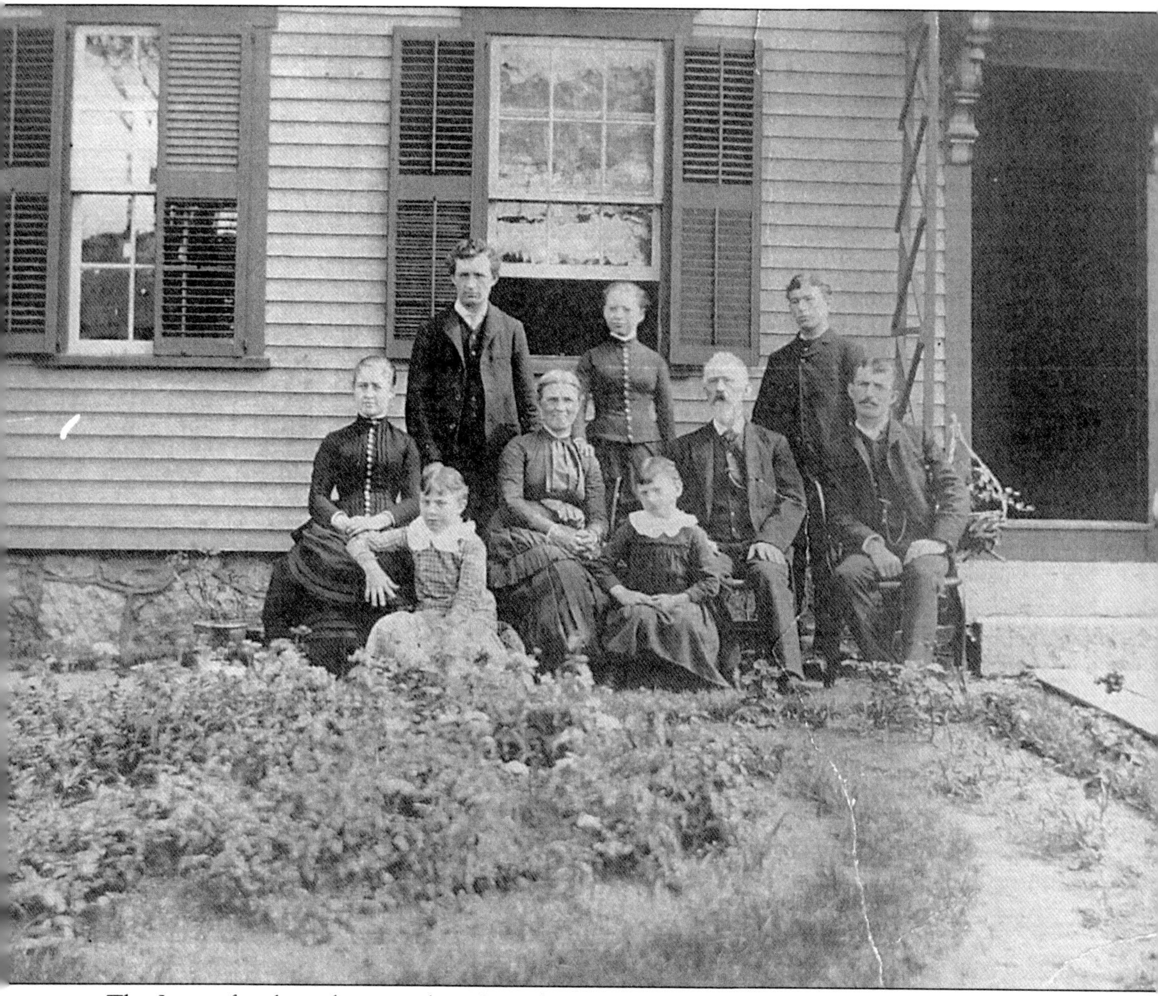

The Lyons family gathers on their front lawn in about 1886. The Lyons were among a wave of Irish immigrants who came to Peace Dale during and after the Irish potato famine of 1848. Patrick Lyons's store, "Est. P. Lyons," was located where the Wakeco Service Center is now, and the house is across the street. Patrick came from County Clare, and his wife, Julia, came from Kilkenney. Shown here are, from left to right, as follows: (front row) Alice Lyons and Nellie Lyons, though which is which is uncertain; (middle row) Julia Theresa Lyons (1870–1929), Julia Houghney Lyons (1843–1887), Patrick Lyons (1837–1908), and William J. Lyons (1865–1921); (back row) P. Joseph Lyons (1866–1935), Mary Lyons (1872–1930), and Edmund Lyons (1869–1937), who ran his father's store and was active in community affairs. (Courtesy of Fred Lyons and Janice Lyons Staruch.)

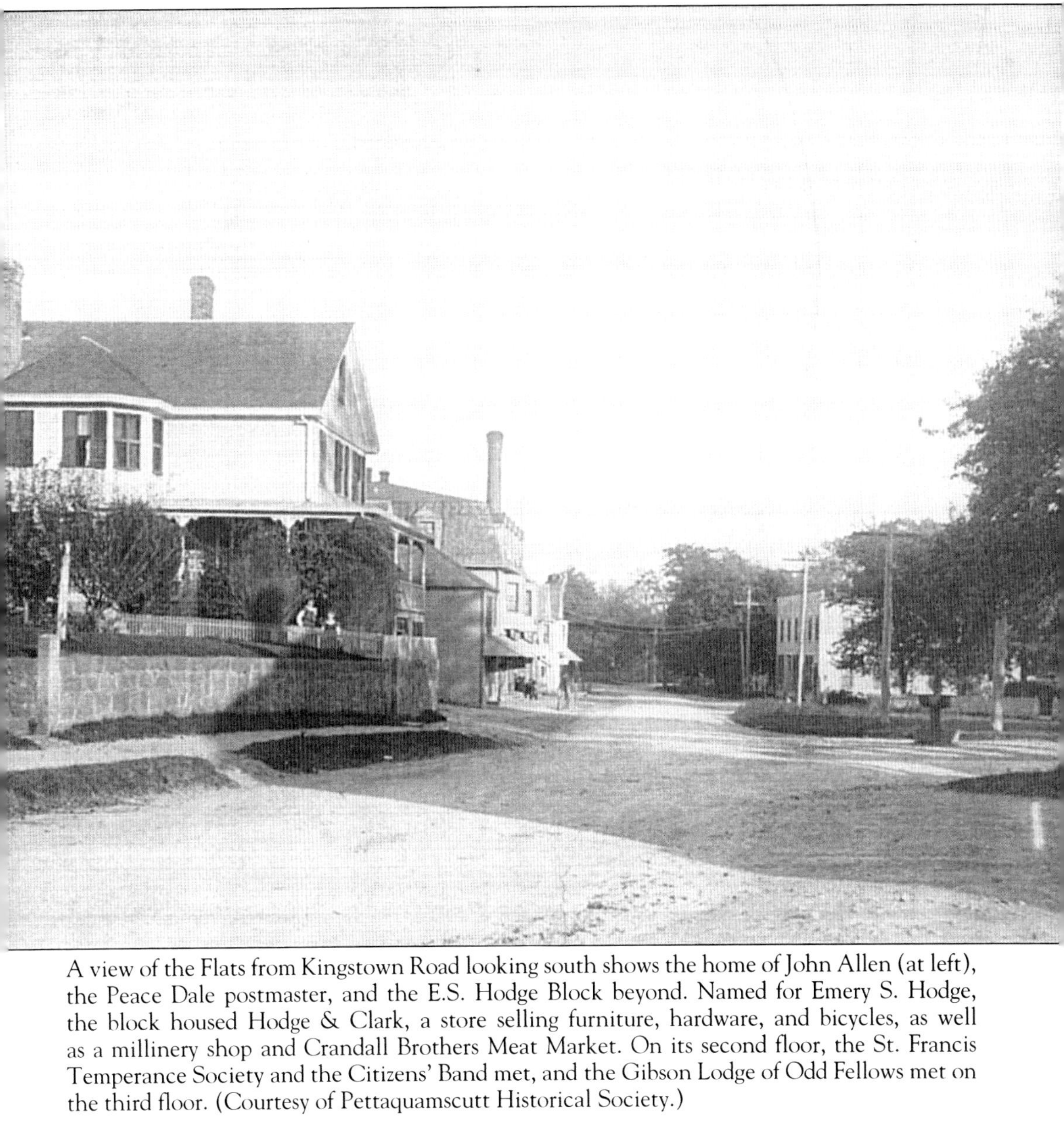

A view of the Flats from Kingstown Road looking south shows the home of John Allen (at left), the Peace Dale postmaster, and the E.S. Hodge Block beyond. Named for Emery S. Hodge, the block housed Hodge & Clark, a store selling furniture, hardware, and bicycles, as well as a millinery shop and Crandall Brothers Meat Market. On its second floor, the St. Francis Temperance Society and the Citizens' Band met, and the Gibson Lodge of Odd Fellows met on the third floor. (Courtesy of Pettaquamscutt Historical Society.)

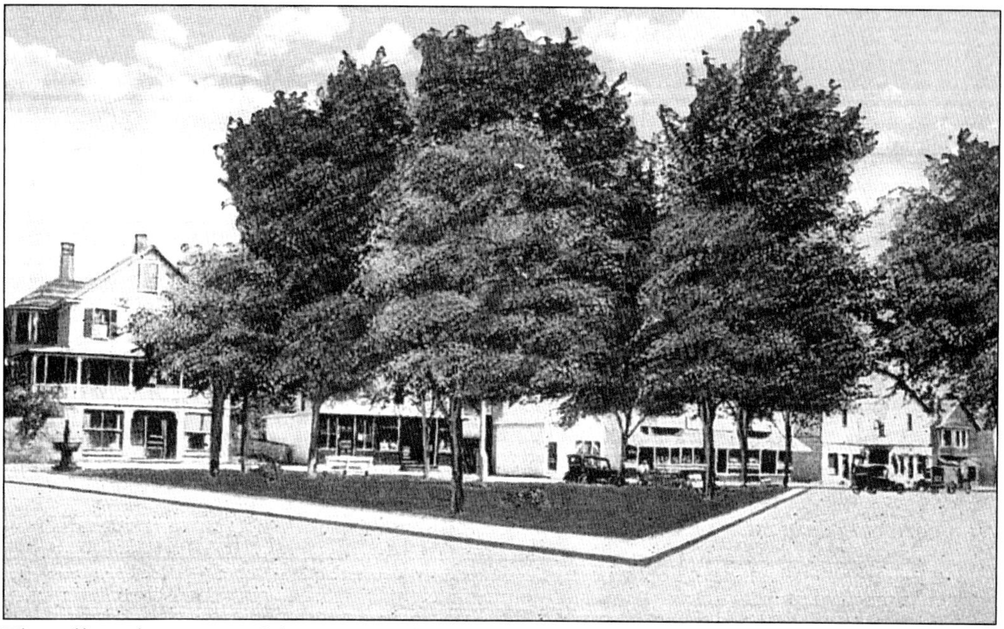

This offers a later view of the rotary at the Flats from a postcard postmarked 1935. Between the turn of the century (at the chapter's start) and this photograph, trees have grown to ring the traffic circle. Note the water fountain at the left. (Courtesy of Shirley and Donald Southwick.)

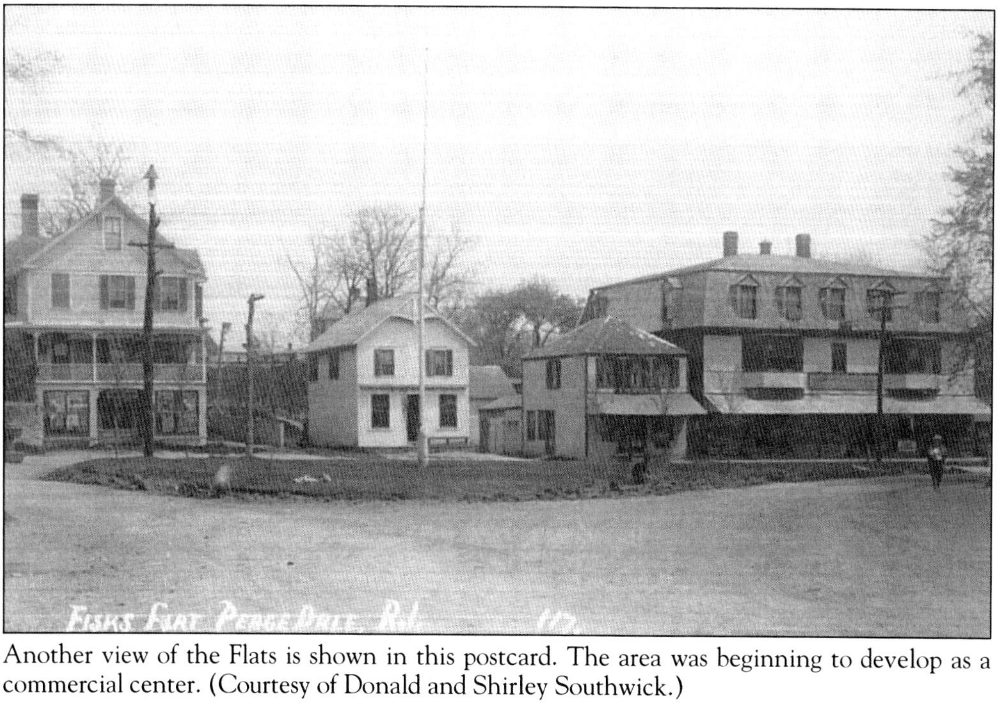

Another view of the Flats is shown in this postcard. The area was beginning to develop as a commercial center. (Courtesy of Donald and Shirley Southwick.)

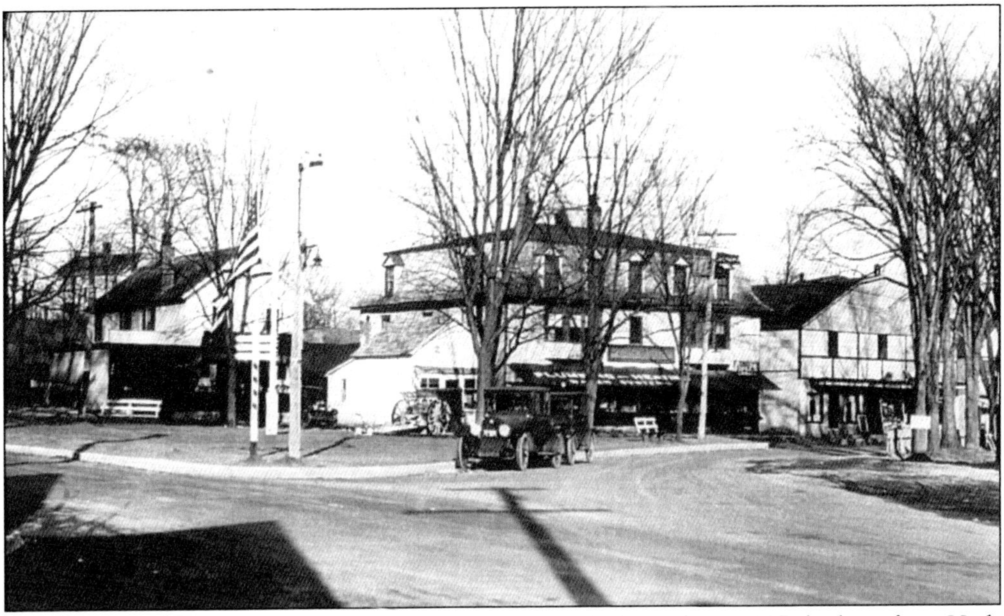

This is a view of the rotary at Peace Dale Flats, probably from about 1927, looking from High Street. The Peace Dale Opera House can be seen in the distance. Frank J. Fagan built the establishment, variously called "Fagan's Opera House" and the "Peace Dale Theatre," in 1921 using lumber from an abandoned mill at Mooresfield. Frank's uncle, Daniel Fagan, supervised the construction. The opera house was the site of community dances, matinees, fairs, and South Kingstown basketball games. It closed in the early 1950s and was razed about a decade later. (Courtesy of Gary Dinonsie.)

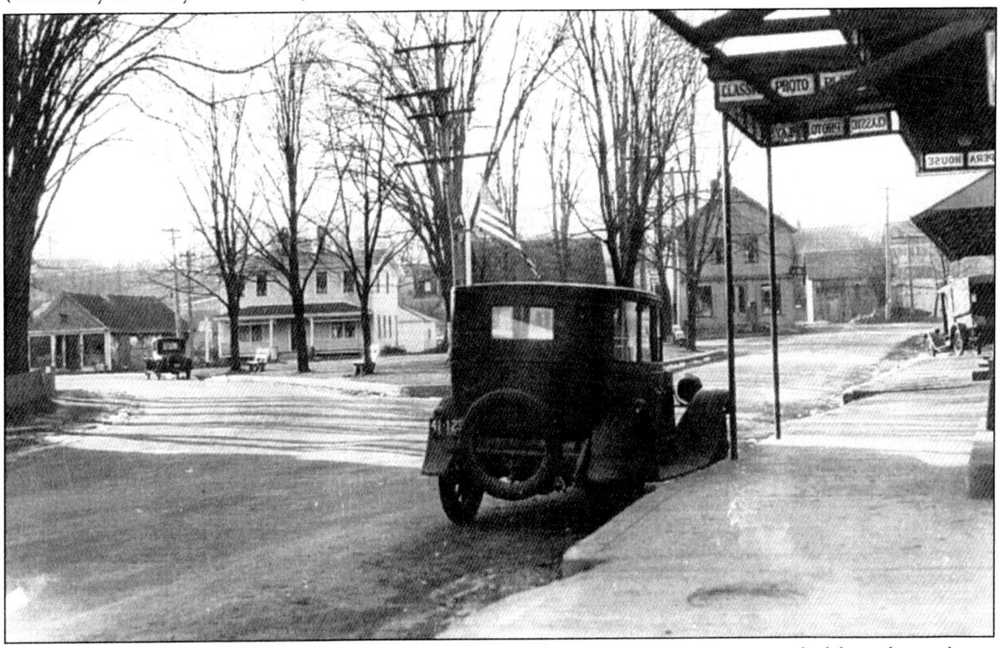

This view of the Flats from Kingstown Road looking northwest was probably taken about 1927. Patsy Dinonsie's dry goods store can be seen at the extreme left corner. (Courtesy of Gary Dinonsie.)

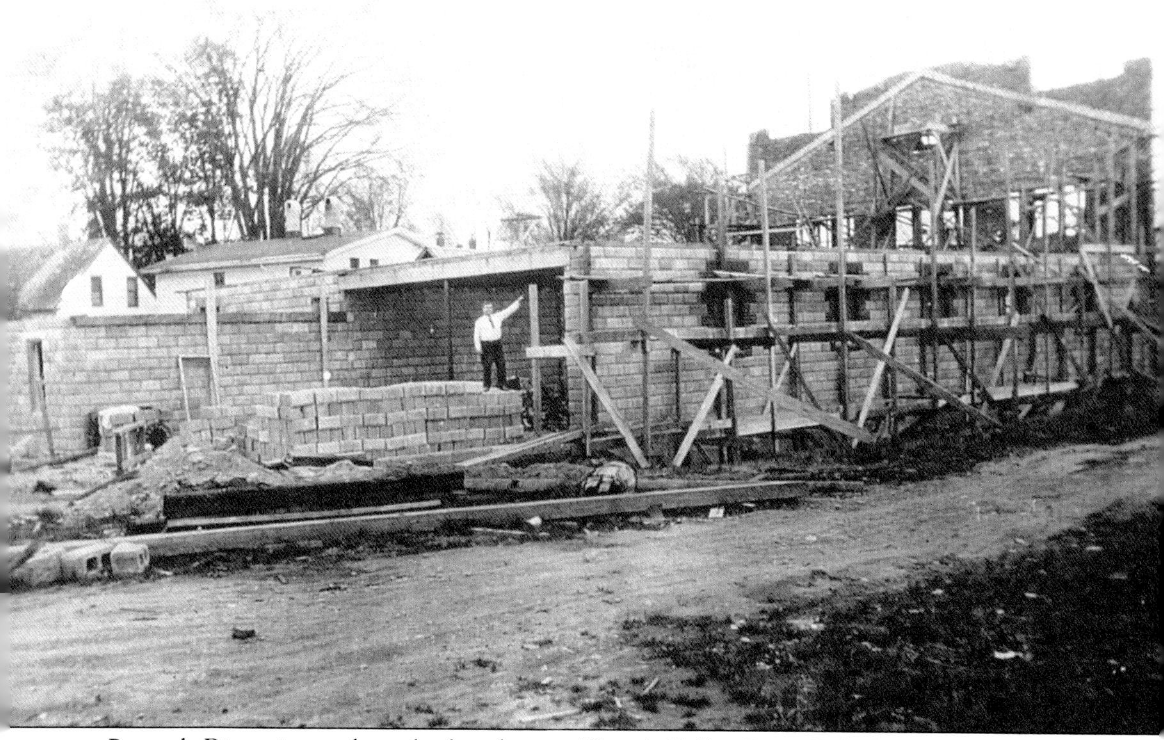

Pasquale Dinonsie stands on the foundation of Patsy's Hall in Peace Dale during its construction in 1929. Dinonsie, who came from Italy in 1906, epitomized the successful immigrant, opening a dry goods store where Patsy's Liquors is now. (Courtesy of Gary Dinonsie.)

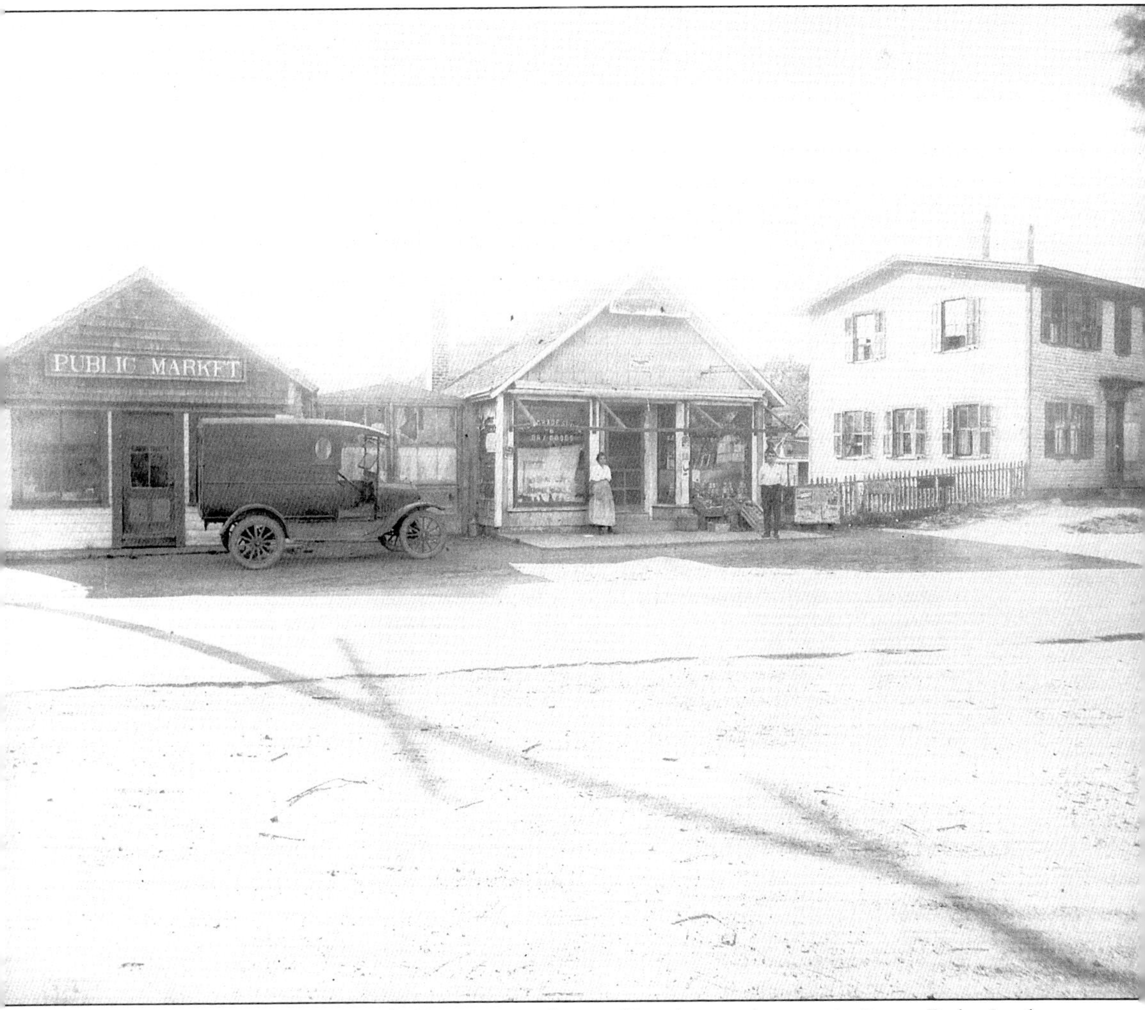

This 1918 photo shows Pasquale Dinonsie in front of his dry goods store in Peace Dale. In the 1915 street directory, his advertisement detailed "Remnants of all kinds, confectionary, cigars, tobacco, etc." Next door is the Public Market, which, in 1915, was operated by Henry T. Allen. (Courtesy of Gary Dinonsie.)

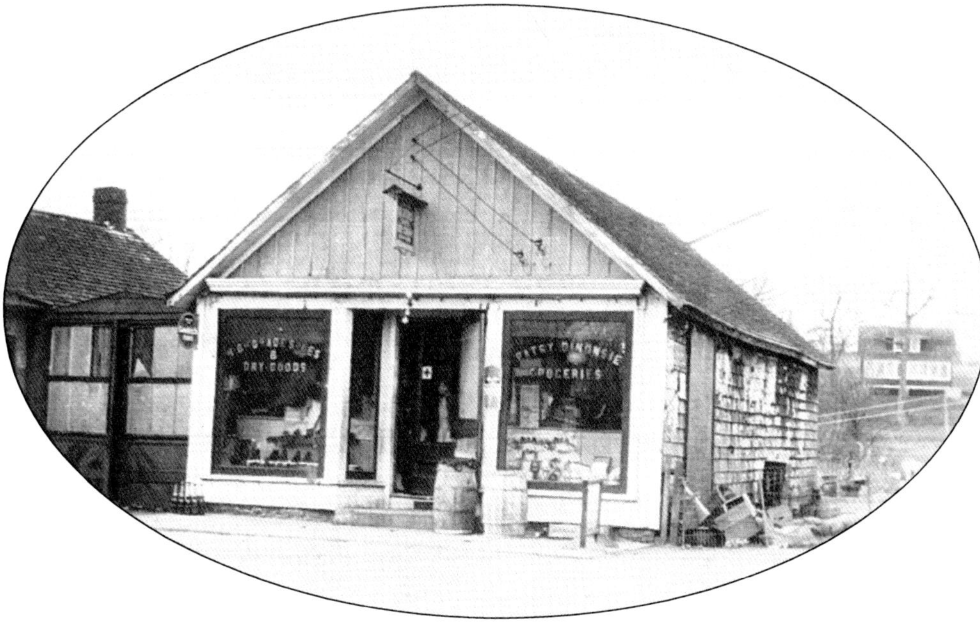

Pasquale "Patsy" Dinonsie sold "high grade shoes," dry goods, and groceries from this store on High Street in the 1930s. Note the barrels out front and what appear to be soft drink bottles at the building's left corner. (Courtesy of Gary Dinonsie.)

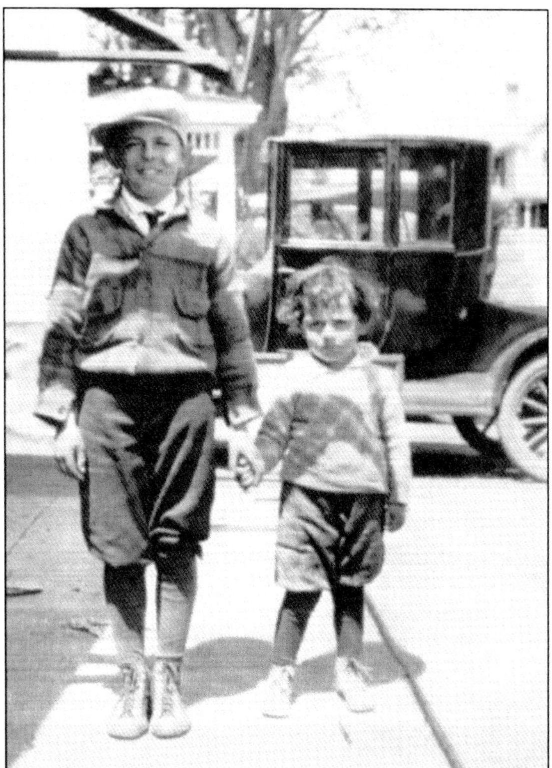

Gary Dinonsie's father, John Dinonsie (left), and John's brother Pat can be seen outside Patsy's store, probably in the late 1920s. Both are sons of Pasquale Dinonsie, who came from Italy in 1906 to build a thriving business in Peace Dale. (Courtesy of Gary Dinonsie.)

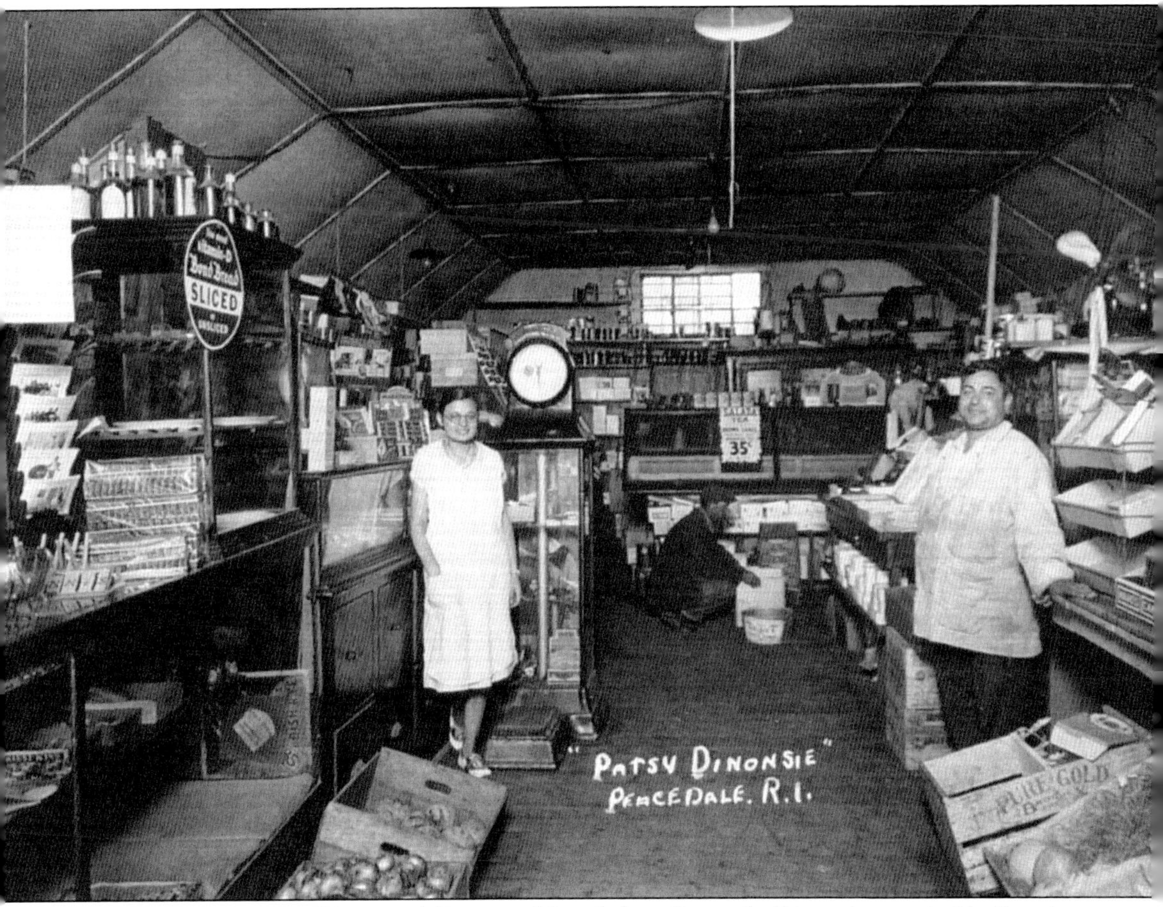

In this picture, Grace (Dinonsie) Pesta and her father, Pasquale Dinonsie, are inside Patsy's Dry Goods in October 1931. The gentleman in the rear center is unidentified. Bond Bread and Salada tea are among the brands advertised inside. (Courtesy of Gary Dinonsie.)

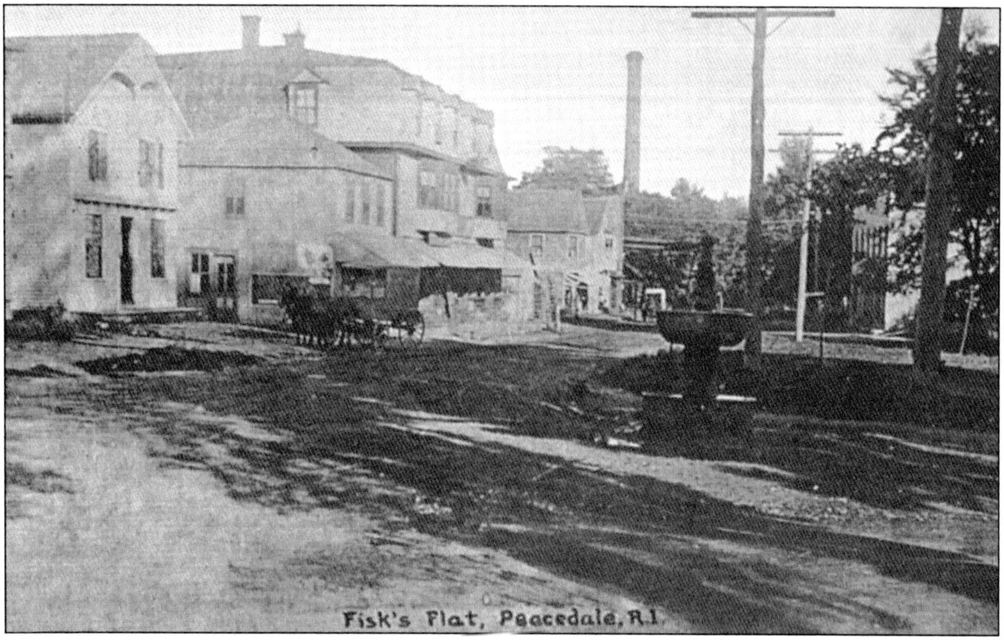

This early view of Peace Dale Flats appears to be before the flat-iron building was constructed in 1899. In the background, the mill's stack, the true center of village life, rises above everything. (Courtesy of Donald and Shirley Southwick.)

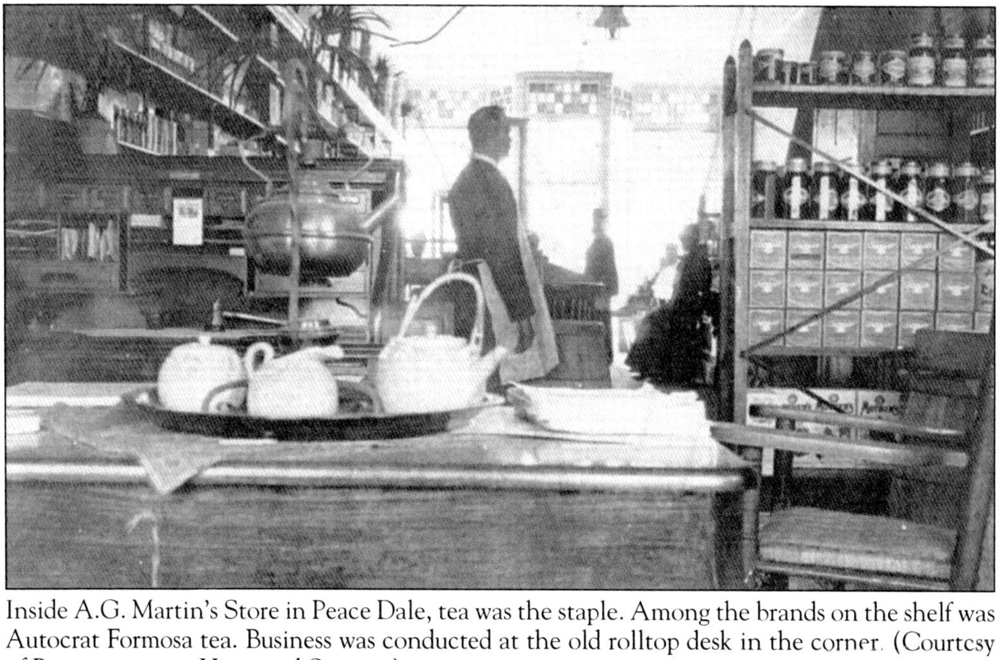

Inside A.G. Martin's Store in Peace Dale, tea was the staple. Among the brands on the shelf was Autocrat Formosa tea. Business was conducted at the old rolltop desk in the corner. (Courtesy of Pettaquamscutt Historical Society.)

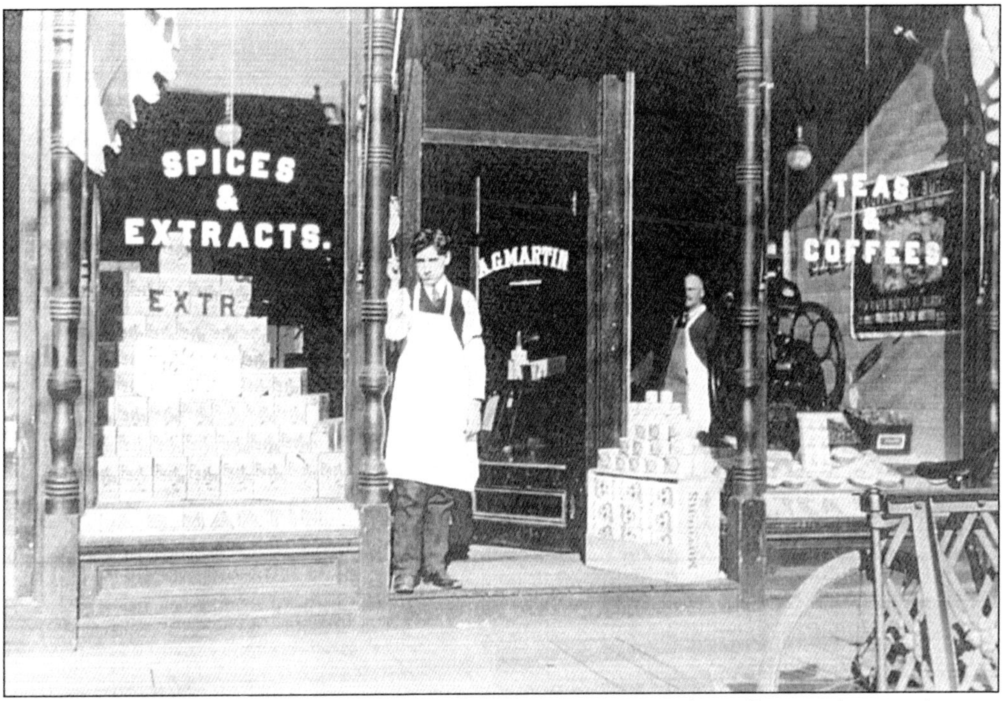

A worker stands outside A.G. Martin's Store in Peace Dale. Note the coffee-grinding machine in the window. The store appears to have been located next door to a dentist's office, but little else is known about this photo, which was taken by George Crandall. (Courtesy of Pettaquamscutt Historical Society.)

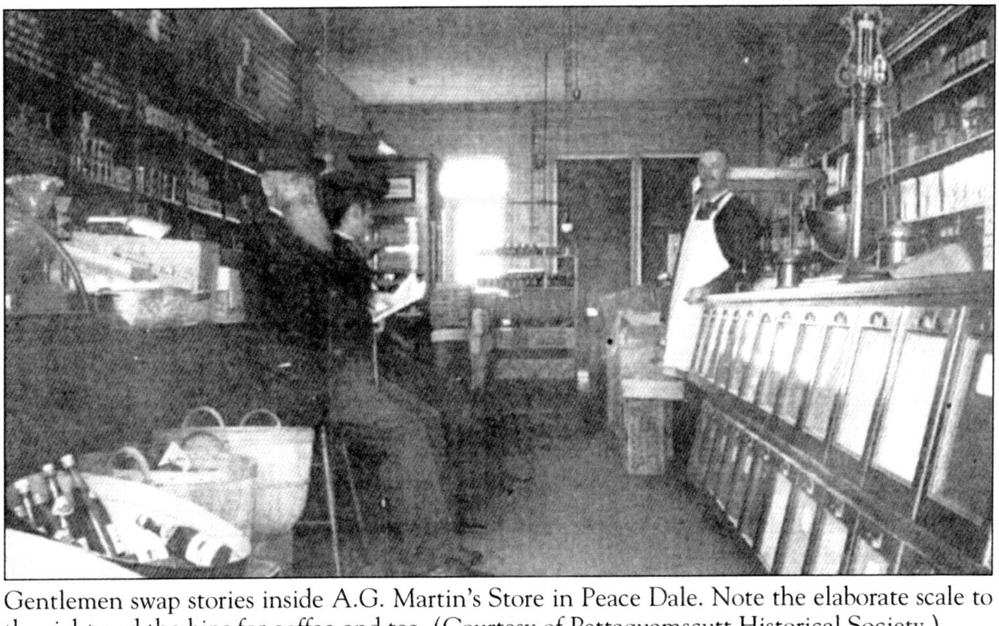

Gentlemen swap stories inside A.G. Martin's Store in Peace Dale. Note the elaborate scale to the right and the bins for coffee and tea. (Courtesy of Pettaquamscutt Historical Society.)

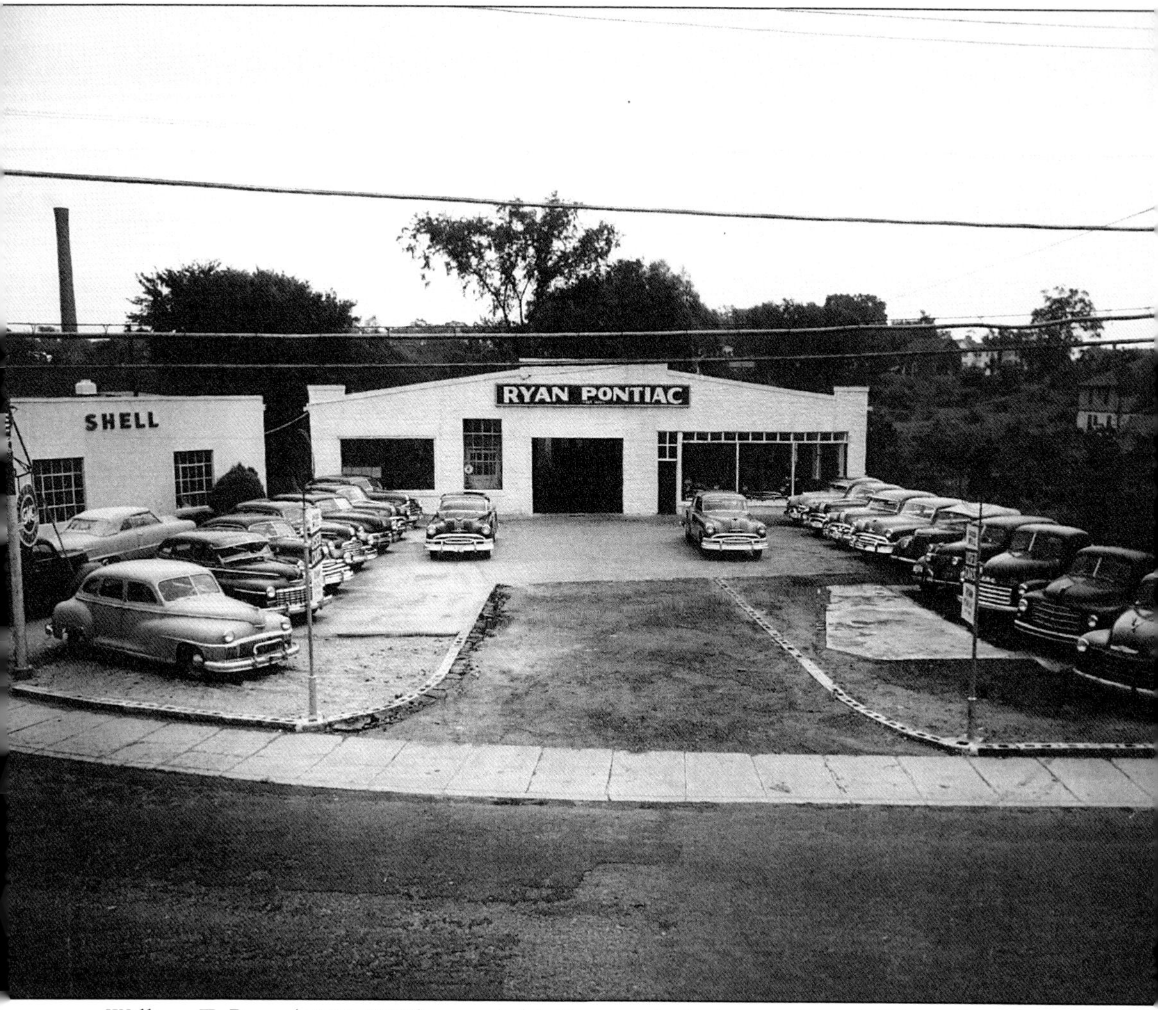

William T. Ryan (1896–1973) started this Pontiac dealership in about 1924 at what was then 203 High Street. The Hazard family, for whom he had worked as a chauffeur, loaned him the money to start his business, according to his son Robert. He started out repairing cars and eventually sold Pontiacs, GMC trucks, and used vehicles. This photograph was taken in 1954. In 1960, Ryan advertised "Pontiac-British Vauxhall-GMC trucks" and "Good Will Used Cars." Today the building, located at 519 High Street, is owned by Scuncio Motors Inc. and is operated by Ronnie's Towing and Auto Repair. (Courtesy of Robert Ryan.)

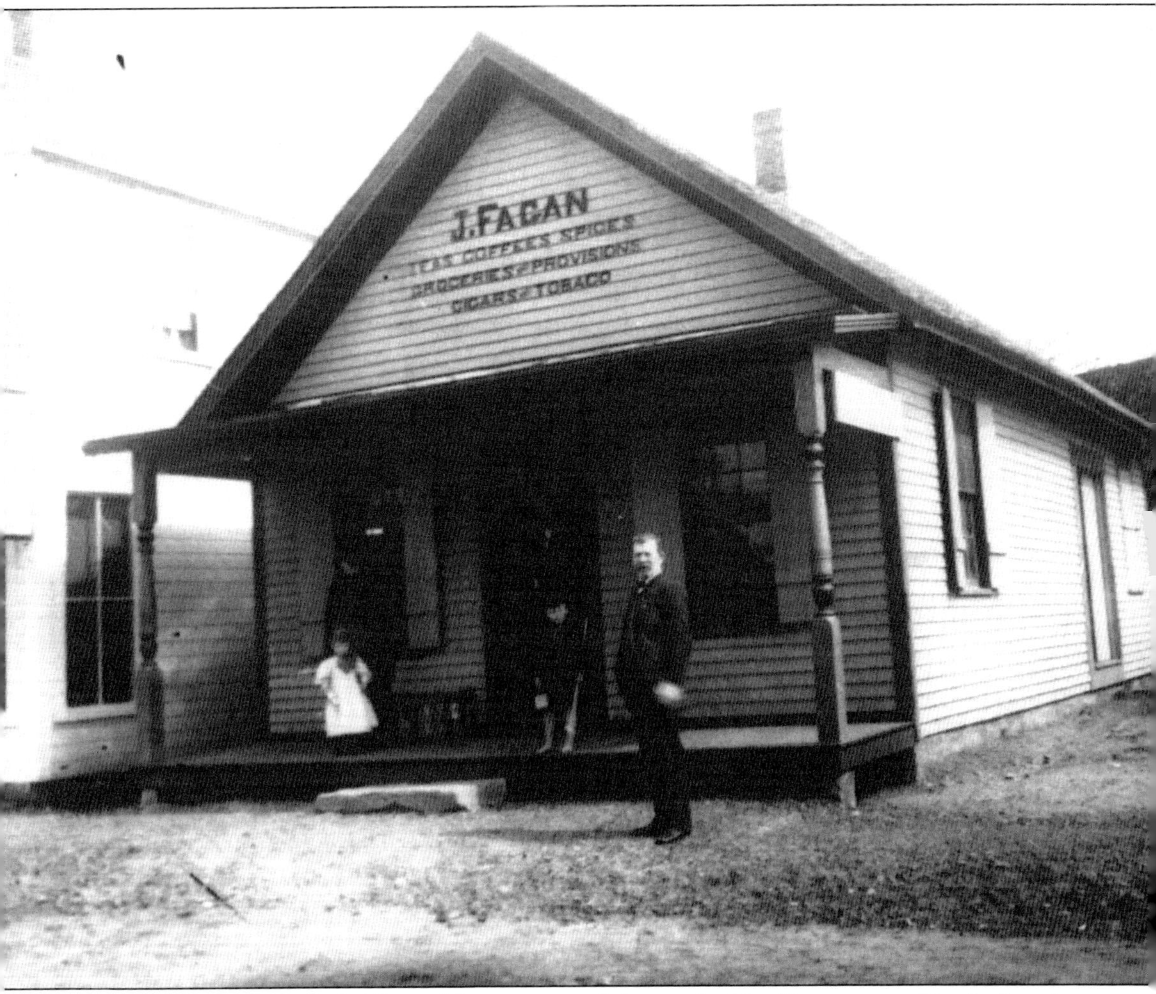

Fagan's Store on Peace Dale Flats sold groceries and dry goods. The Narragansett Pier Railroad passed on this hill behind the store. (Courtesy of David Gates.)

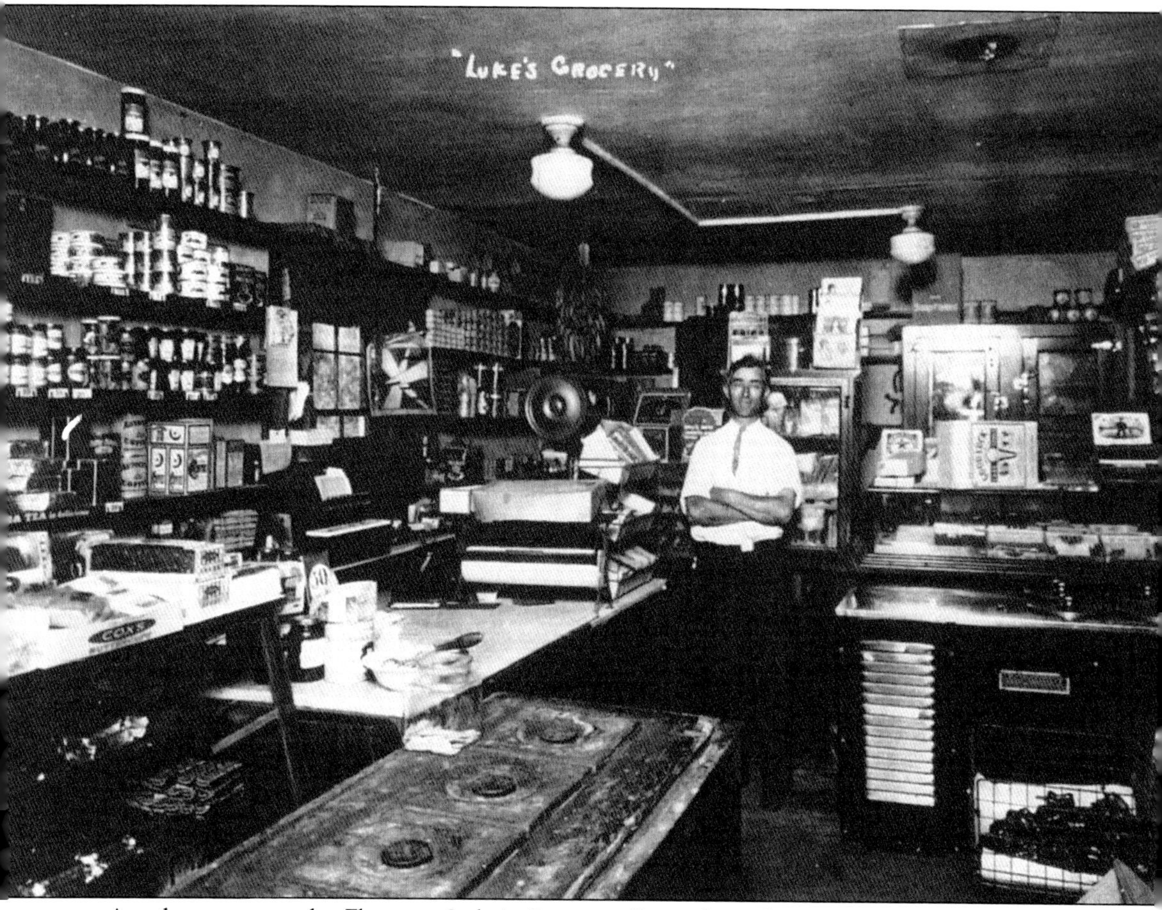

Another store on the Flats was Luke's Grocery. Canned goods, penny candy, and ice cream were among the goods sold here. (Courtesy of John and Marie Champion.)

Six

VILLAGE LIFE

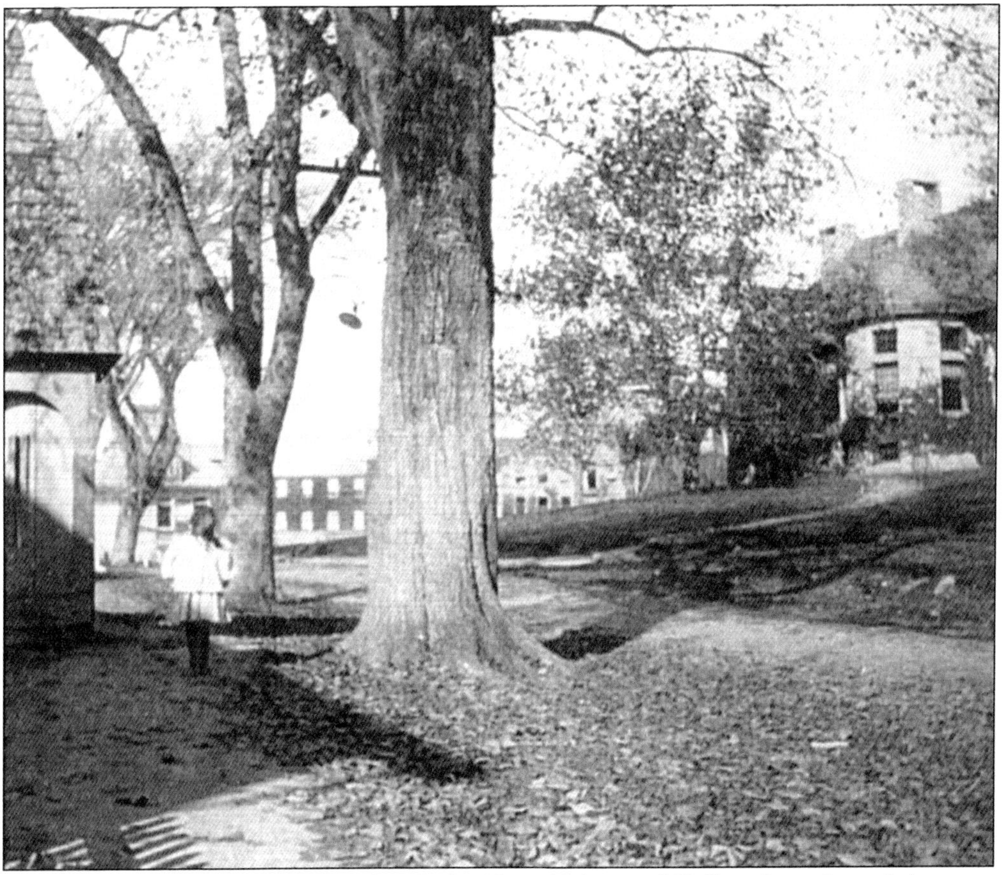

A girl walks down Kingstown Road with the Hazard Memorial Hall to the right and the town pump on the left. Called East Road in the early 1900s, this street winds through Peace Dale like a spool of thread unwound by a kitten. The village's history takes similar twists and turns. (Courtesy of Peace Dale Library.)

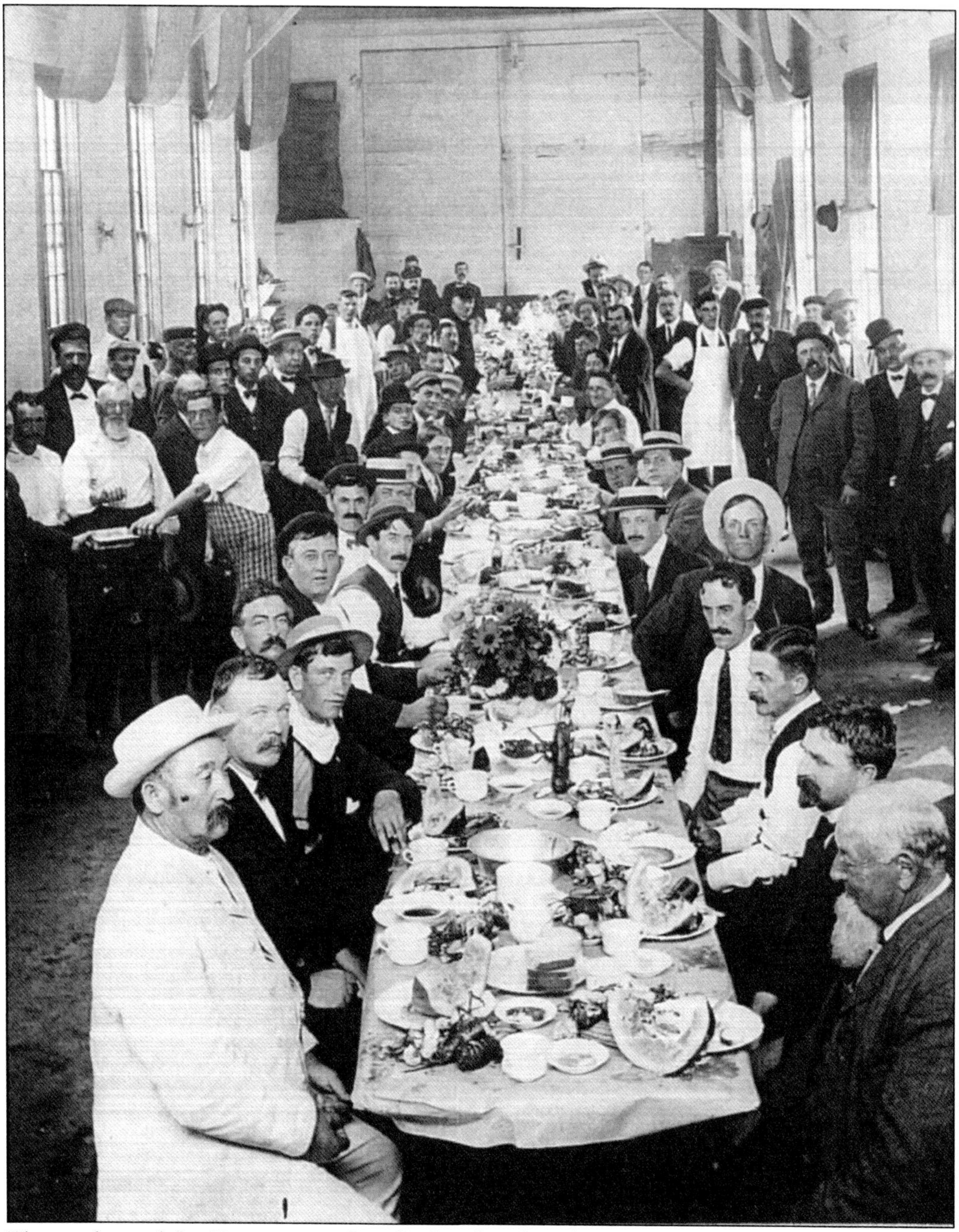

The workers of the Narragansett Pier Railroad gathered in September 1906 for their annual clambake in the large paint shop across from the Peace Dale Train Station on Railroad Avenue. A special table had been built for the occasion to seat more than 100 railroad workers and their guests. The *Narragansett Times* reported that they dined on chowder, clams, bluefish, lobsters, sweet potatoes, brown bread, white bread, coffee, and watermelon, with cigars after dinner. W.A. Brown made the chowder, Elisha Gardiner supervised the clams' preparation, and "Photographer Rowsell secured some good pictures of the party while at dinner," *The Times* related in its October 5 issue. "Altogether it was the best time the railroad men have held for 20 years and the largest numbers present." (Courtesy of Pettaquamscutt Historical Society.)

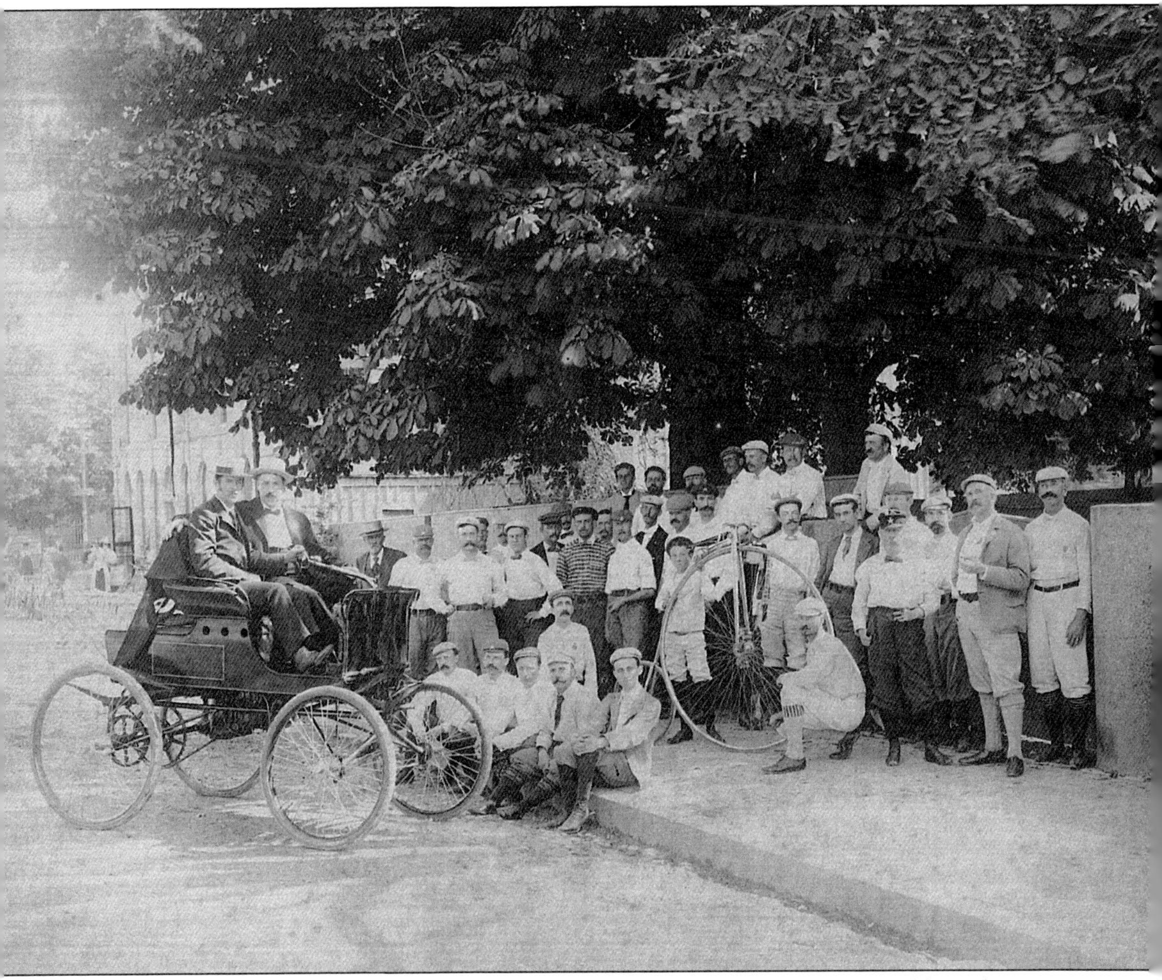

This photograph, inscribed with an 1894 date, may show bicyclist R.B. Grubbs, who, on September 5, 1894, stopped in the village during a 1,400-mile trip through the Northeastern states from Washington, D.C. A clerk in the department of agriculture, Grubbs set a grueling pace on his Victor bicycle, making Philadelphia from D.C. in 14.5 hours. "He found the roads from Westerly to Cross' Mills horrid, but with those in this town he had no fault to find," reported the *Narragansett Times*. He left the *Times* office hoping to reach Fall River by 11 o'clock that evening. (Courtesy of Pettaquamscutt Historical Society.)

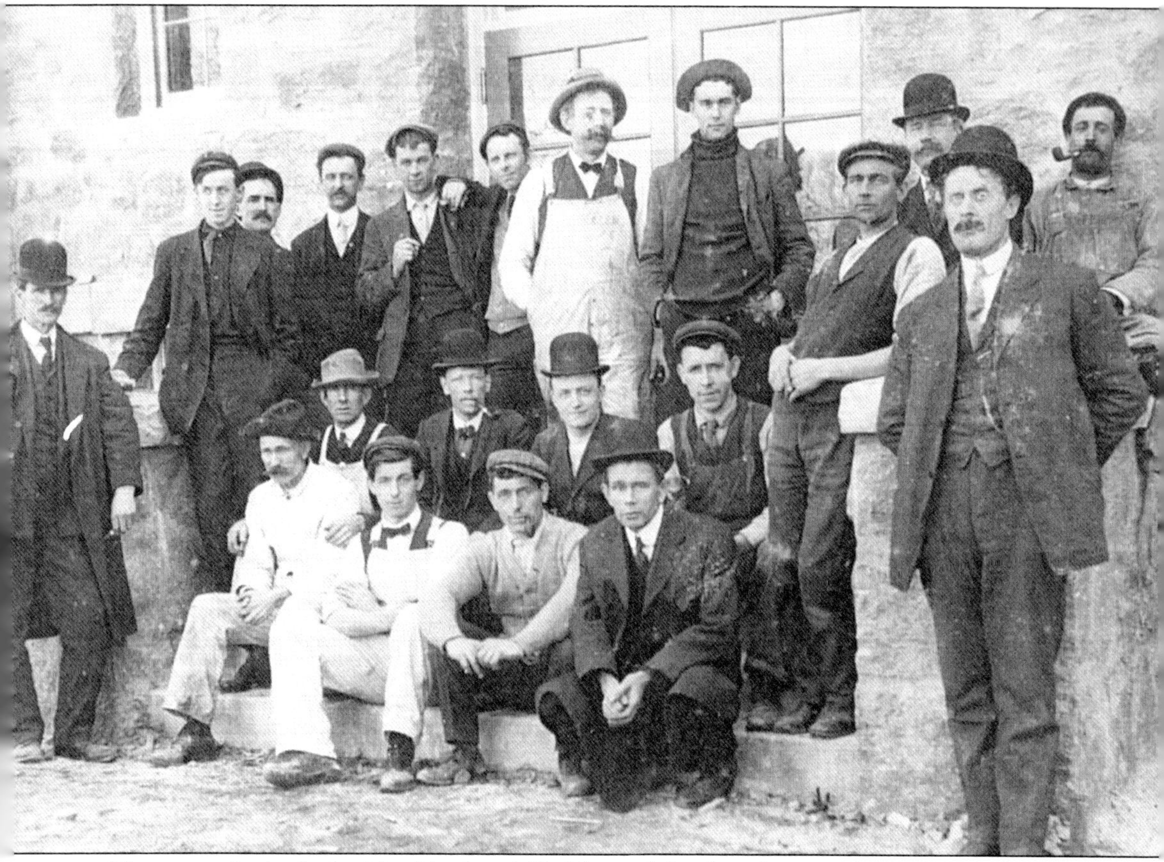

The men who built the Neighborhood Guild posed for this photograph some time during the 1908–09 construction. The contractor was Woodbury and Leighton of Boston, and the building was designed by R. Clipston Sturges, also of Boston. Of split stone with wide bands of mortar, the Guild was designed to be a centerpiece of village life, with baths and showers for men and women, a laundry "for any of the village people who may prefer to do their home laundrying there," a dining room for female mill workers to spend the noon hour, and a large cooking room, the *Narragansett Times* reported. The building also was designed with the domestic science and manual training classrooms that were the Guild's primary function. Guild workers were given living accommodations on the second floor, which contained seven large bedrooms, a dining room, a large dressing room, a sitting room, and a butler's pantry, as well as separate apartments for the janitor and his family. "The building cannot fail to be not only an ornament to the village, a suitable memorial to Mr. [John Newbold] Hazard and a monument as well to the generous impulses of those who have planned for something of use for the whole community, besides being a boon to Miss Trowbridge and her efficient corps of Guild workers," the *Narragansett Times* predicted in 1908. (Courtesy of Pettaquamscutt Historical Society.)

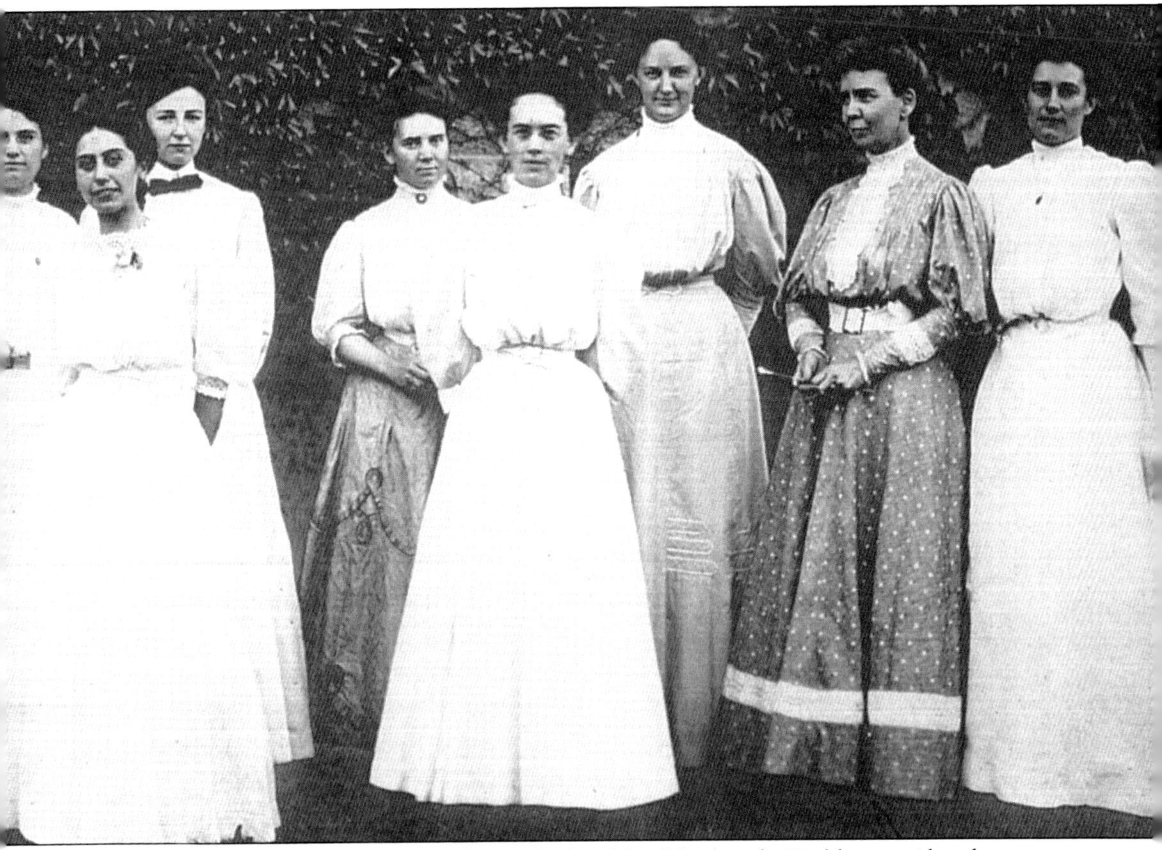

These women lived on the top floor of the Neighborhood Guild, considered proper accommodations for working women who had no husbands to support them. They were, from left to right, as follows: (front row) Miss Anna Darby, a teacher who later became Mrs. Bushnell; Miss Lottie Trowbridge, sewing teacher at the Guild; Miss Edith Carpenter, secretary to Rowland Gibson Hazard; Miss Rose Sherman, librarian at Peace Dale Library; Miss Elizabeth E. Trowbridge, director of domestic science at the Guild and later a domestic science teacher at the high school; and Miss Marion Lenore Flint, a Latin and French teacher at South Kingstown High School who left in 1910 to study in Europe; (back row) Miss Cummings, the village nurse; and an unidentified Peace Dale Grammar School teacher. (Courtesy of Pettaquamscutt Historical Society.)

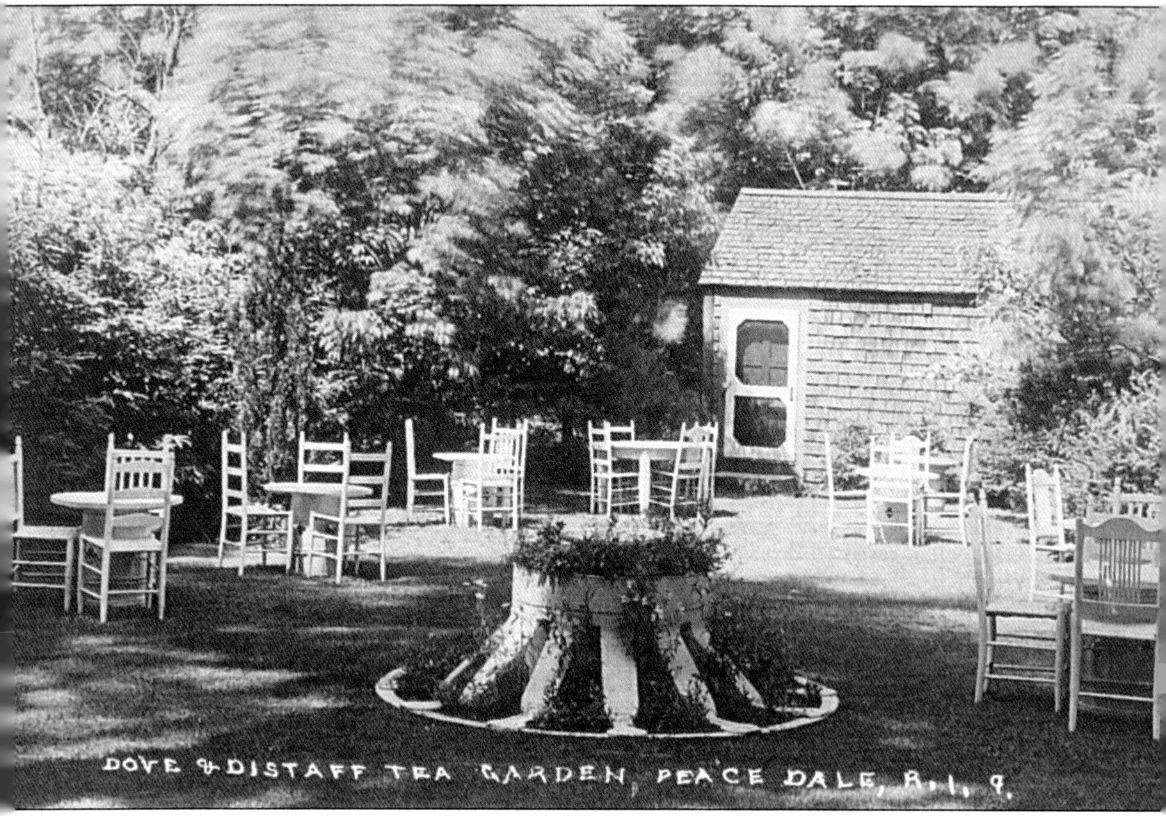

The Dove & Distaff was a craft guild and tea room that Dotha Bushnell, sister of Mrs. Rowland G. Hazard, and Minnie Merrill, Mrs. Hazard's sister-in-law, opened in 1913 at what is now the Gates Insurance Agency on Columbia Street. The tea room was run by Margaret and Adelaide Watson, who made $1,200 for the village women who had brought fare to be sold. First located in two rooms at the Neighborhood Guild, Dove & Distaff relocated to an unused wool storage room across the street, where the ladies put the best feminine touch possible on their surroundings. Wooden barrels from the mill became tables, for instance, and the flower arrangement above was, in fact, an old mill wheel. Oliver Stedman, in his account, recalls affluent women from Narragansett Pier arriving in chauffeured cars to have tea and fancy cakes. Started partly as a way to appease the Hazards' restless workforce, the cooperative featured women's crafts. A brochure from the time mentions linens, baskets, rugs, sweaters, old glass and china, and La Luz pottery, as well as homemade cakes, rolls and jellies, special luncheons, and children's and picnic lunches to order. The Depression spelled the end of the business, which continued in private homes before its demise in 1941. Caleb Davis used the name for his furniture restoration business, taking the name with him when he moved to Wakefield. (Courtesy of Donald and Shirley Southwick.)

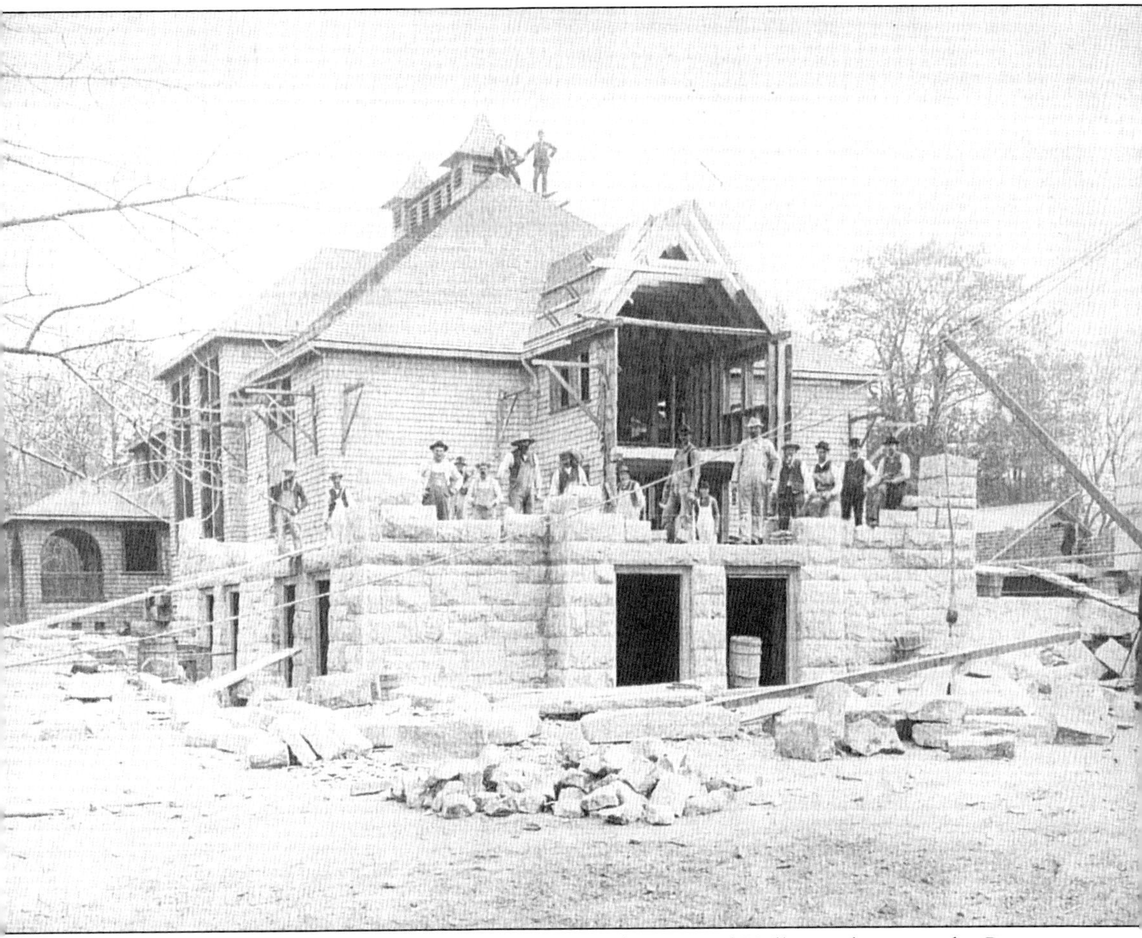

Stone masons pose with their handiwork at the Hazard Memorial Hall, now home to the Peace Dale branch of the South Kingstown Public Library. Dedicated in 1891, the building was the work of local men. Kneeland Partelow supervised the stonework, and Louis F. Bell was in charge of the carpenters. F.W. Angell was the architect. The Hazards almost exclusively used local workmen on their many building projects. (Courtesy of Pettaquamscutt Historical Society.)

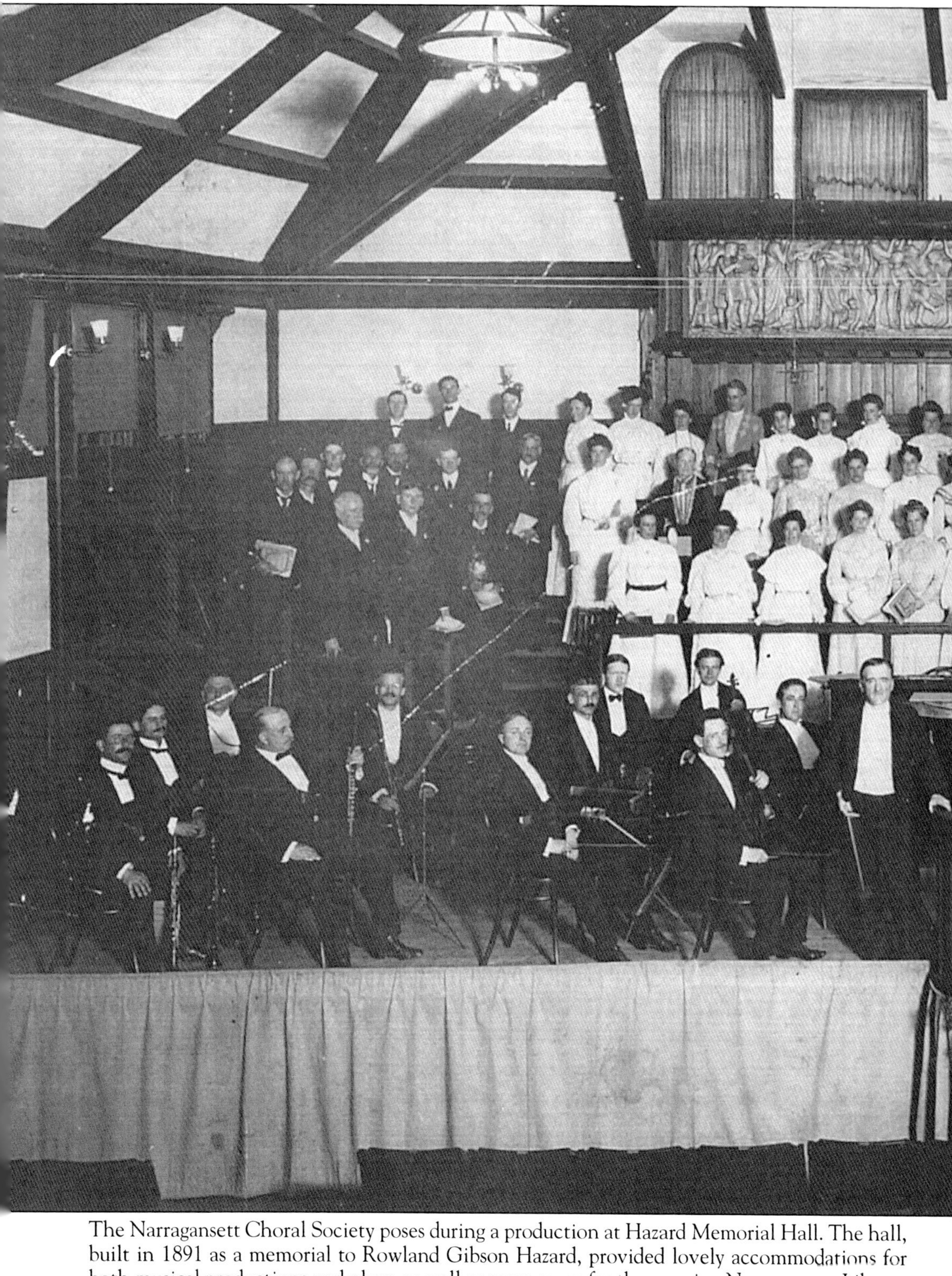

The Narragansett Choral Society poses during a production at Hazard Memorial Hall. The hall, built in 1891 as a memorial to Rowland Gibson Hazard, provided lovely accommodations for both musical productions and plays, as well as more room for the growing Narragansett Library

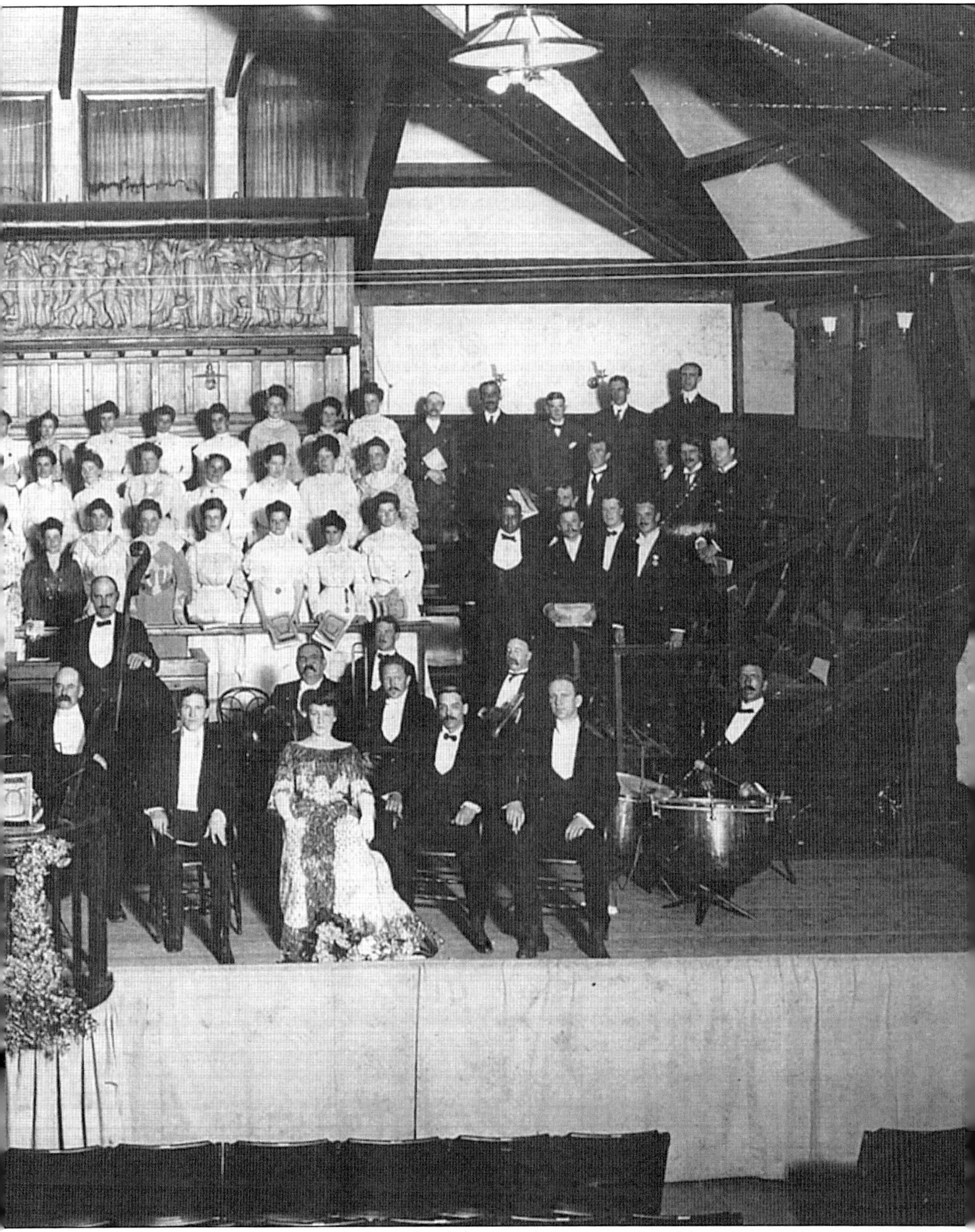

Association, now the Peace Dale branch of the South Kingstown Public Library. (Courtesy of Pettaquamscutt Historical Society.)

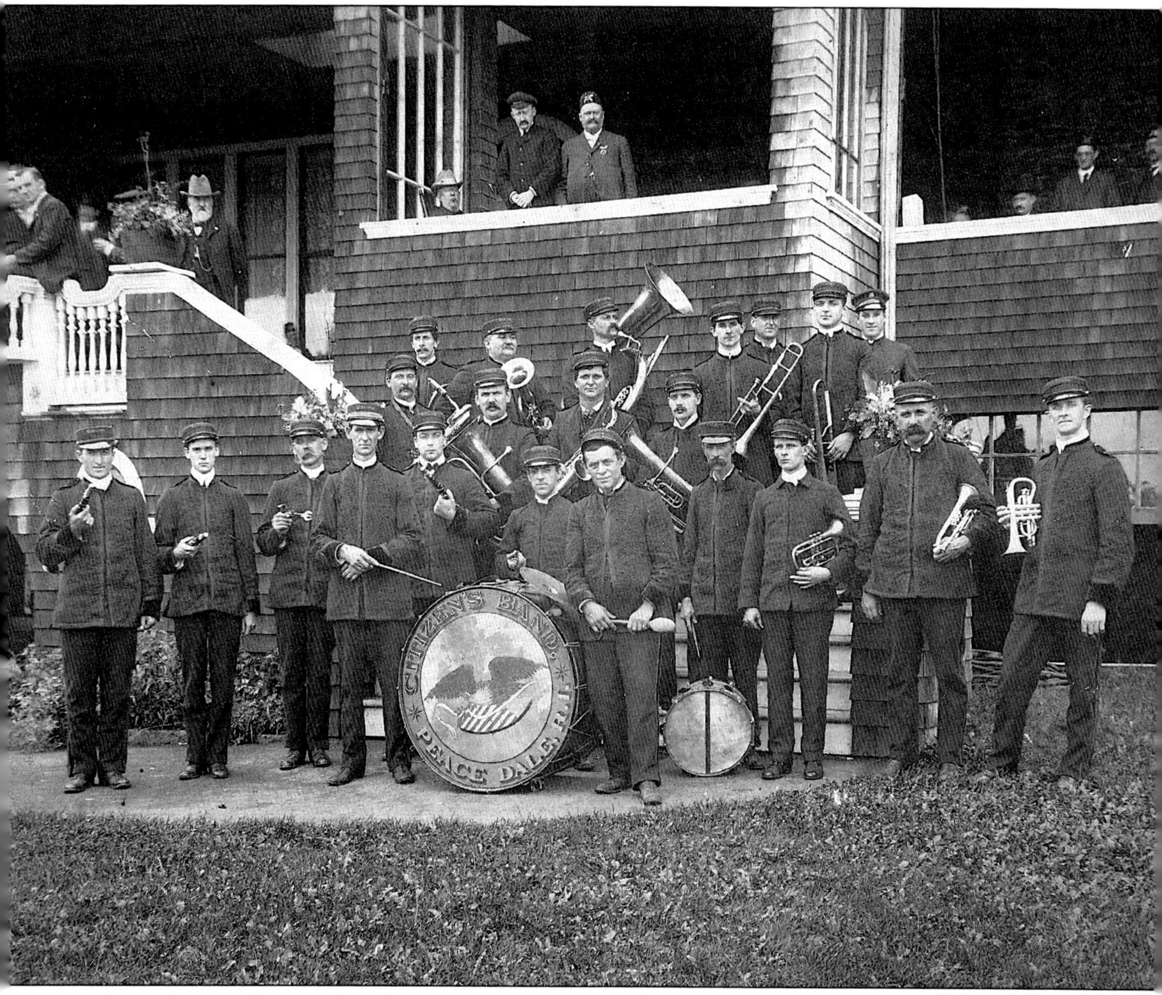

Peace Dale's Citizens' Band is shown here and on the cover in a photograph thought to have been taken around 1904. Frequently booked at the Wakefield Opera House, the band was popular throughout town and played an important role in the age before movies and television. W. Frank Holland was the director, and Paul W. Dixon was the manager. The Citizens' Band was probably the first act to play on the Village Green. On July 31, 1908, the *Narragansett Times* reported that the band "gave a very pleasing open air concert" on that Tuesday evening. In September 1894, the then-"Citizens' Cornet Band" of Peace Dale serenaded T.A. Gardner's home on Main Street in Wakefield on a Saturday evening, according to the *Times*. (Courtesy of Pettaquamscutt Historical Society.)

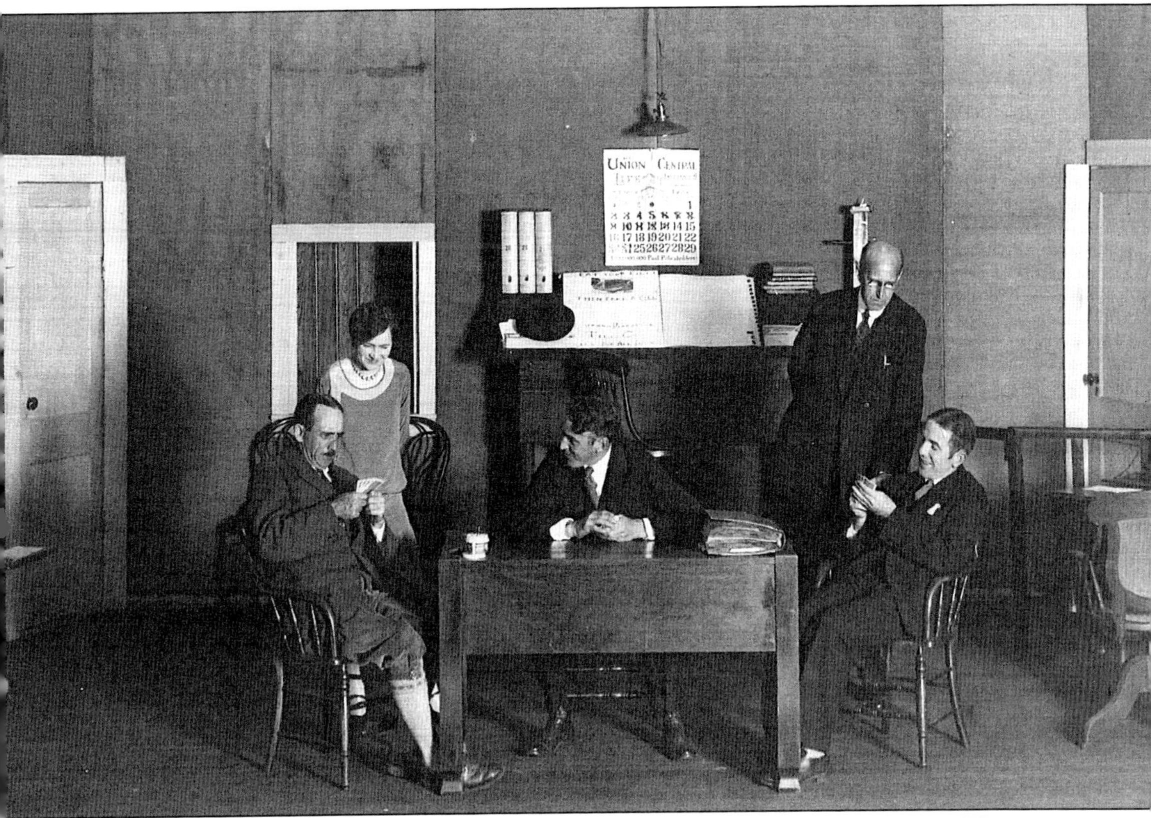

A *Pair of Sixes* was presented October 11, 1927, by the South County Community Players, a group which presented many productions at Hazard Memorial Hall. The *Narragansett Times* reported "fine advance sales" for the show, which it described as "a three-act farce, which will be presented under the auspices of the Hope Masonic Club." The newspaper added this warning: "The Players want it distinctly understood that everyone who is late will be requested to remain standing in the rear of the hall until the end of the first act." The actors are, from left to right, A.E. Thomas, K. Crandall, T.P. Hazard, John Allen, and Dick Taft. (Courtesy of Pettaquamscutt Historical Society.)

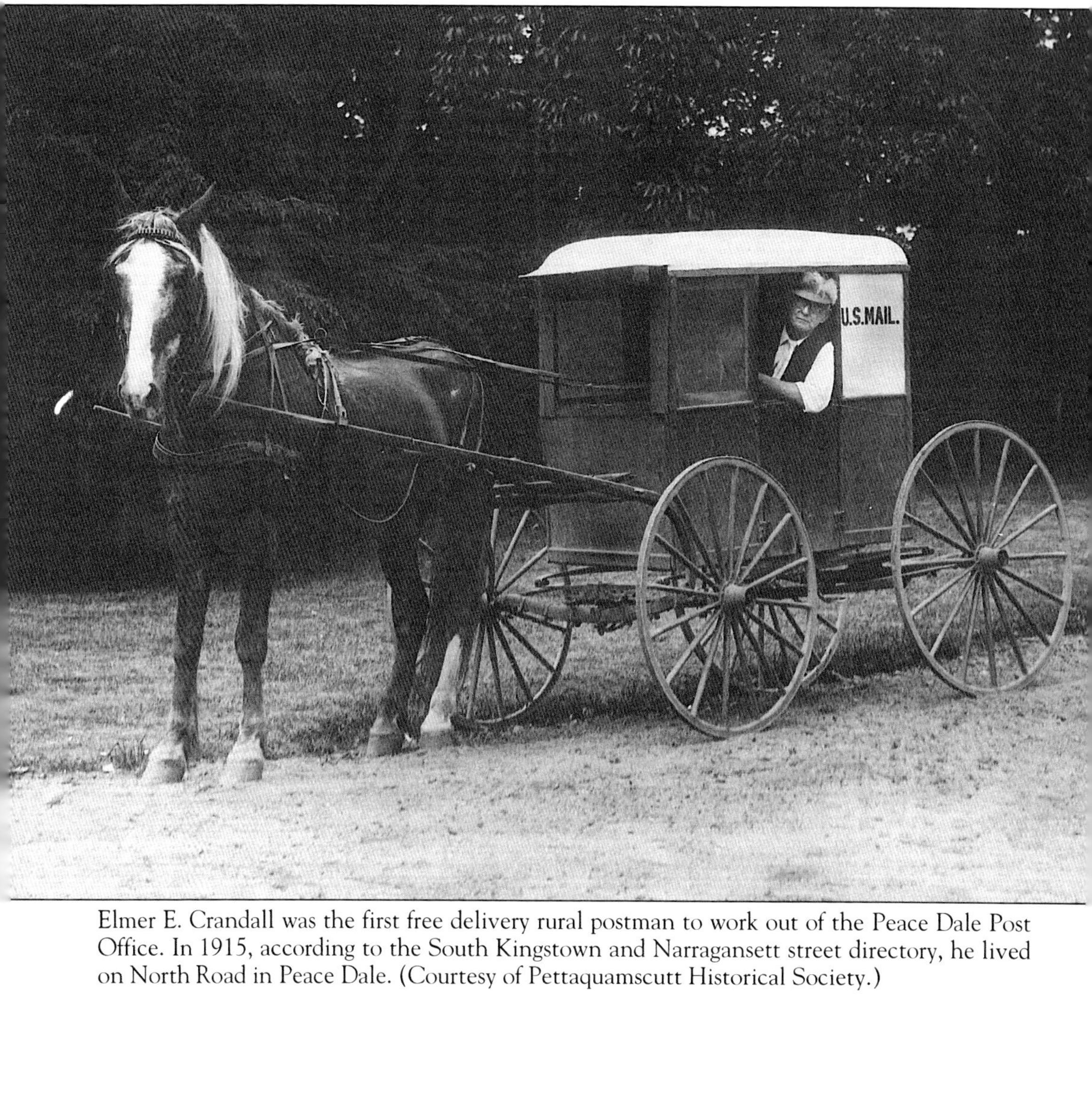

Elmer E. Crandall was the first free delivery rural postman to work out of the Peace Dale Post Office. In 1915, according to the South Kingstown and Narragansett street directory, he lived on North Road in Peace Dale. (Courtesy of Pettaquamscutt Historical Society.)

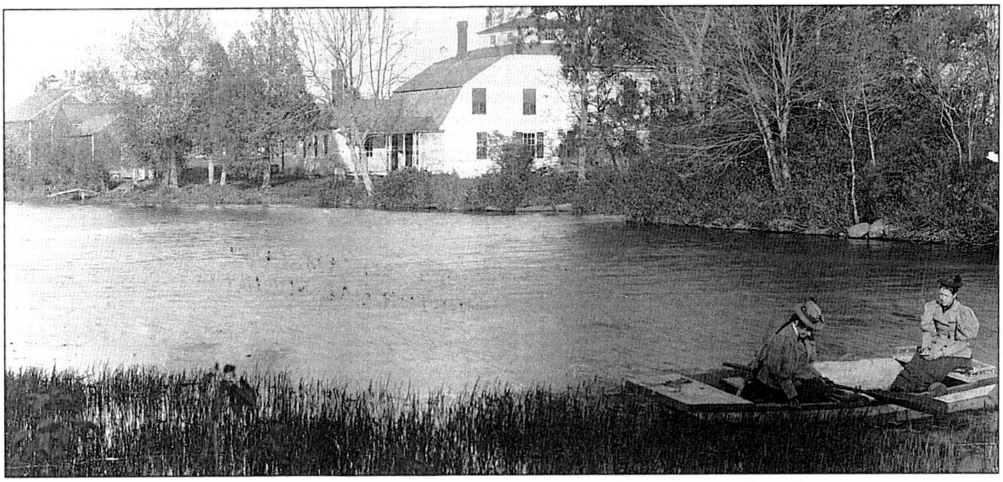

Ladies enjoy a peaceful row on Peace Dale Pond. Water has always played an important role in Peace Dale, making manufacturing possible but also bringing beauty to the village as the various streams and tributaries wind their way toward the Saugatucket River. (Courtesy of Pettaquamscutt Historical Society.)

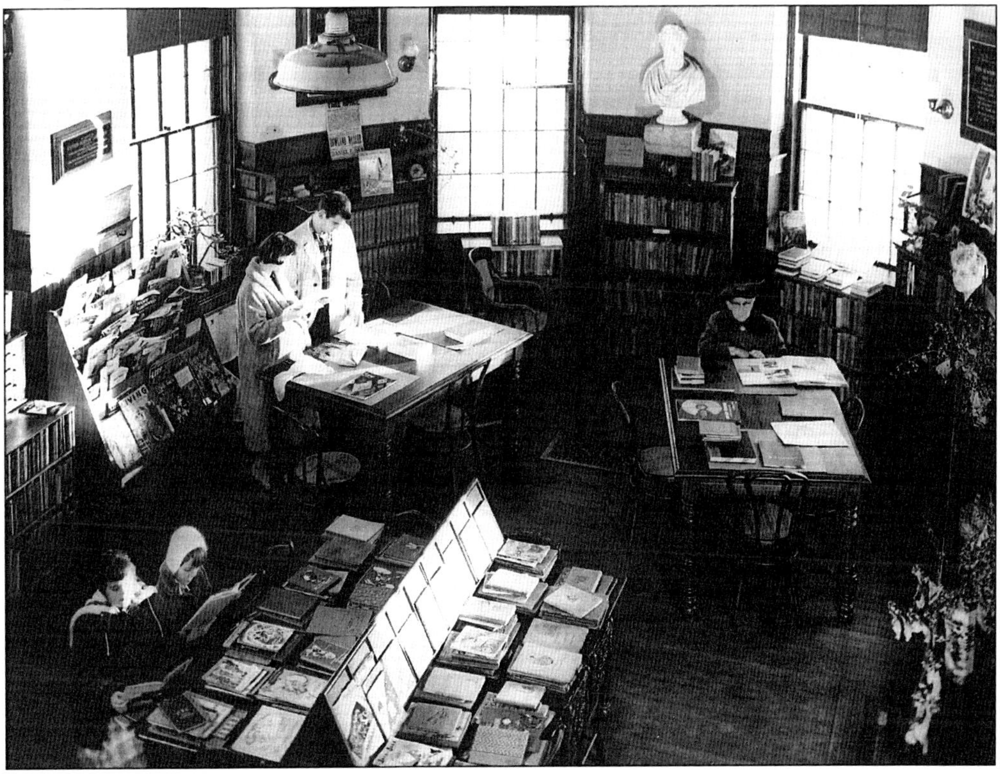

Peace Dale Library has been the intellectual heart of Peace Dale since the Narragansett Library Association was formed in 1853. The library moved into rooms in what is now the Peace Dale Office Building in 1857 and then to Hazard Memorial Hall upon its construction in 1891. Although much has changed since this vintage 1940s picture, the library—now part of the South Kingstown Public Library system—still provides its patrons with a quiet place for that supreme pleasure, reading. (Courtesy of Peace Dale Library.)

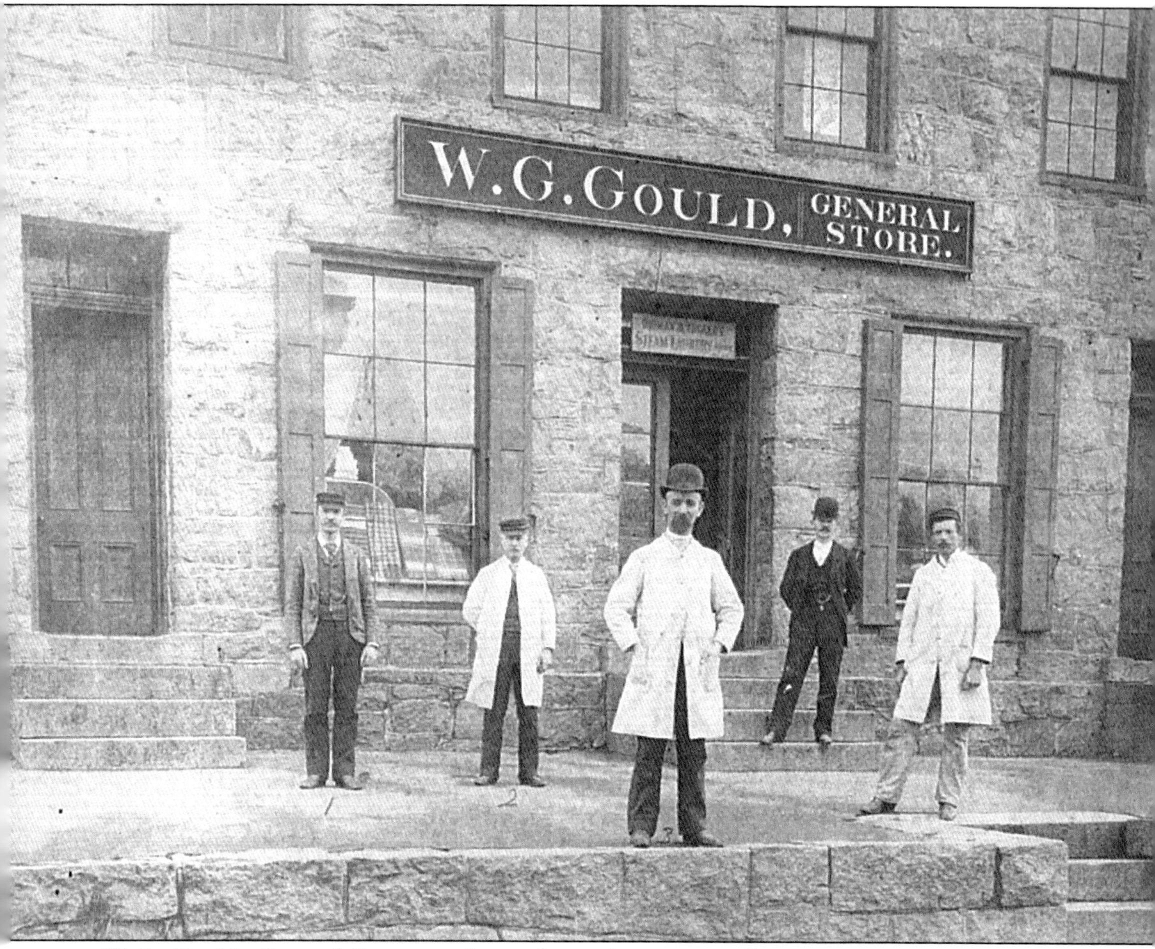

W.G. Gould, General Store was located in what is now the Peace Dale Office Building. Workers from the store pose outside the store facing Kingstown Road. They are, from left to right, Thomas Arnold, George Helliwell, William Gould, and two unidentified workmen. This photograph was donated to the Pettaquamscutt Historical Society by Mrs. Richard Helliwell. (Courtesy of Pettaquamscutt Historical Society.)

Seven

Church Life

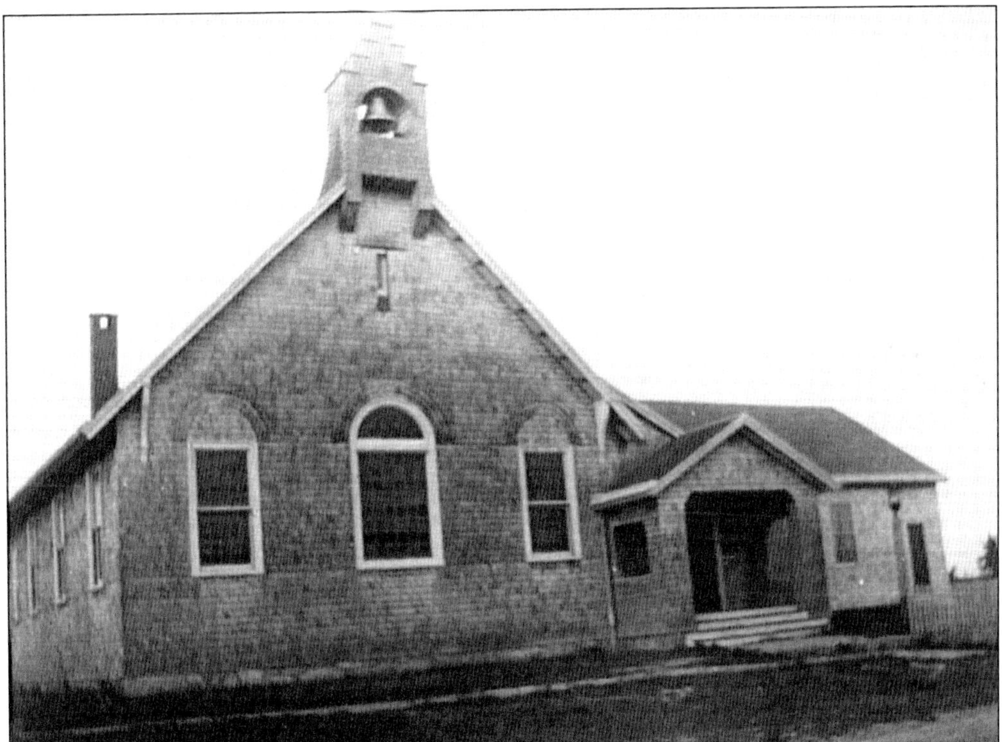

The Rocky Brook Advent Christian Church was formed in 1851 by a splinter group of nine believers from the Wakefield Baptist Church. The group met first at a schoolhouse in Rocky Brook and then, in 1852, built its church on land donated by Isaac P. Hazard. The church, located on Sweet Fern Lane, is still active. (Courtesy of Pettaquamscutt Historical Society.)

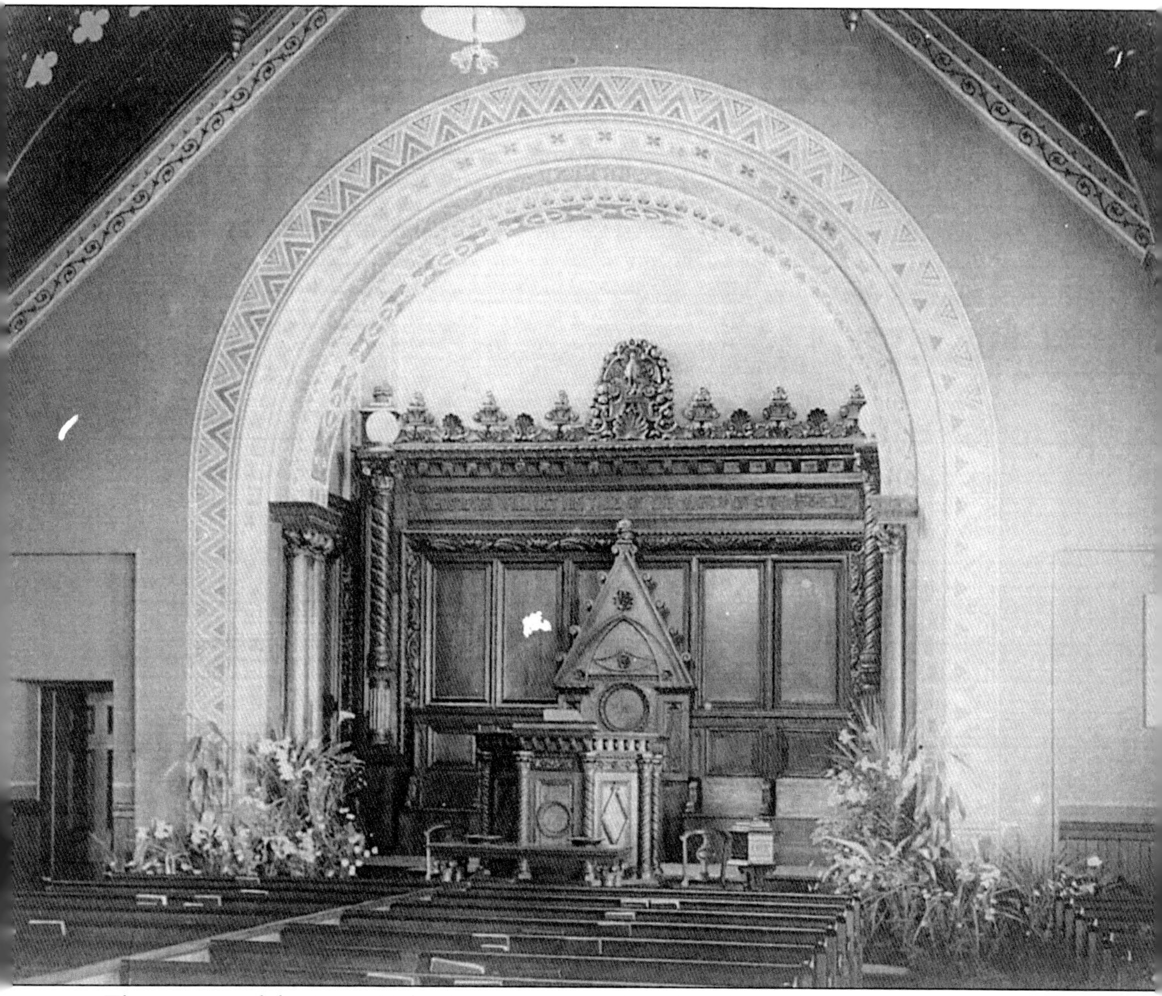

The interior of the Peace Dale Congregational Church is shown here probably at Easter near the turn of the century. The church was organized as the Second Congregational Church of South Kingstown in 1857, its 13 original members meeting first at Oakwoods and later in what is now the Peace Dale Office Building. The present church on Columbia Street was built between 1870 and 1872 of stone and with a slate roof. John LaFarge designed the interior. Rowland Hazard built the church and, later, an addition dedicated in 1895 in memory of his wife, Mrs. Margaret Hazard. A second memorial tablet in his memory was placed in the church on December 31, 1898. (Courtesy of Pettaquamscutt Historical Society.)

The Reverend Joseph Warner Fobes was pastor of Peace Dale Congregational Church at the turn of the century. An influential man in community affairs, Reverend Fobes helped negotiate a settlement in the Peace Dale Manufacturing Co. strike of 1906. (Courtesy of Pettaquamscutt Historical Society.)

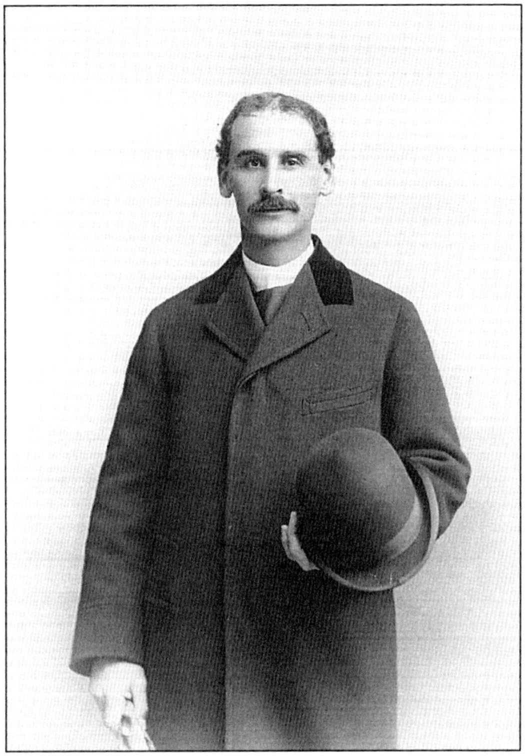

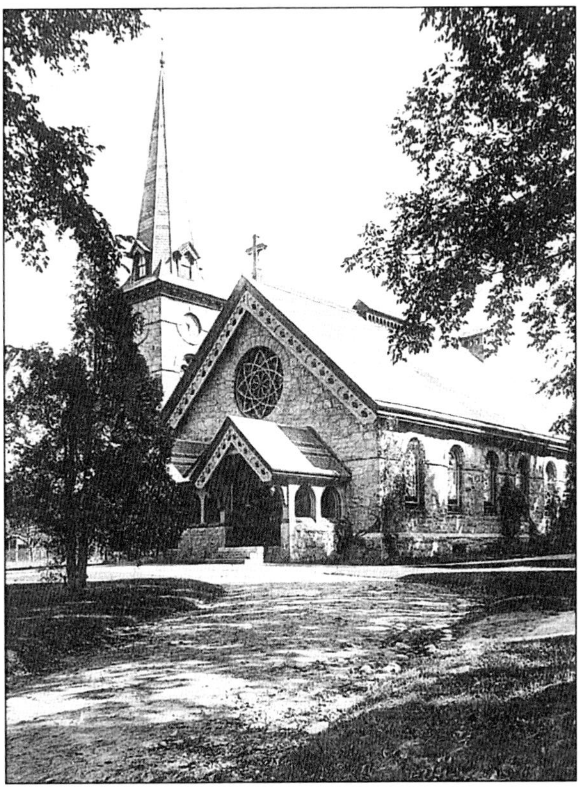

This exterior view of the Peace Dale Congregational Church shows the magnificent rose window of stained glass designed by John LaFarge. Caroline Hazard, in her biography of her father, *A Precious Heritage*, wrote that this window "presented special difficulties to country stone masons," as did the roof timbers to local carpenters. (Courtesy of Pettaquamscutt Historical Society.)

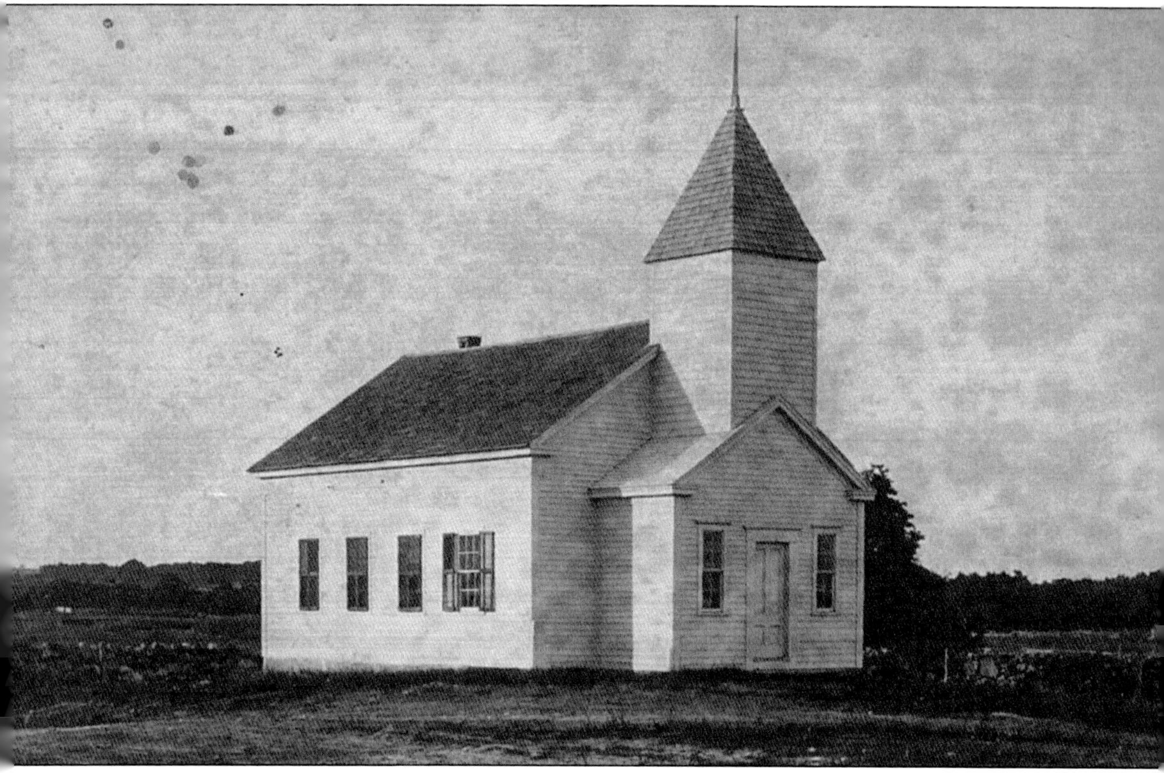

The Curtis Corner Baptist Church, with Elder Silas Leonard as pastor, was built in 1843 for about $1,000. A faction of worshippers who felt differently about Sabbath worship broke off in about 1877 to build their own Seventh-Day Adventist house a short distance from the original church. (Courtesy of Pettaquamscutt Historical Society.)

Eight

School Days

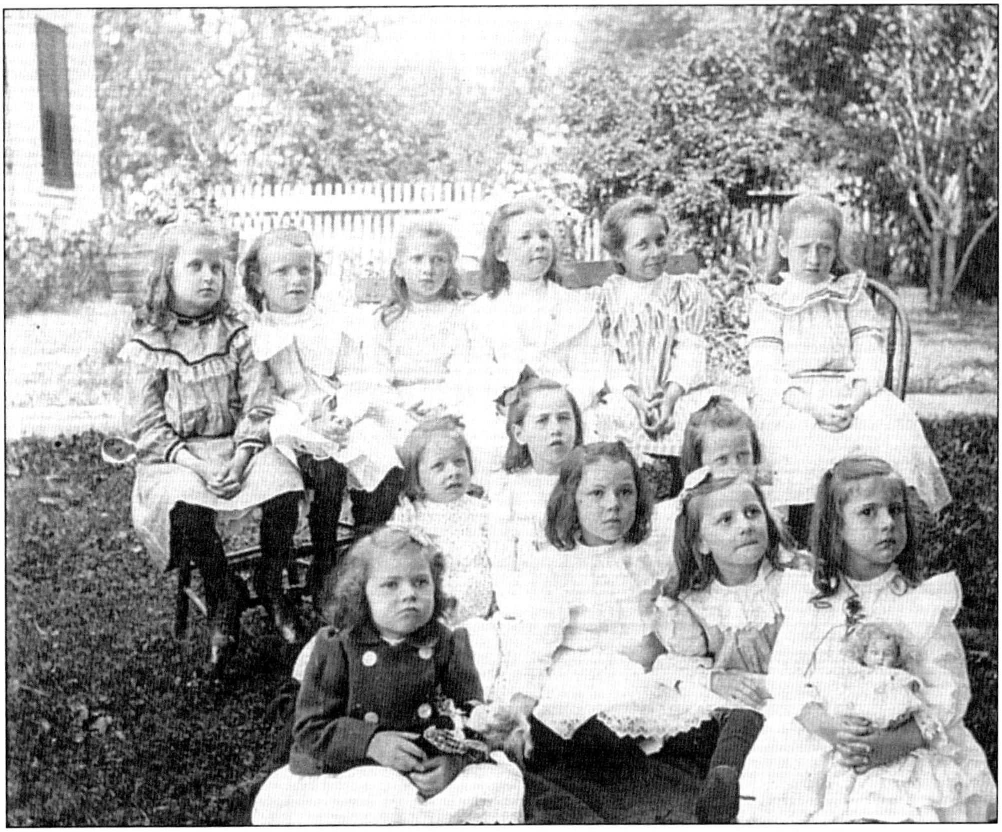

Perhaps nothing symbolizes the Hazards' commitment to education like Stepping Stone Kindergarten, which these girls attended. The kindergarten, one of the first in the United States, was started by Mrs. Margaret Rood Hazard in 1891 after she and her husband spent a summer in Germany. The Hazard family supported education unfailingly and also exercised quite a bit of power over school policy. (Courtesy of Pettaquamscutt Historical Society.)

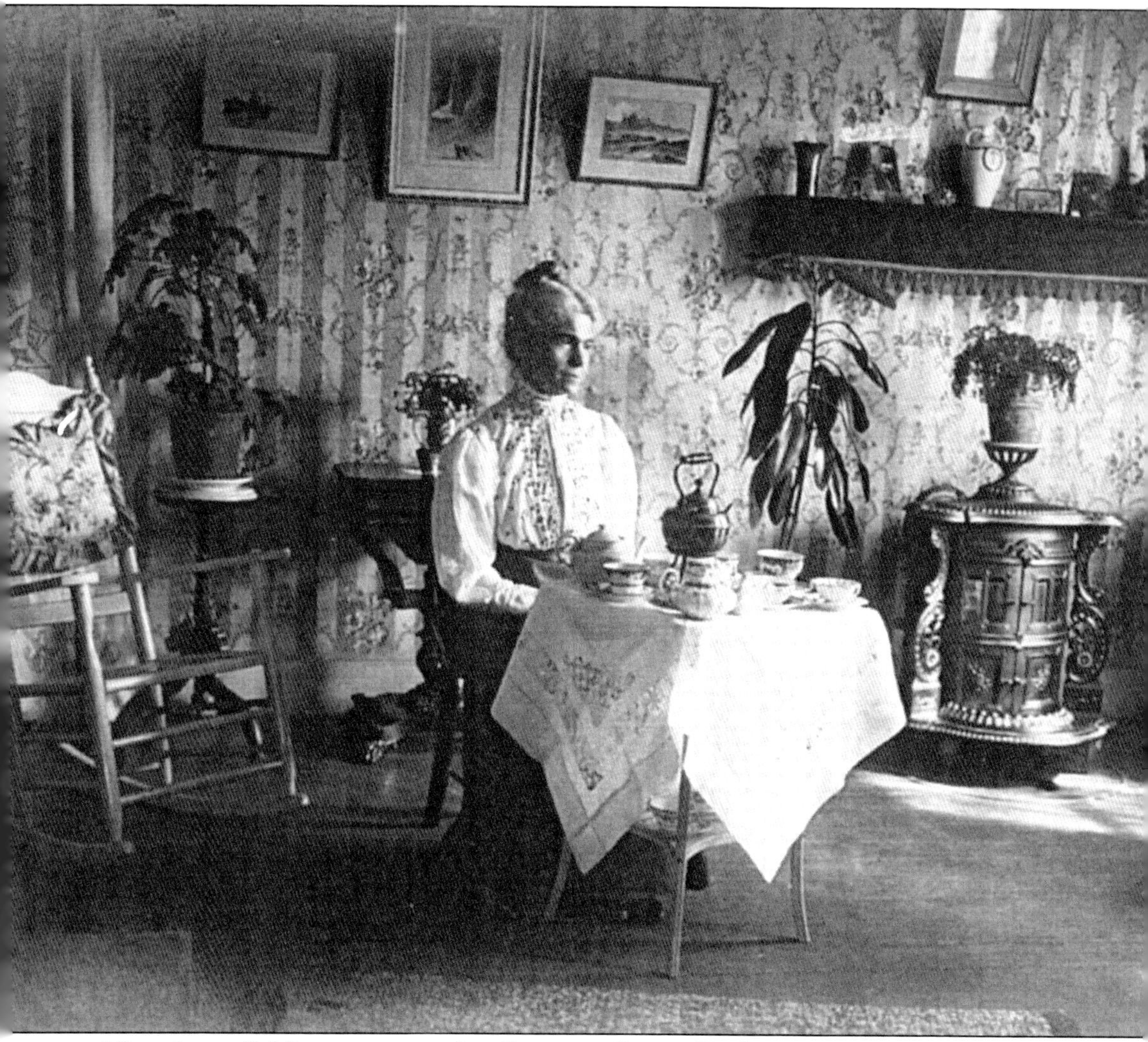

Miss Anna Schliepstein was the Stepping Stone Kindergarten's first teacher when Mrs. Margaret Rood Hazard opened the school on the grounds of the Hazard estate in 1891. Mrs. Hazard returned to Germany in 1913, but World War I prompted her return three years later. Miss Clara Whaley took over in the interim. In his historical accounts, Oliver Stedman recalls how children were fascinated by Miss Schliepstein's German cuckoo clock. (Courtesy of Pettaquamscutt Historical Society.)

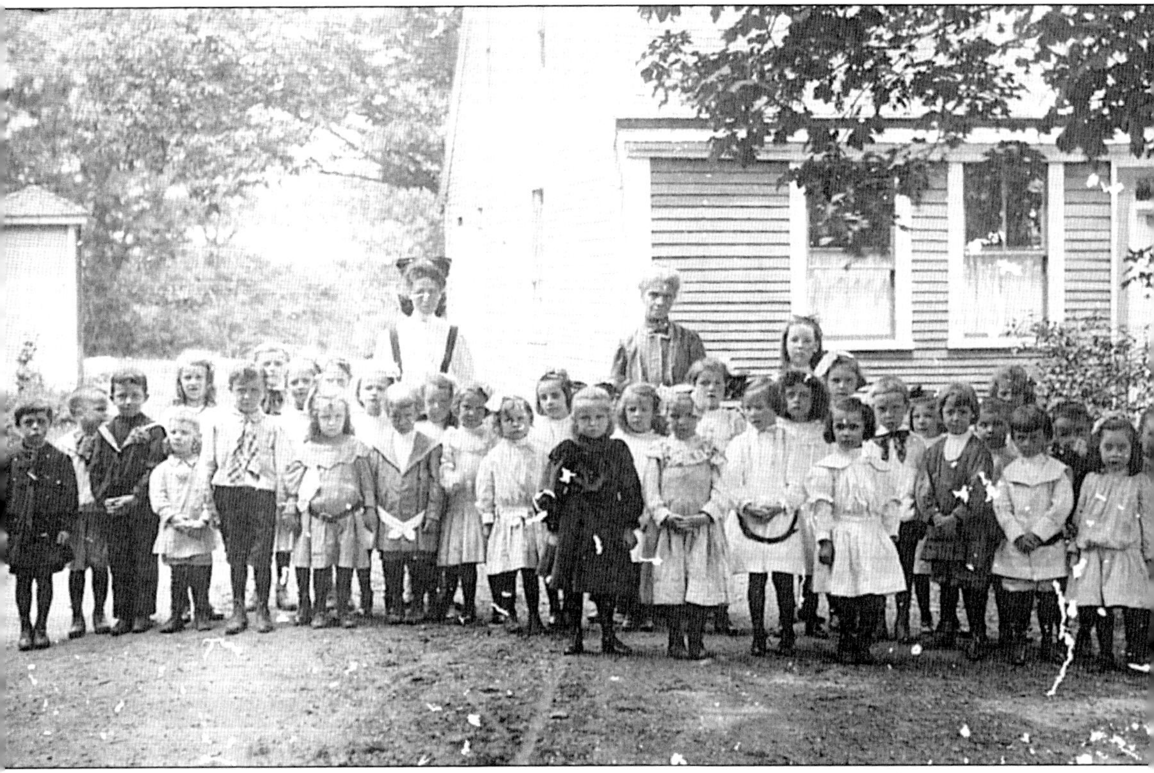

The students of Stepping Stone Kindergarten are shown here *c.* 1905. Later, the kindergarten was moved to a new building on Spring Street, where today it houses the town's Creative Activities program. The students are, from left to right, as follows: (front row) Mark Quigley, Bill Sweet, Whitney Green, Agnes O'Brien, Gladys Gardner, Mary Farrell, ? Cook, Christabel Arnold, Shirley Pelkey, Marian Hennessey, Theodore Holland, Nancy Arnold, Henry Pontefract, Irene Yost, and Betty Reid; (back row) Roy Huddleston, Ruth Curtis, Margaret Holland, Mary McCarthy, and Laura Burdick. The teachers were Miss Anna Schliepstein and Miss Tilley Kelley. (Courtesy of Pettaquamscutt Historical Society.)

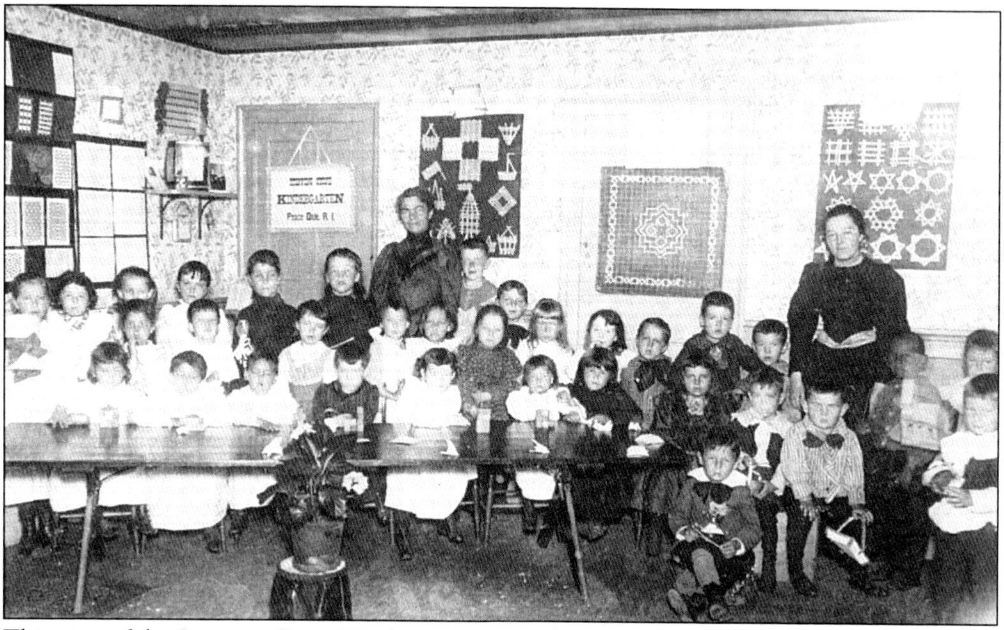

This view of the Stepping Stone Kindergarten was taken about 1895. Miss Schliepstein is at the left. (Courtesy of Pettaquamscutt Historical Society.)

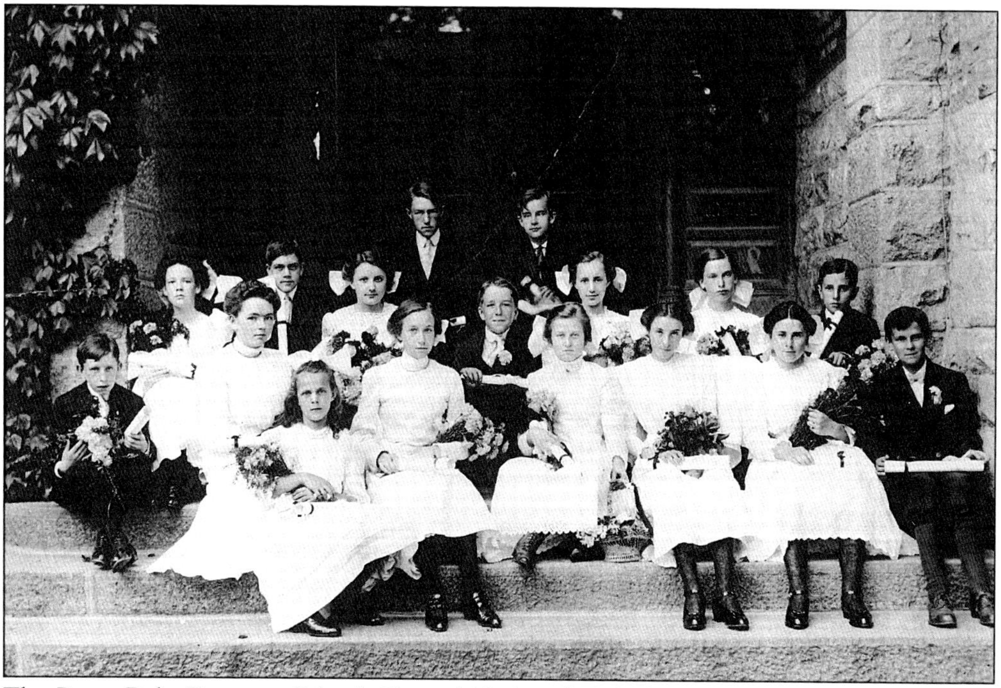

The Peace Dale Grammar School Class of 1910 included, from left to right, Nancy McRae Arnold, Gertrude Mabel Cooke, John Thomas Farrell, Francis Joseph McGrath, Hope Marjorie Rodman, Merle Elizabeth Watson, Alma Atkinson, Eliza Marion Crandall, Helen Gould, John Francis Mullen, James Bernard Stickley, Leon Trebby Brown, Sarah Rodman Dixon, Martha Amelia Lanphear, Emily Louise Potter, Halsey Harrington Smith, and Sydney Wilde. (Courtesy of Pettaquamscutt Historical Society.)

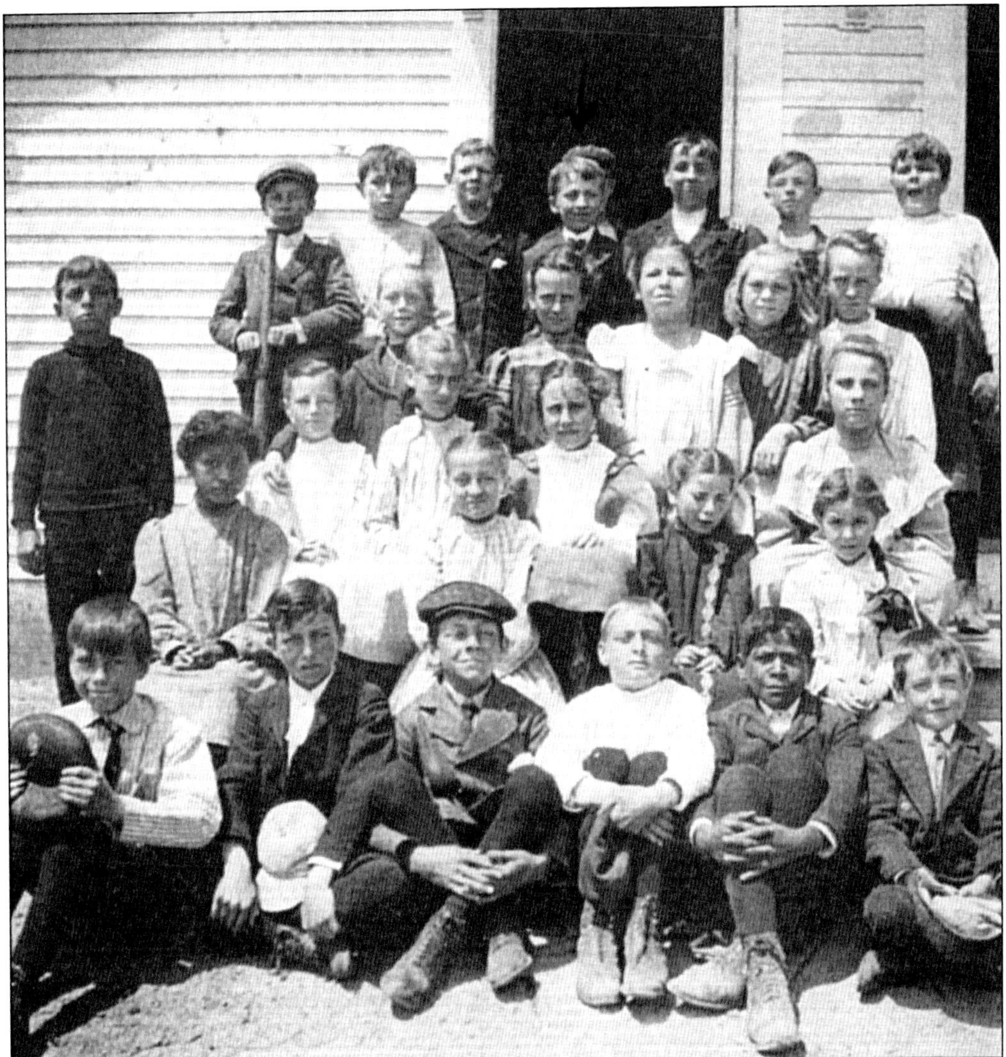

The boys and girls of the Rocky Brook School pose for a portrait near the turn of the century. The school closed in 1923 when the new Peace Dale Grammar School was opened, but, before that, it was quite crowded for several years. In 1902–1903, four pupils were turned away for lack of room, according to the school committee's annual report. The year the school closed, its teachers were Eliza C. Dawley, E. LaFreniere, Clara R. Stedman, and Gladys F. Whitford. (Courtesy of Betty Tucker.)

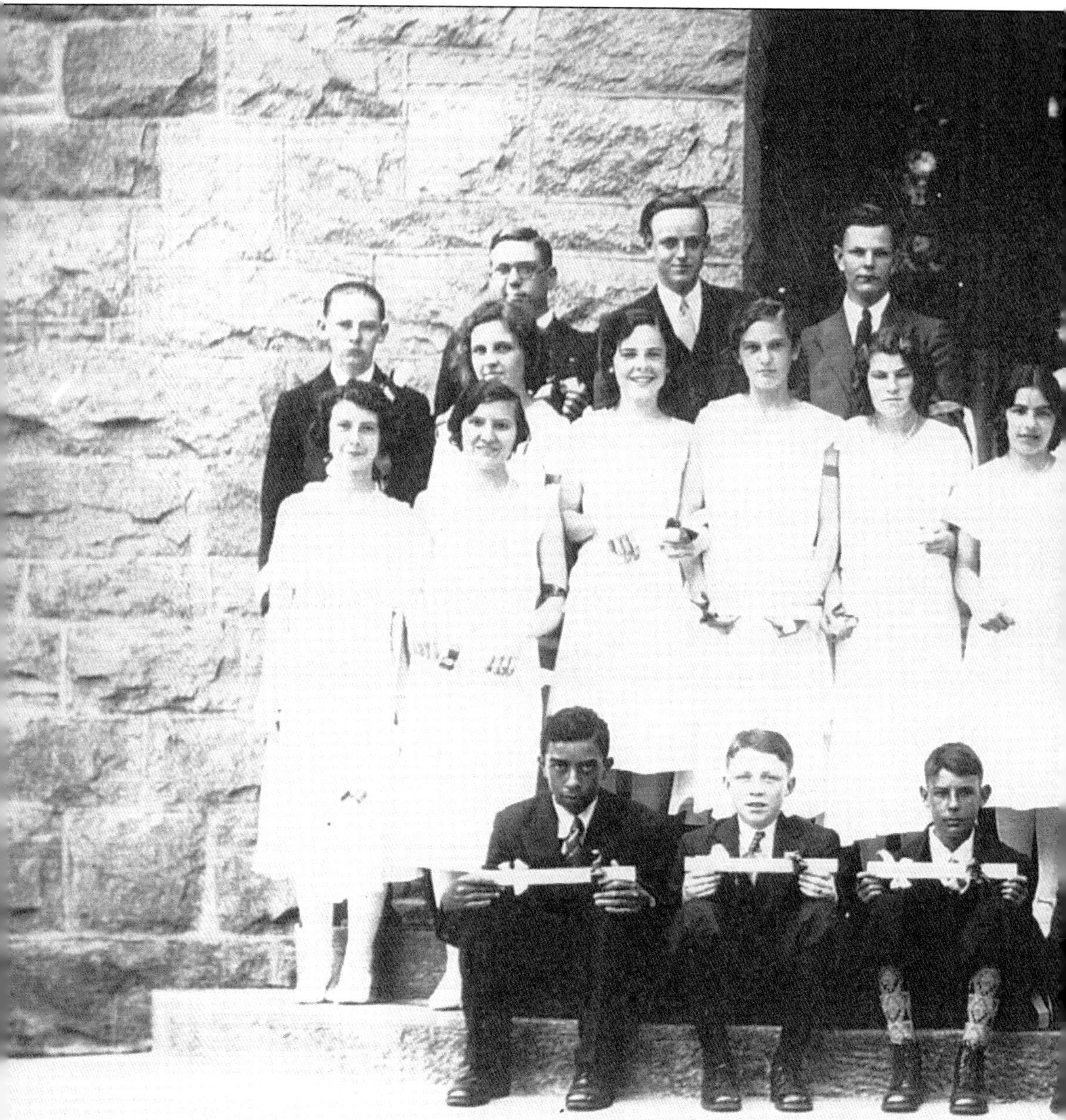

Peace Dale Grammar School graduates pose at Hazard Memorial Hall. They are, from left to right, as follows: (front row) Joseph Monroe, Thomas Egan, Alfred Houde, James Tully, Robert Thompson, William McNally, Richard Paquin, and Norris Pucella; (middle row) Clara (Wilson) Smith, Frances Hurlbert Ferraro, Velma (Eddy) Stadnick, Harriot (Eaton) Schalet, Elizabeth Holloway, Celtina (Whitaker) Taylor, Mary DeSista, Ida (Colleti) Palm,

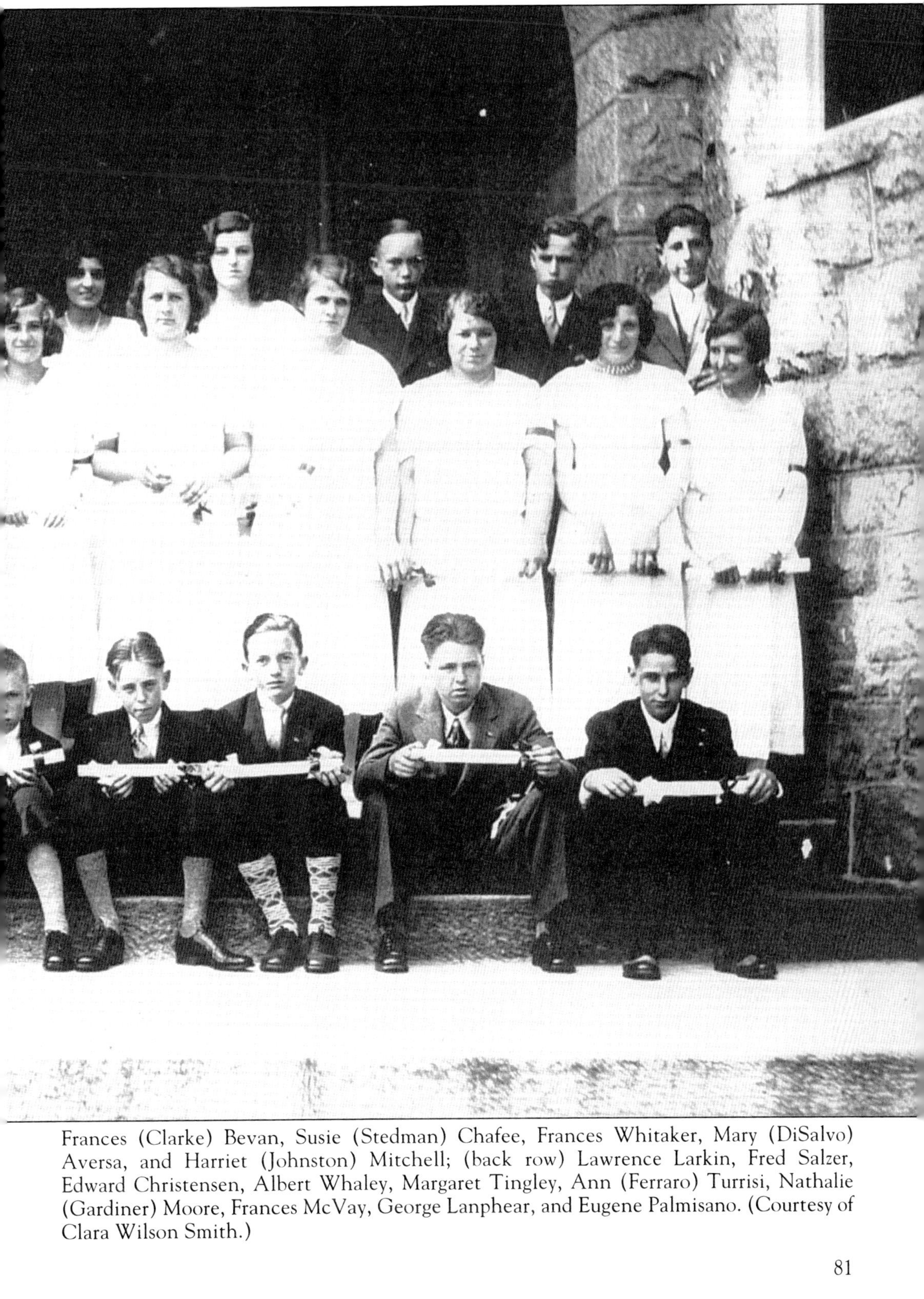

Frances (Clarke) Bevan, Susie (Stedman) Chafee, Frances Whitaker, Mary (DiSalvo) Aversa, and Harriet (Johnston) Mitchell; (back row) Lawrence Larkin, Fred Salzer, Edward Christensen, Albert Whaley, Margaret Tingley, Ann (Ferraro) Turrisi, Nathalie (Gardiner) Moore, Frances McVay, George Lanphear, and Eugene Palmisano. (Courtesy of Clara Wilson Smith.)

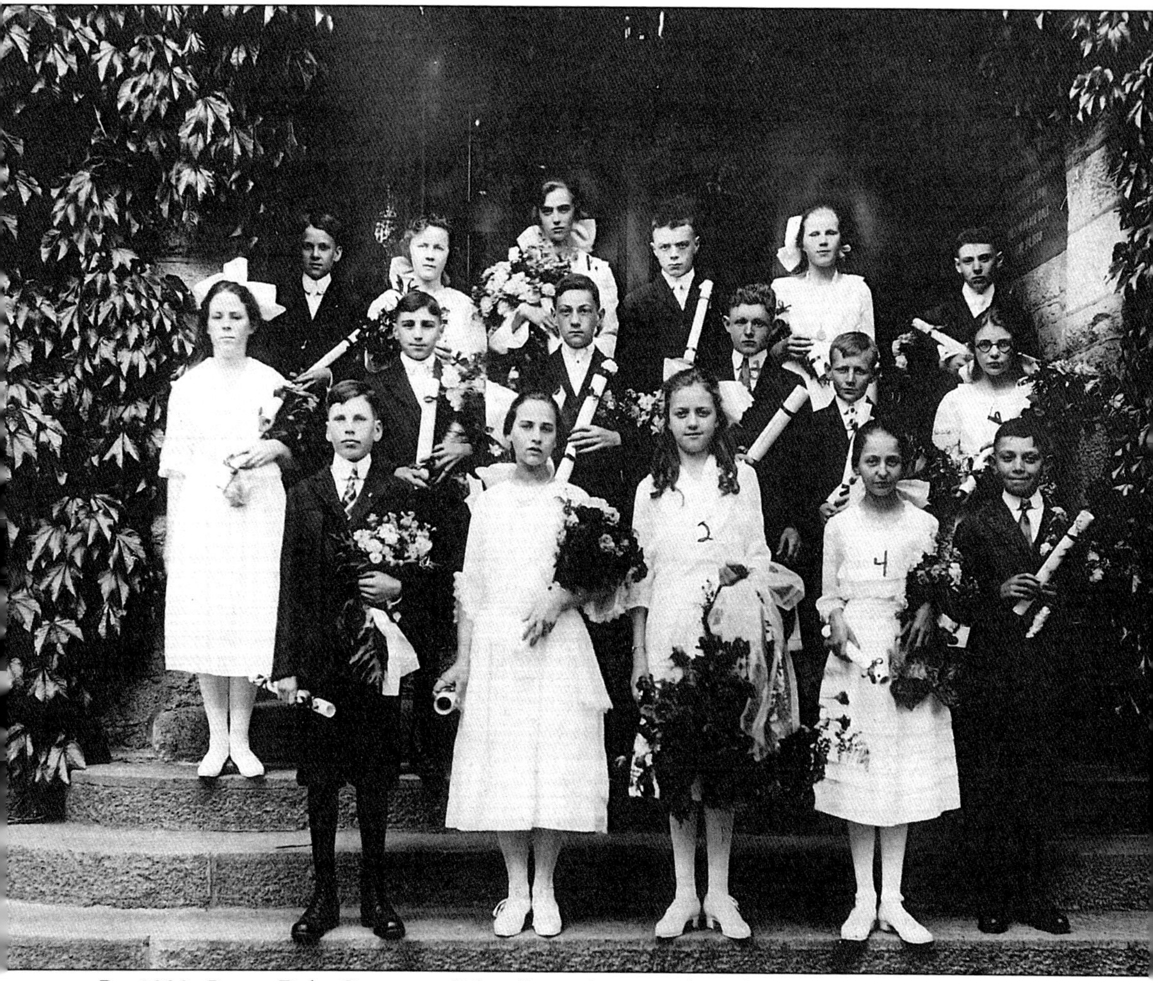

By 1920, Peace Dale Grammar School's graduating class displayed different fashions. The graduates are, from left to right, as follows: (front row) Harold Northup, Alexina Roy, Jennie Curtis, Gladys Coggeshall, and Joseph Feola; (middle row) Margaret Murney, Mino Beatrice, James Quinlan, Harold Watson, James Cronkshaw, and Ruth Gwynne; (back row) John Helliwell, Nina Mellor, Joanna Sims, Frank Maguire, Hazel McGann, and Robert Coggeshall. (Courtesy of Pettaquamscutt Historical Society.)

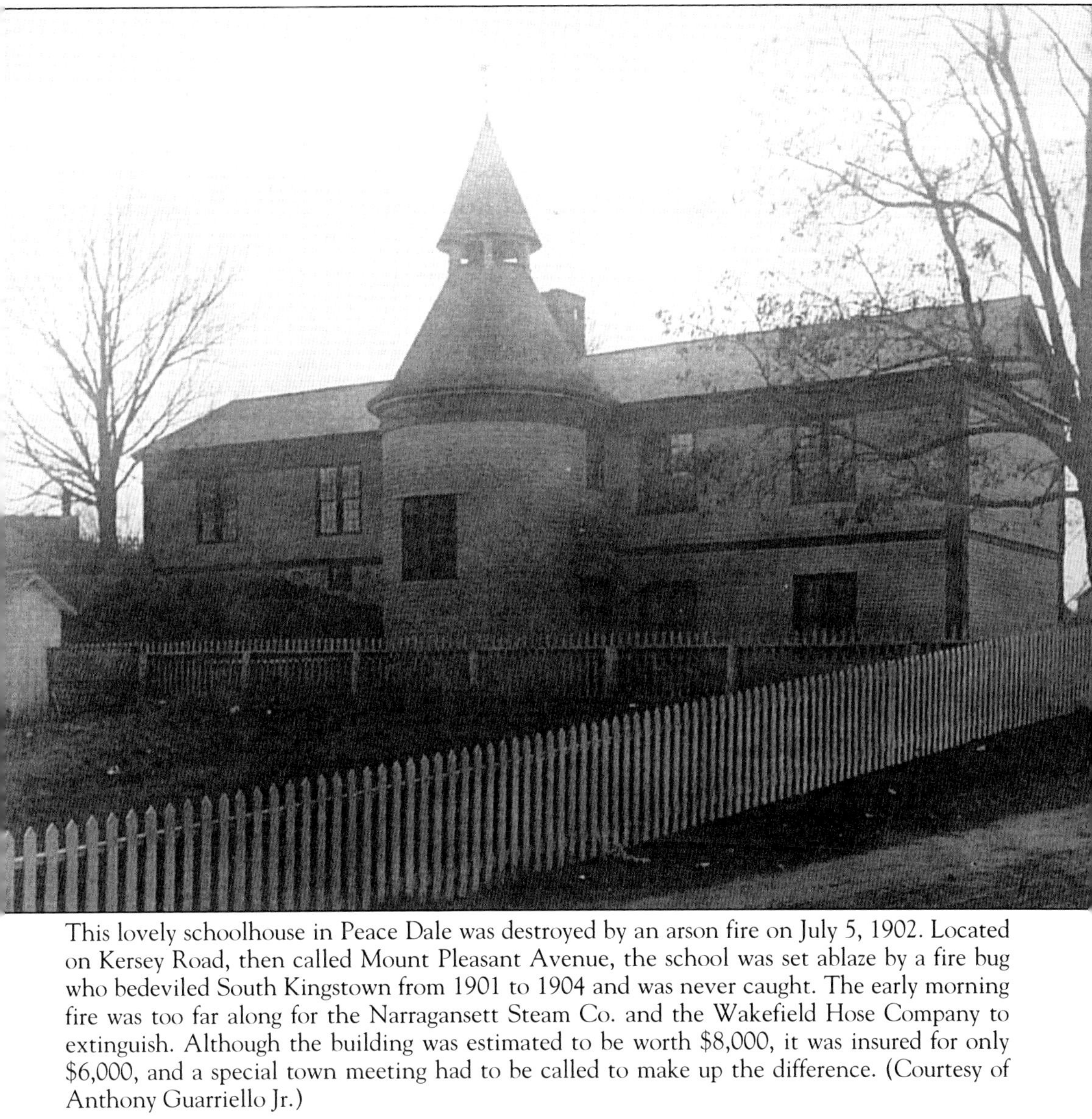

This lovely schoolhouse in Peace Dale was destroyed by an arson fire on July 5, 1902. Located on Kersey Road, then called Mount Pleasant Avenue, the school was set ablaze by a fire bug who bedeviled South Kingstown from 1901 to 1904 and was never caught. The early morning fire was too far along for the Narragansett Steam Co. and the Wakefield Hose Company to extinguish. Although the building was estimated to be worth $8,000, it was insured for only $6,000, and a special town meeting had to be called to make up the difference. (Courtesy of Anthony Guarriello Jr.)

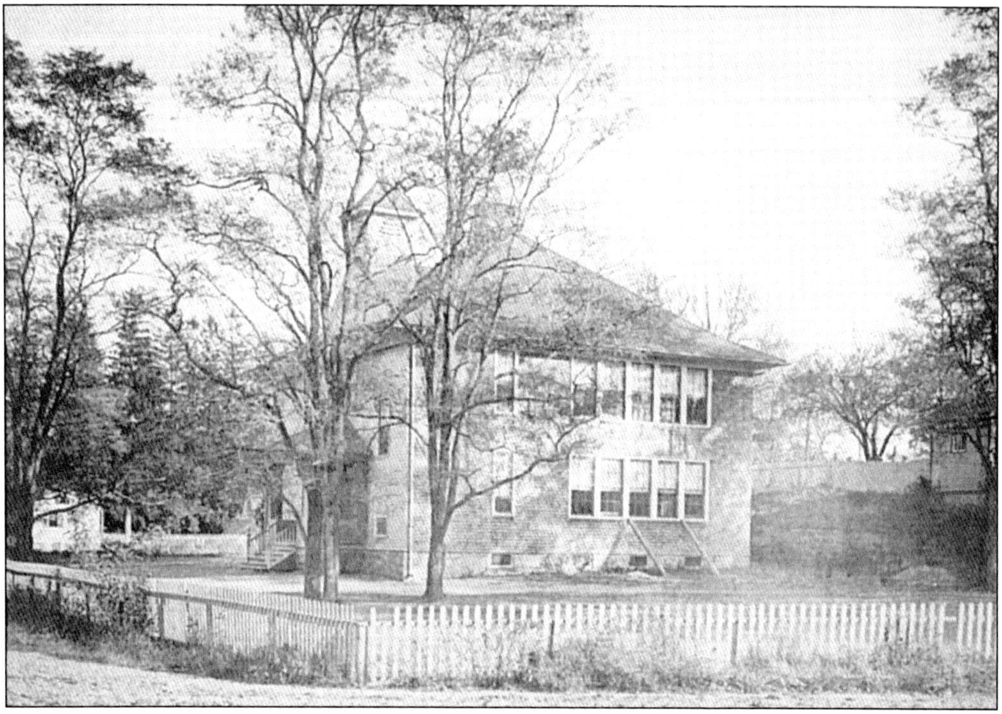

Students attended class in the Sunday school rooms of the Peace Dale Congregational Church and Hazard Memorial Hall in the fall term of 1902 in the wake of a fire that destroyed the Peace Dale Grammar School in 1902. The new school, pictured above, was ready for occupancy in January 1903. The *Narragansett Times* called the new school "a very substantial and convenient building." (Courtesy of Pettaquamscutt Historical Society.)

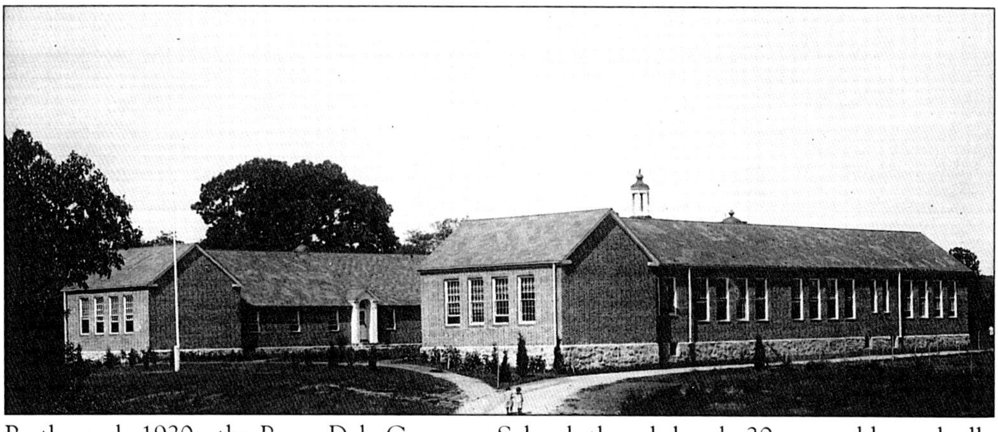

By the early 1920s, the Peace Dale Grammar School, though barely 20 years old, was badly overcrowded, as was Rocky Brook School. This brick schoolhouse was built farther down Kersey Road to replace both in 1923. The school committee, in its annual report, noted that the school was costing the public only about $30,000 "through the initiative and untiring efforts of Mr. Sumner Mowry and the generosity of Mrs. J.W. Fobes and of other members of that public-spirited family, whose gifts have hitherto enriched the town with several public buildings . . ." The new school contained nine classrooms, a principal's office, and a basement that served as a combined playroom, kitchen, and boiler room. (Courtesy of Pettaquamscutt Historical Society.)

Nine

The Mansions

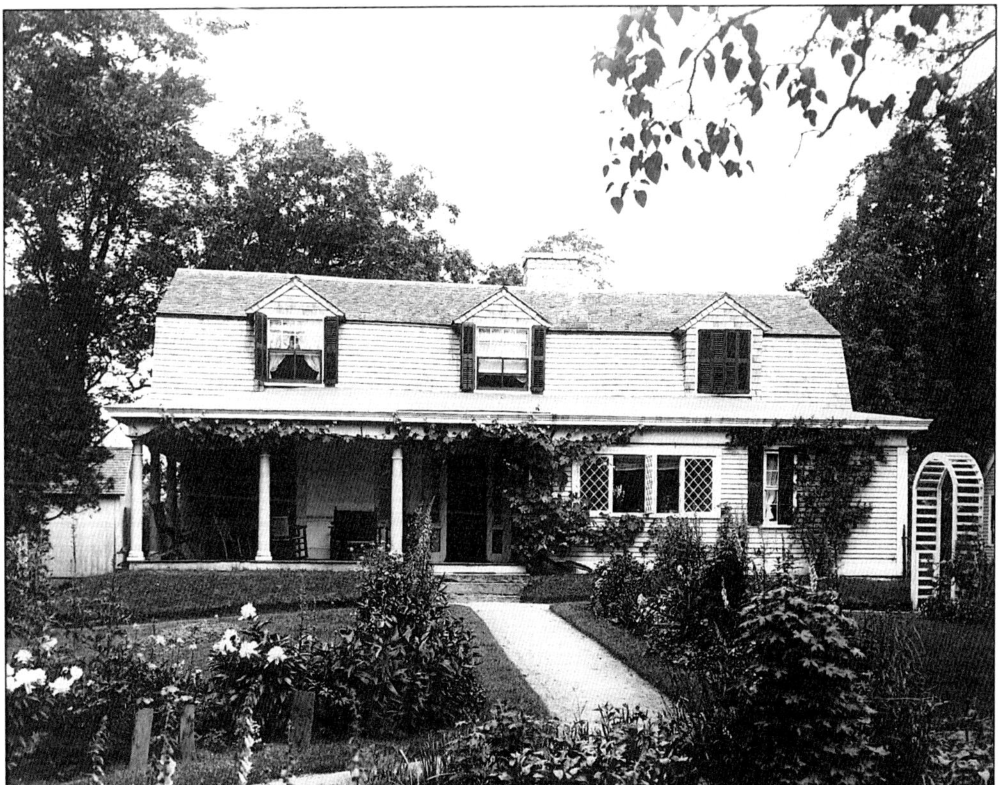

The Homestead, purchased by Peace Dale Manufacturing Co. founder Rowland Hazard in 1805, was the first of many grand Hazard houses in Peace Dale. The more money the Hazards' manufacturing interests made, the more opulent their lifestyle became. This photograph was taken about 1905 by Dexter W. Hoxie. (Courtesy of Pettaquamscutt Historical Society.)

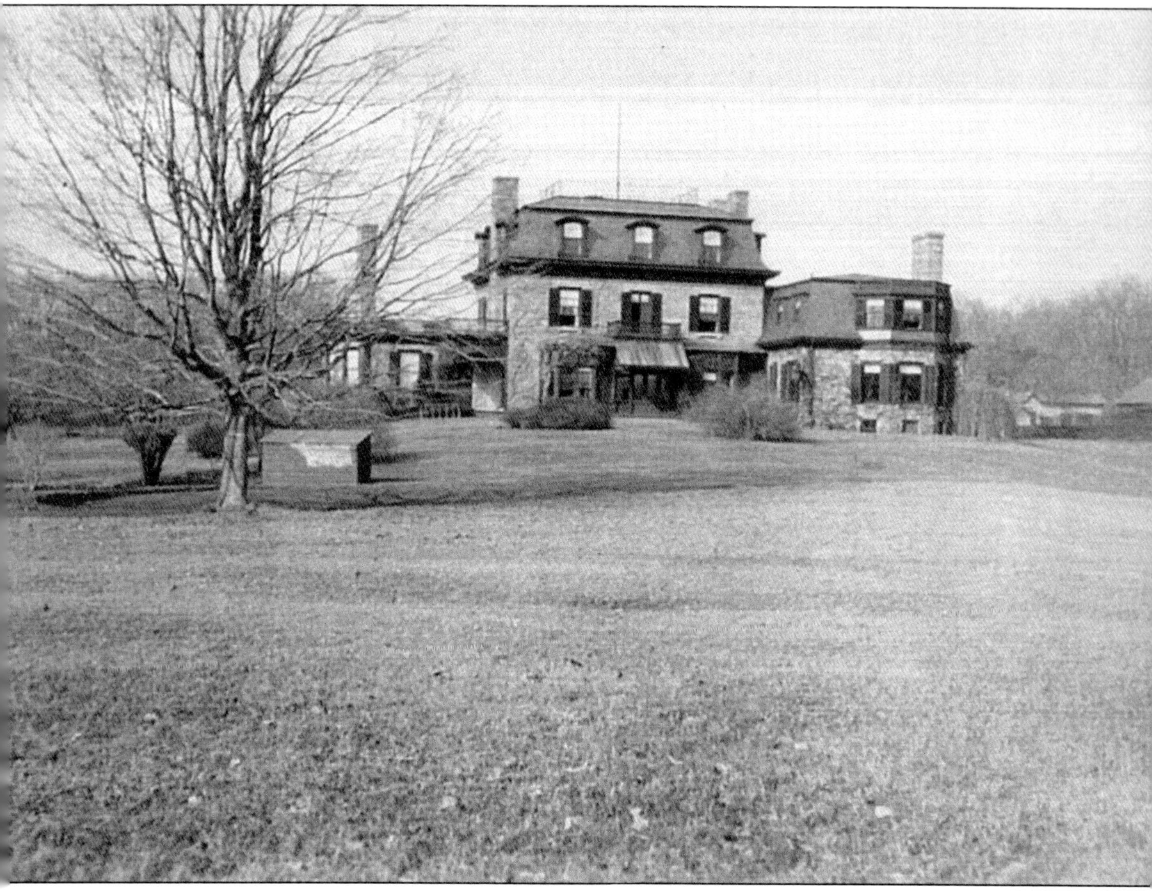

Built in 1853–55 for Rowland Hazard and enlarged and renovated in 1887, Oakwoods was the center of Hazard family life. It was here that the Peace Dale Congregational Church was organized. The Hazards were forever tinkering with and redesigning their houses. When the lines for the house were originally laid out by Rowland Hazard in 1853, he set them by the North Star although the plans were later altered slightly. Narragansett Indian Joshua Noka is credited with the stonework, and Thomas A. Tefft was the original architect. (Courtesy of Pettaquamscutt Historical Society.)

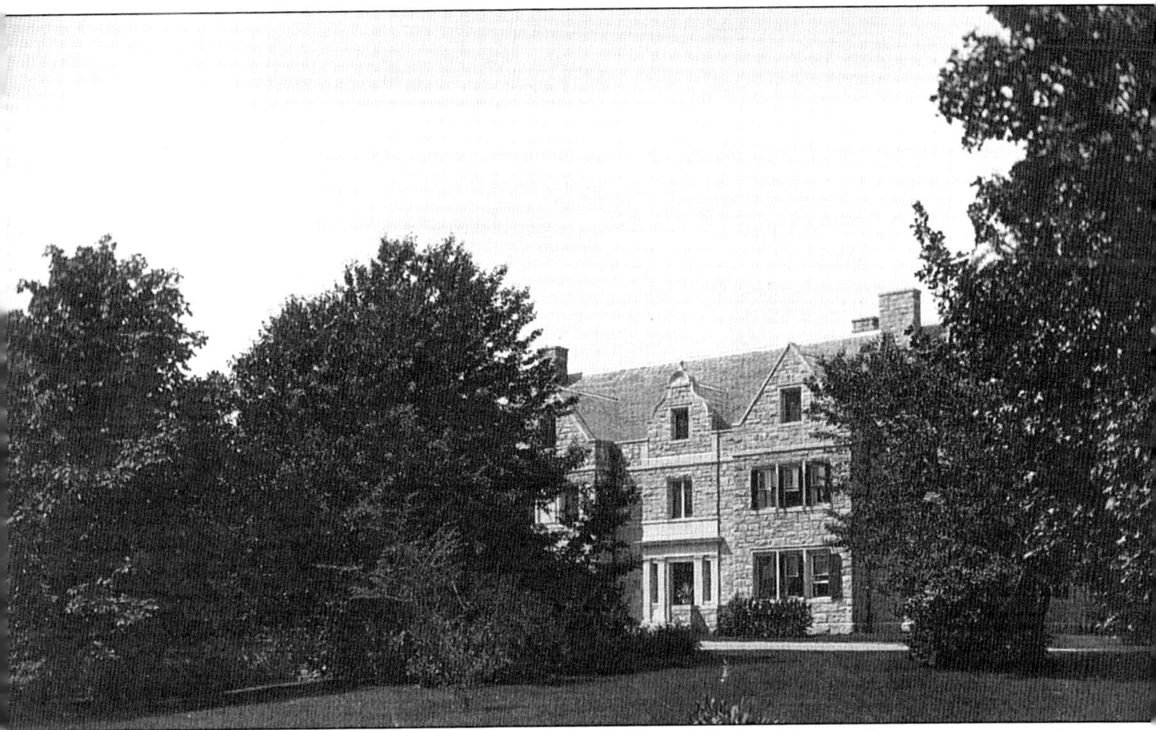

Holly House, shown here in a c. 1907 photograph, was built about 1855 and then transformed into a much grander house by Charles McKim of McKim, Mead and White. Caroline Hazard's grandparents moved into the house after it was built and, like Oakwoods, it was torn down in 1948 when The Oaks subdivision was developed. (Courtesy of Pettaquamscutt Historical Society.)

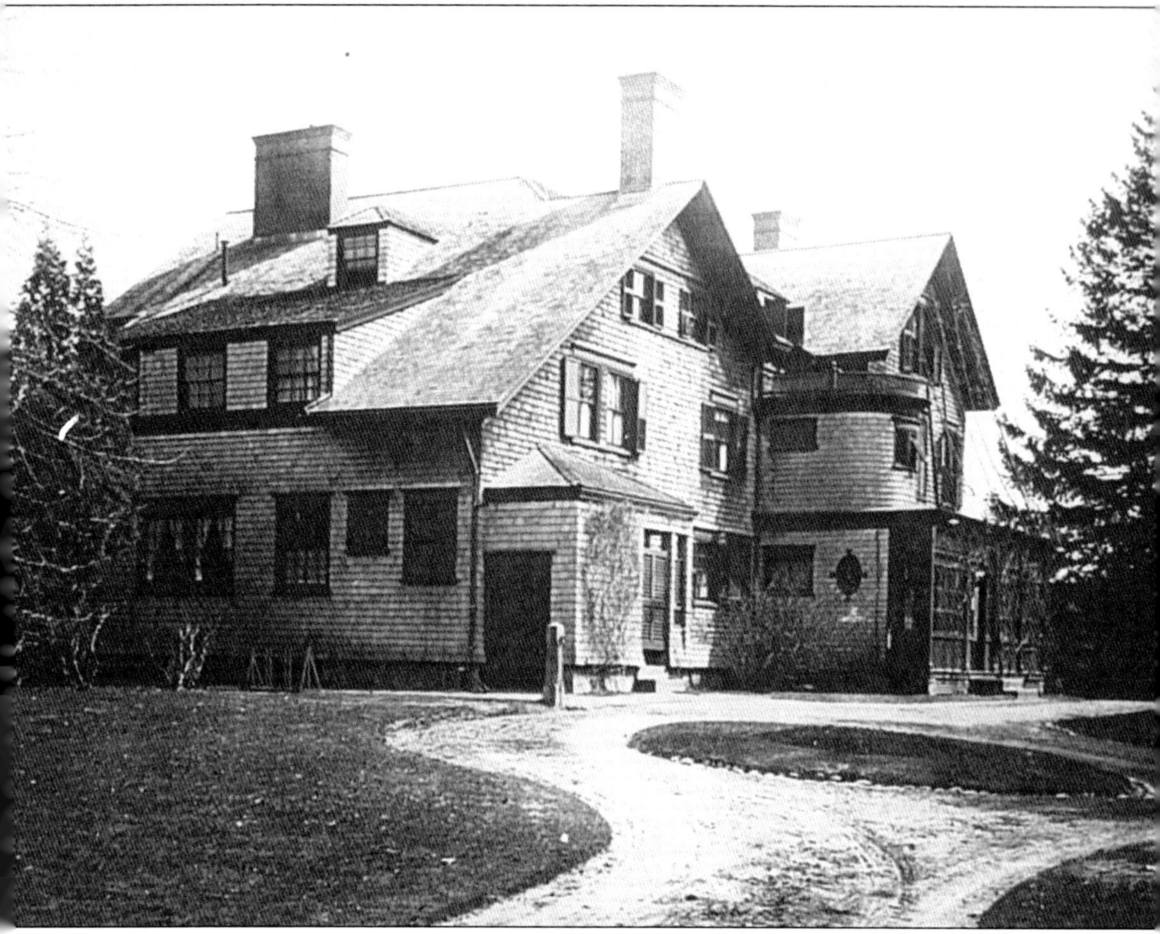

Lily Pads, which still stands today at the junction of North and Kersey Roads, was built some time before 1870 by John Newbold Hazard. It was for him that the Neighborhood Guild was dedicated. Today it houses offices and has been added on to and extensively remodeled. (Courtesy of Pettaquamscutt Historical Society.)

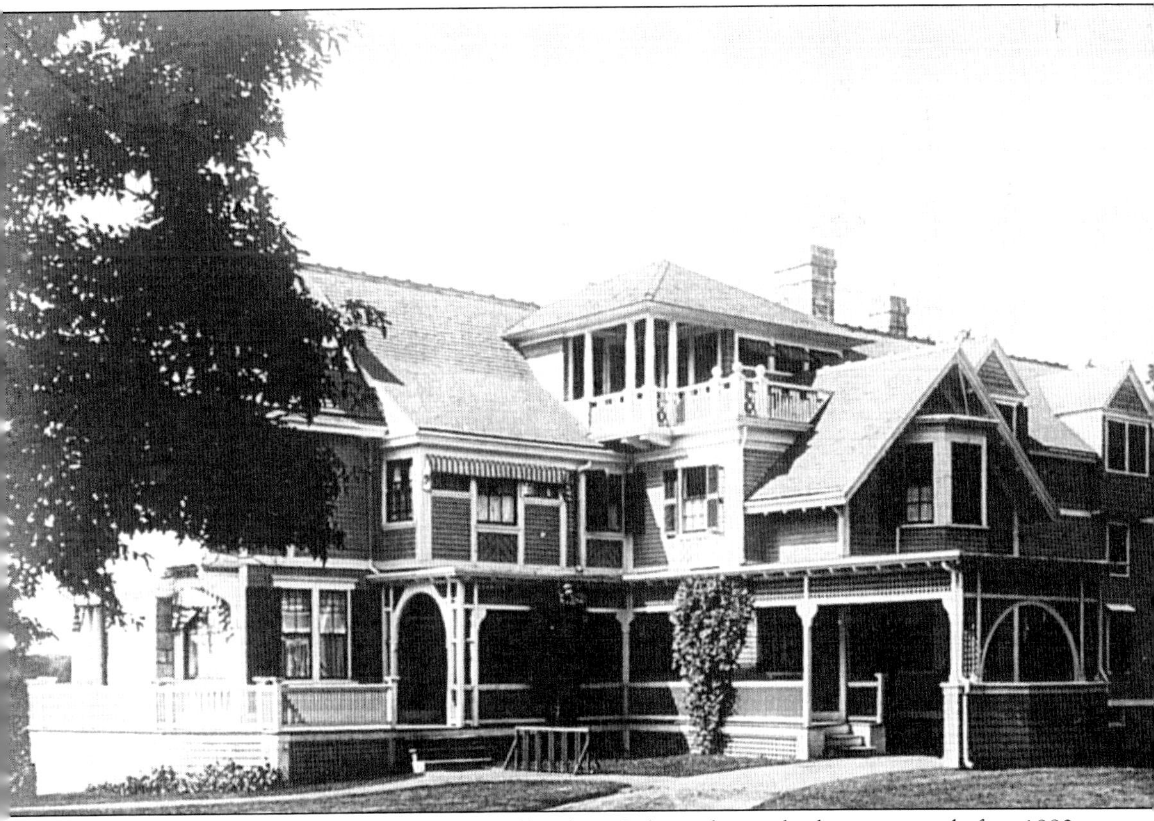

The Acorns, so named because it was smaller than Oakwoods, was built some time before 1880 and later remodeled for Helen Hazard in 1894–95. Helen was Rowland Gibson Hazard's sister, and she later married Nathaniel Bacon. Their son, Leonard Bacon, won the Pulitzer Prize for poetry in 1941. (Courtesy of Pettaquamscutt Historical Society.)

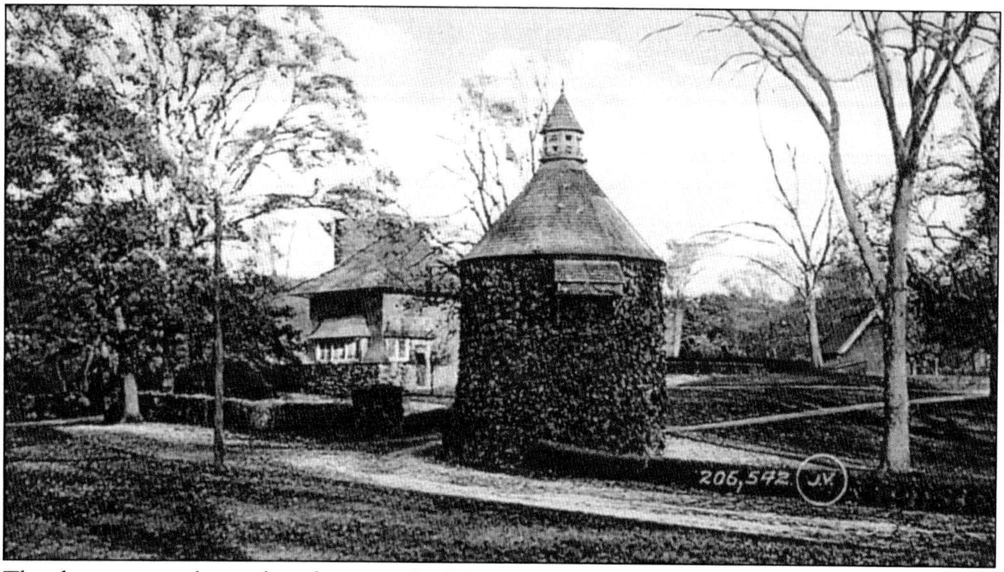

This dovecote was located on the grounds of the Holly House estate. (Courtesy of Pettaquamscutt Historical Society.)

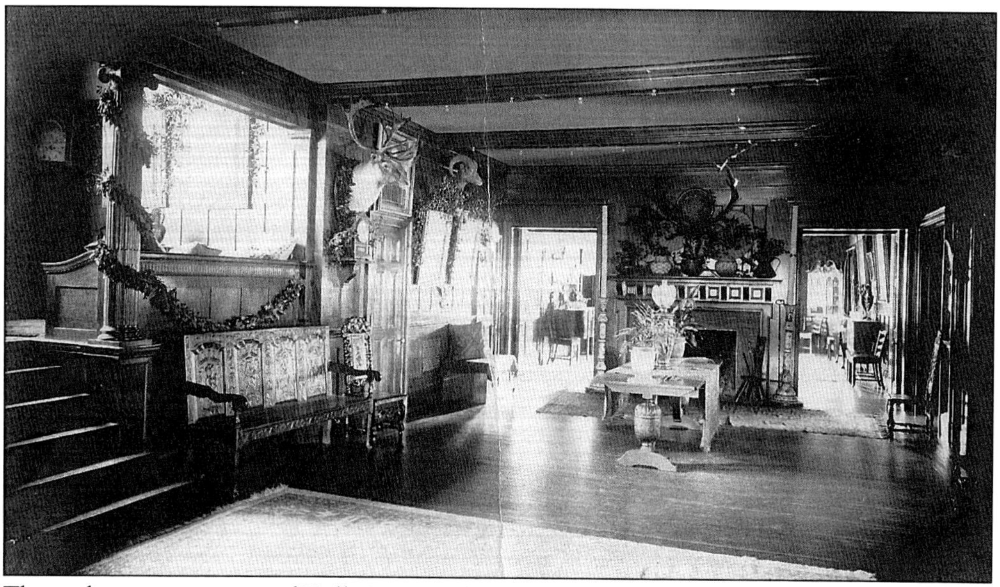
This is the ornate interior of Holly House. The house was built in the style of an English Tudor country house. (Courtesy of Pettaquamscutt Historical Society.)

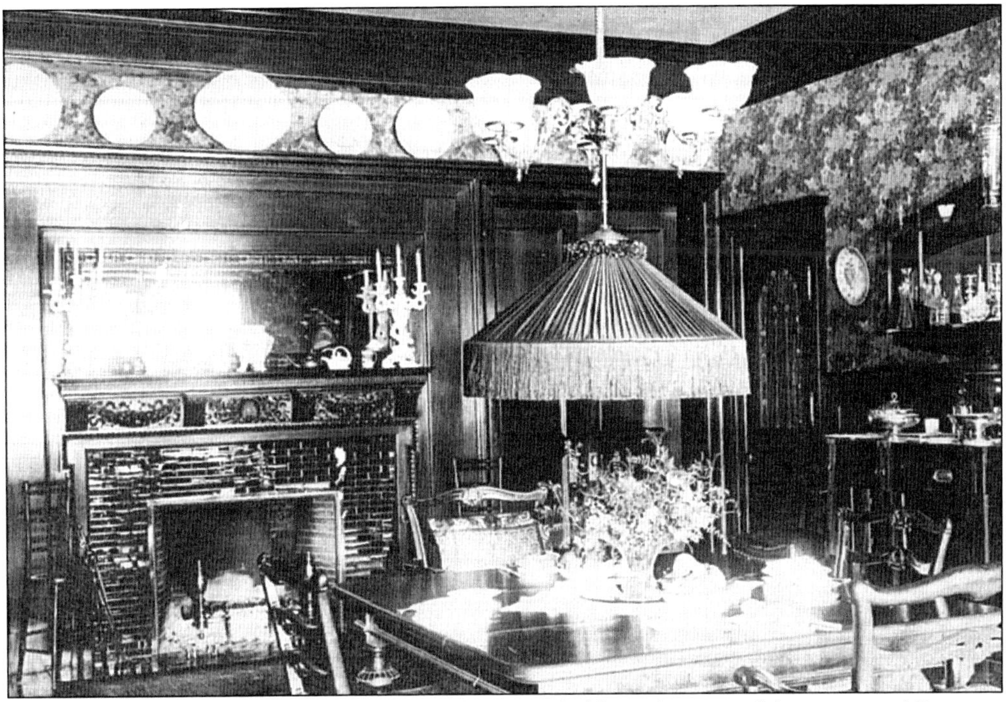

The dining room at Holly House is pictured here probably at the turn of the century. (Courtesy of Pettaquamscutt Historical Society.)

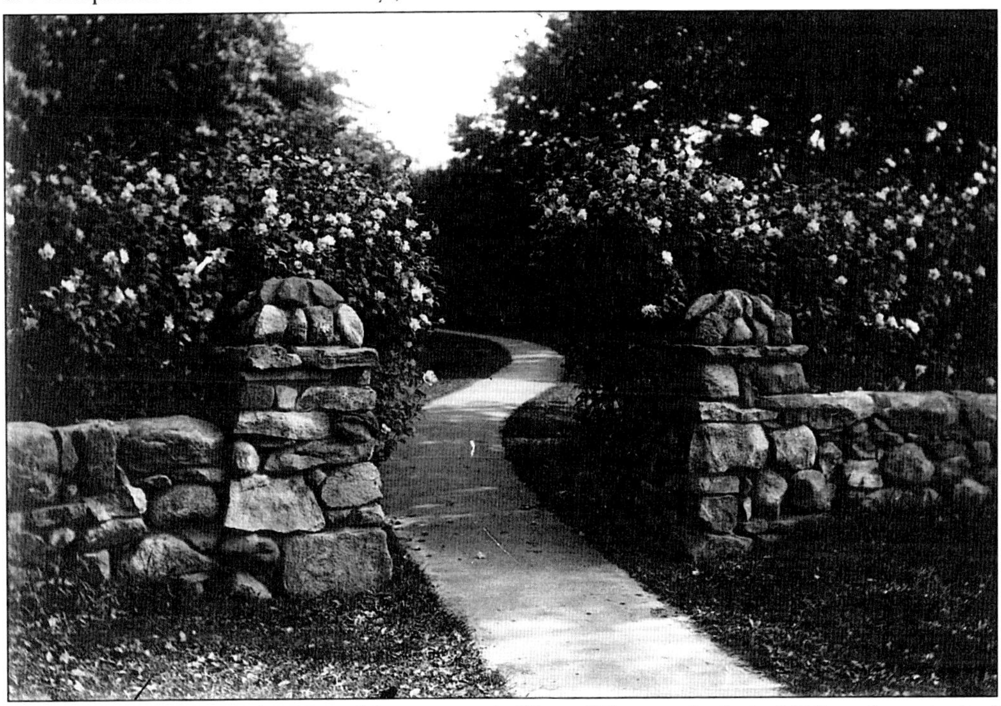

This is an entrance to the Hazards' compound. Water Way was built in 1889 as the principal entrance to Oakwoods and the Acorns, and an old road between the two estates was abandoned. (Courtesy of Anthony Guarriello Jr.)

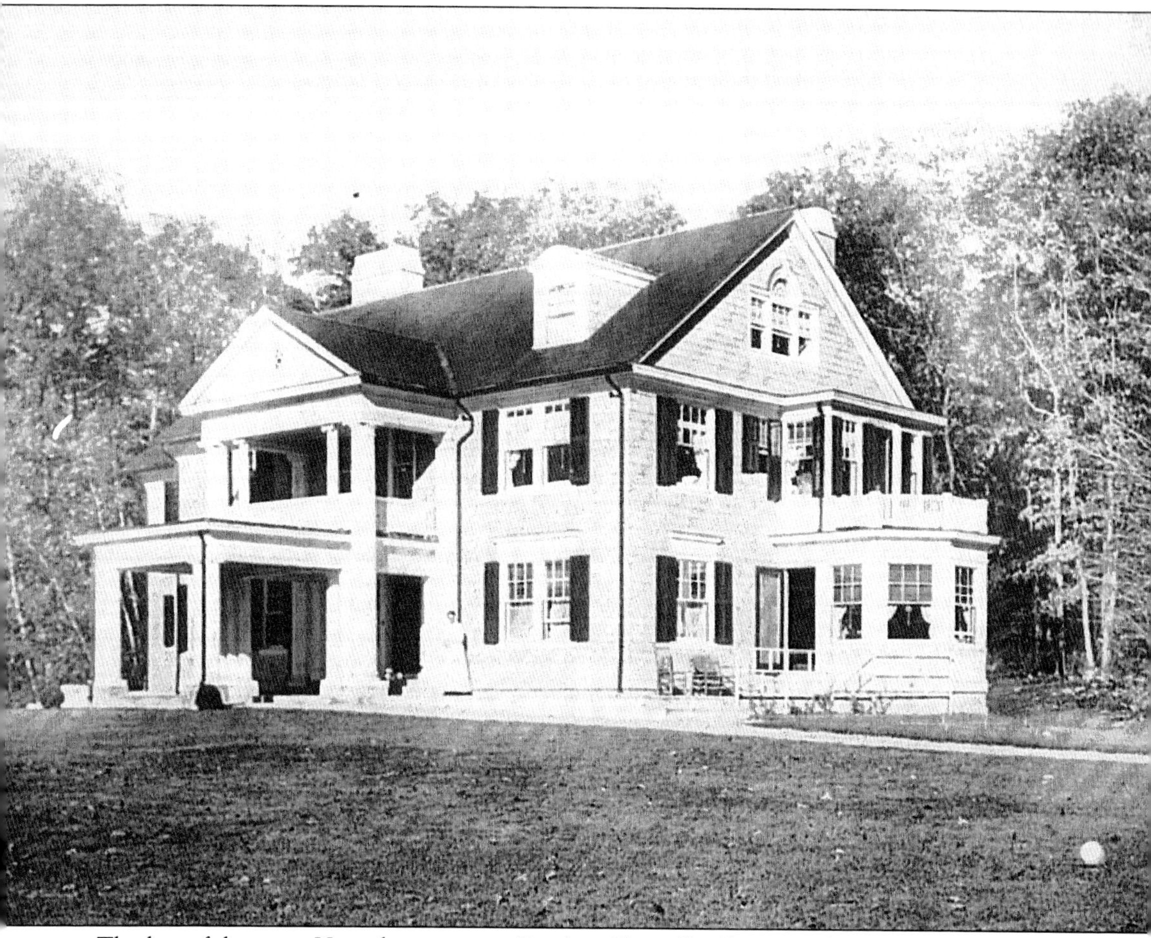

The last of the great Hazard estates was Caroline Hazard's. She named it Scallop Shell because the seashell was one of her favorite icons—one of her books of poetry was entitled *A Scallop Shell of Quiet*—and it was a symbol on the Hazard coat of arms. The house was built in 1910 under the supervision of contractor Louis F. Bell. Miss Caroline had just retired as president of Wellesley College, and she had turned over Oakwoods to her recently married nephew, Rowland Hazard. The author of essays, poetry collections, and a biography of her father entitled *A Precious Heritage*, Caroline was active in local affairs, helping to found South County Hospital in 1920. She died at her winter home in Santa Barbara, California, on March 18, 1945. Scallop Shell was converted into a nursing home and then torn down in 1976 to make way for a new building, which the Mahoney family still operates as a nursing home and daycare center under the Scallop Shell name. (Courtesy of Pettaquamscutt Historical Society.)

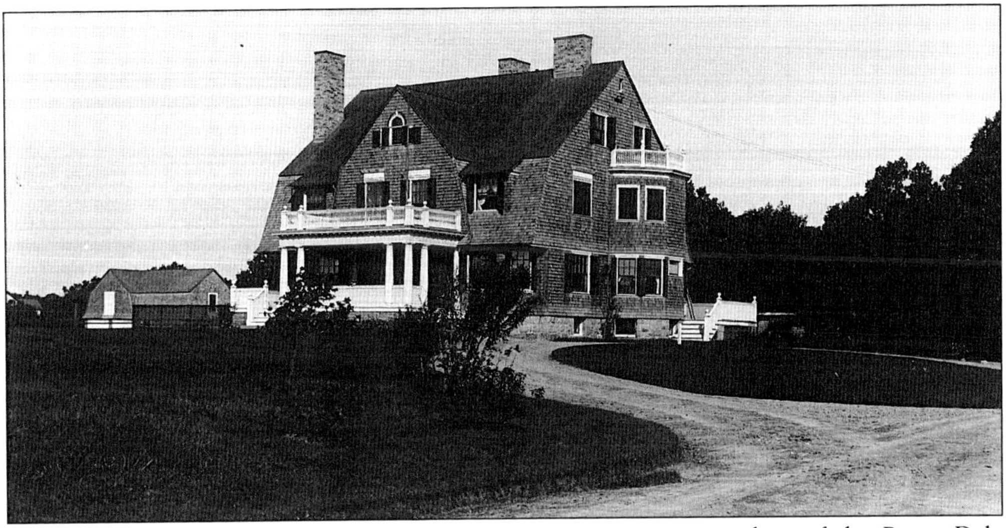

This elaborate house was home to William C. Greene, superintendent of the Peace Dale Manufacturing Co. It stood approximately where Rose Circle is now, off Church Street. In the 1880s, the mill superintendent made between $4,000 and $10,000 per year, vastly more than the mill operatives. (Courtesy of Pettaquamscutt Historical Society.)

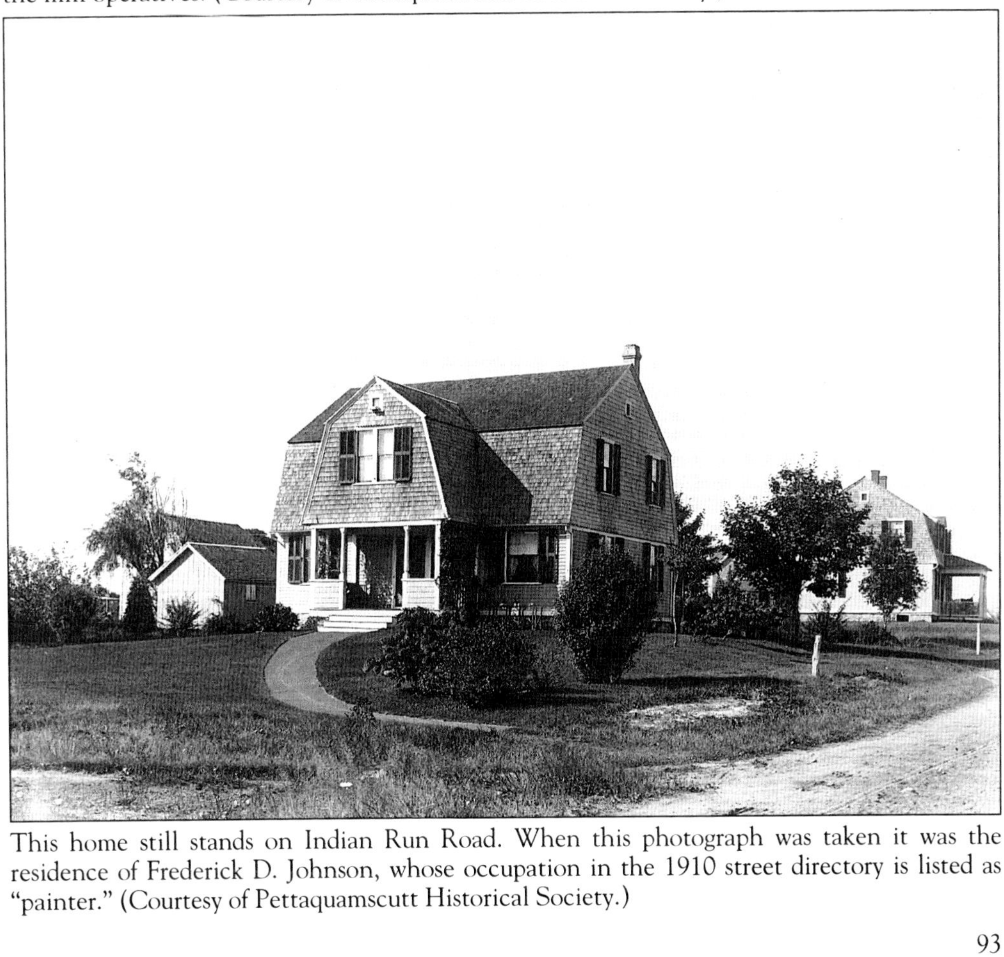

This home still stands on Indian Run Road. When this photograph was taken it was the residence of Frederick D. Johnson, whose occupation in the 1910 street directory is listed as "painter." (Courtesy of Pettaquamscutt Historical Society.)

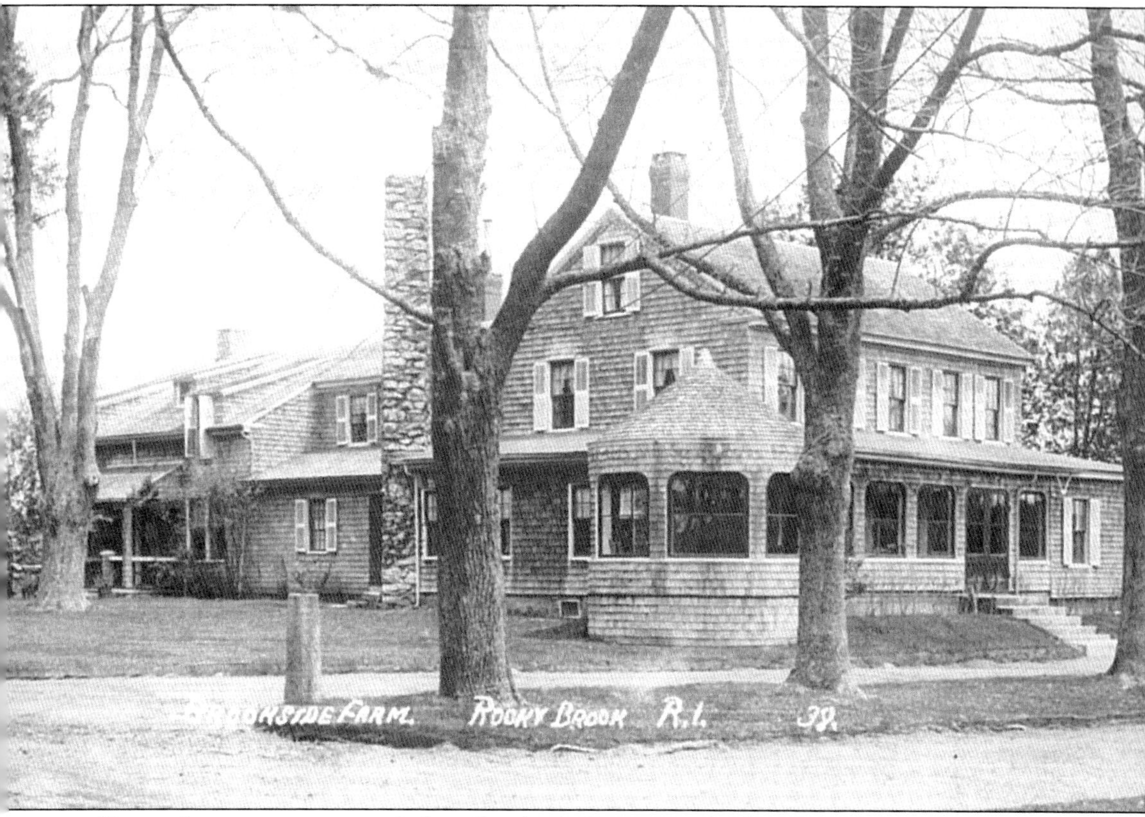

Known by many names, including Brookside Farm, Meadowbrook, and the Pope estate, this home stood off Kingstown Road in the Rocky Brook section. It was built in 1839 by Samuel R. Rodman, who first managed the Hazard mills and later manufactured slave cloth as S.R. Rodman and Sons. Eventually, the Rodman mills were damaged by fire and foreclosed upon, and Rodman's sons went off to fight in the Civil War. Charles H. Pope, a New York broker, bought the house for a summer residence. Still later, it became the Meadowbrook Nursing Home. After sitting vacant for a number of years, it was torn down in the late 1990s to make way for an apartment complex. (Courtesy of Donald and Shirley Southwick.)

Ten

NEXT STOP, PEACE DALE

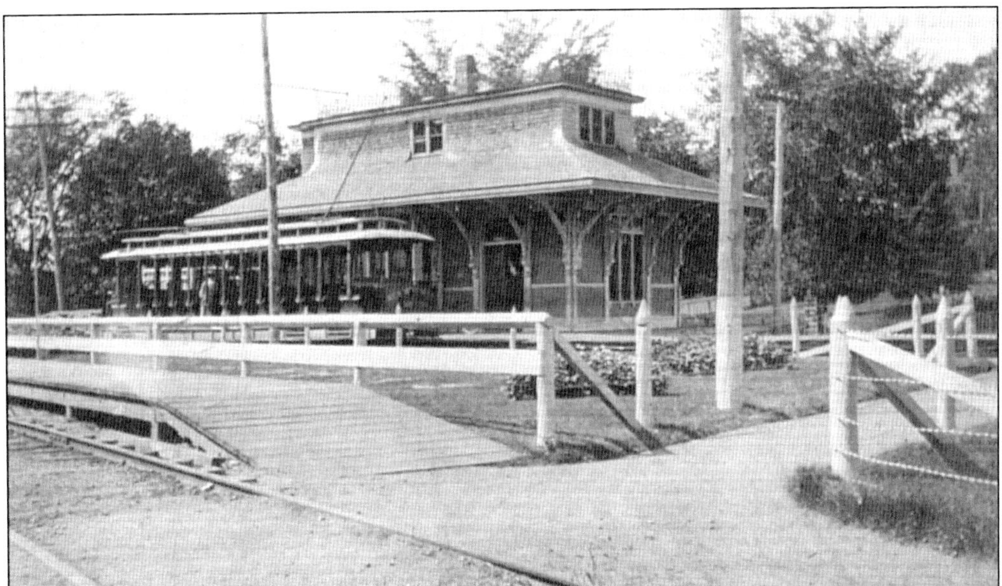

The Peace Dale Train Station was built in 1876 as part of the Narragansett Pier Railroad, which carried wealthy summer visitors from Kingston to Narragansett Pier. The railroad was chartered in 1868 by Rowland Hazard and A. & W. Sprague and carried its first passengers in July 1876. The station is a private residence today. (Courtesy of Pettaquamscutt Historical Society.)

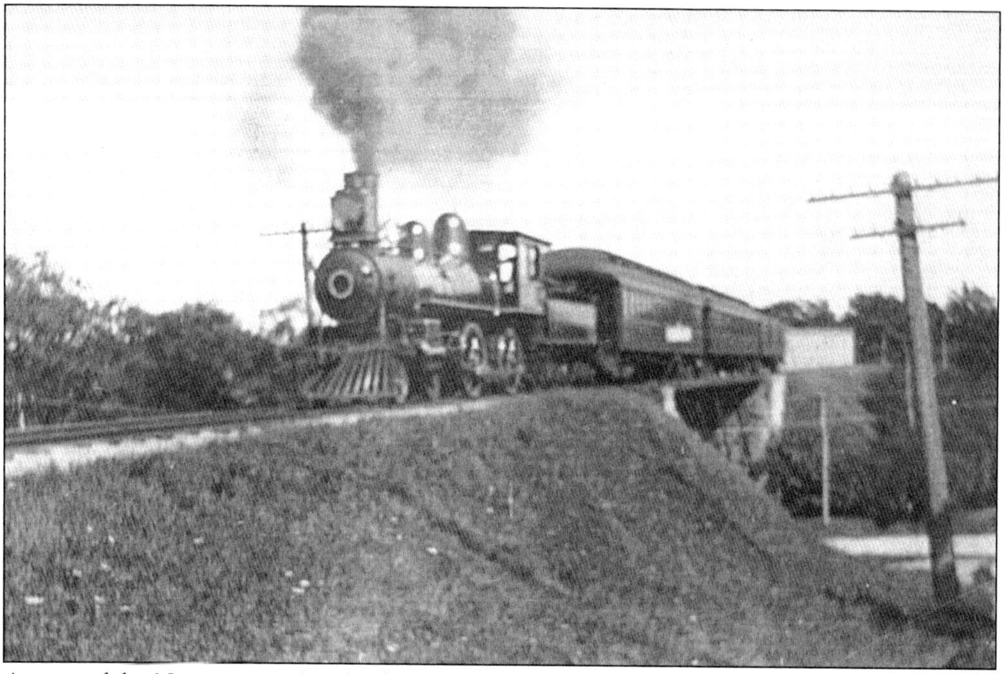

A train of the Narragansett Pier Railroad heads over the Church Street overpass. The railroad altered the landscape of Peace Dale with three overpasses in the vicinity of the Flats. (Courtesy of Pettaquamscutt Historical Society.)

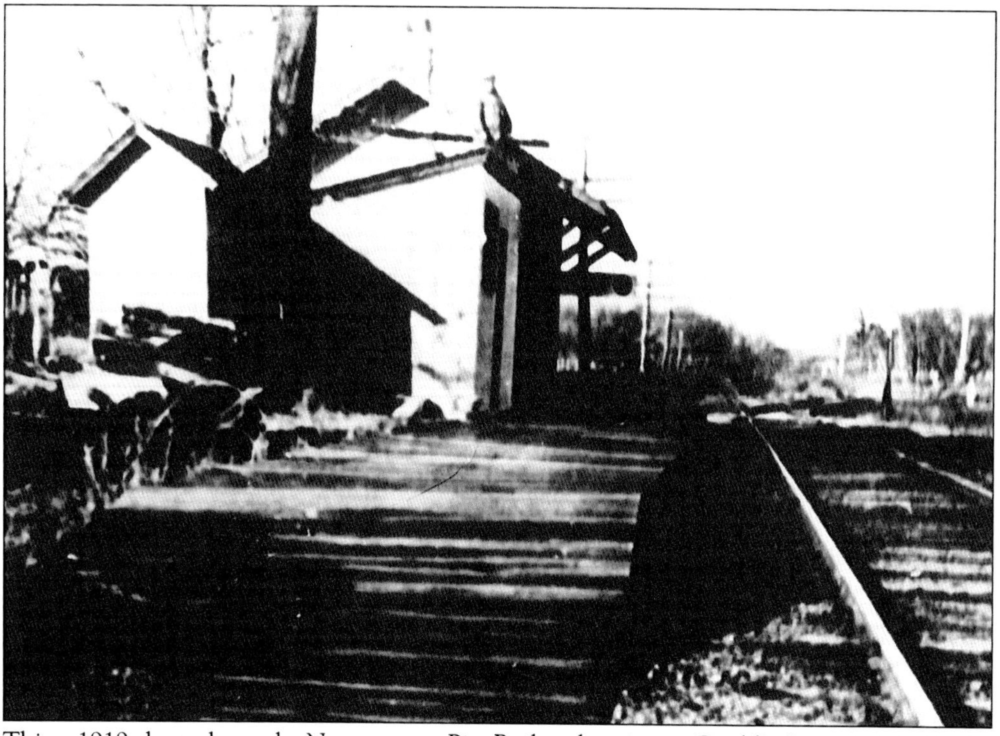

This c. 1919 photo shows the Narragansett Pier Railroad station at Gould's Crossing near Curtis Corner Road. (Courtesy of Peace Dale Library.)

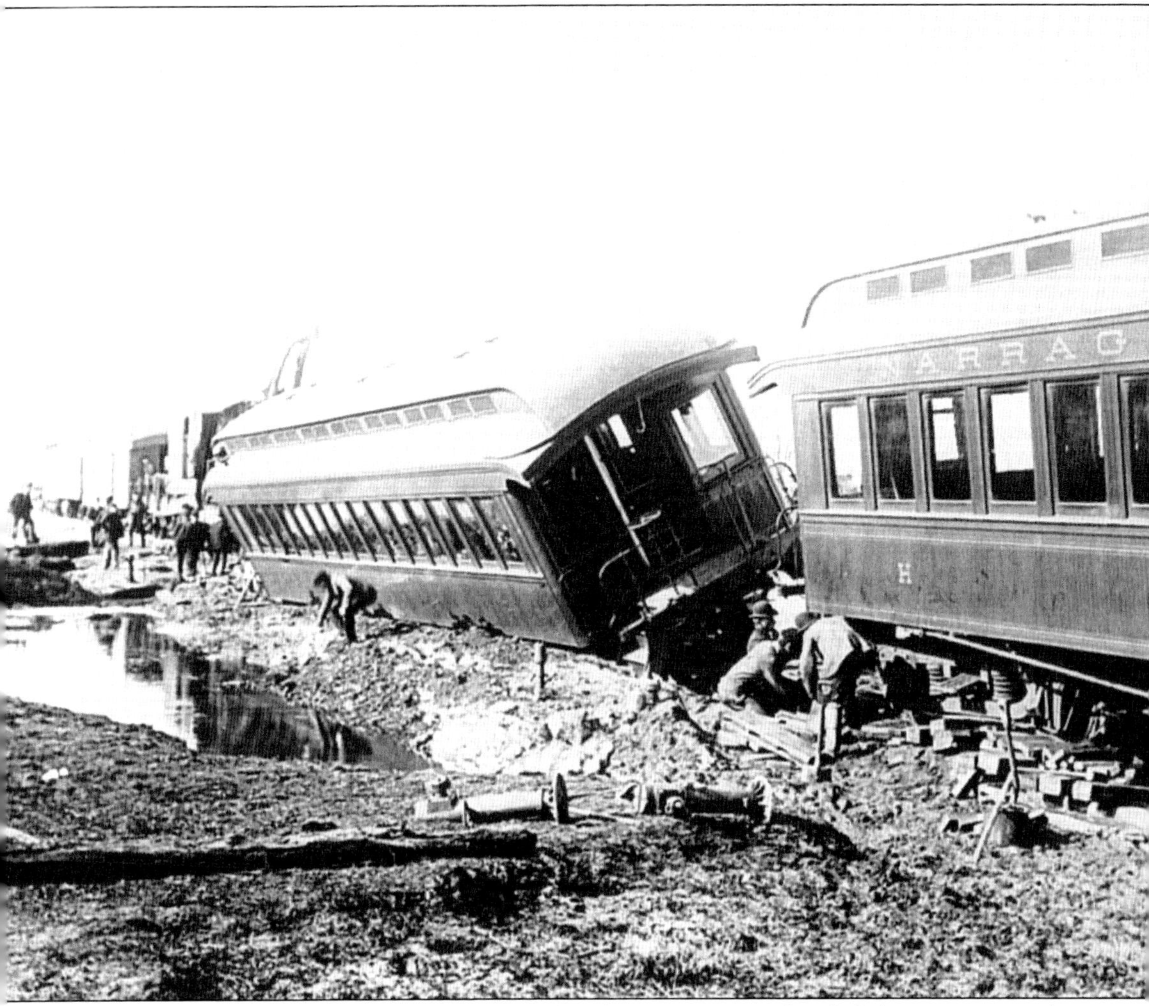

On March 1, 1902, this Narragansett Pier Railroad passenger train derailed about a quarter of a mile east of the Kingston Junction; it was the worst accident the railroad had met with up until that point. Heavy rain the previous night had eroded the track, which gave way as the train crossed over it. The coal tender and two cars ran off the tracks first as the rails broke, and then the engine jumped the track. A crowd gathered as a wrecking train attempted to raise the train back onto the tracks. No one was injured, and the passengers and baggage were taken to the station by carriage. Remarkably, reported the *Narragansett Times*, "Not a window in the whole train was broken." (Courtesy of Pettaquamscutt Historical Society.)

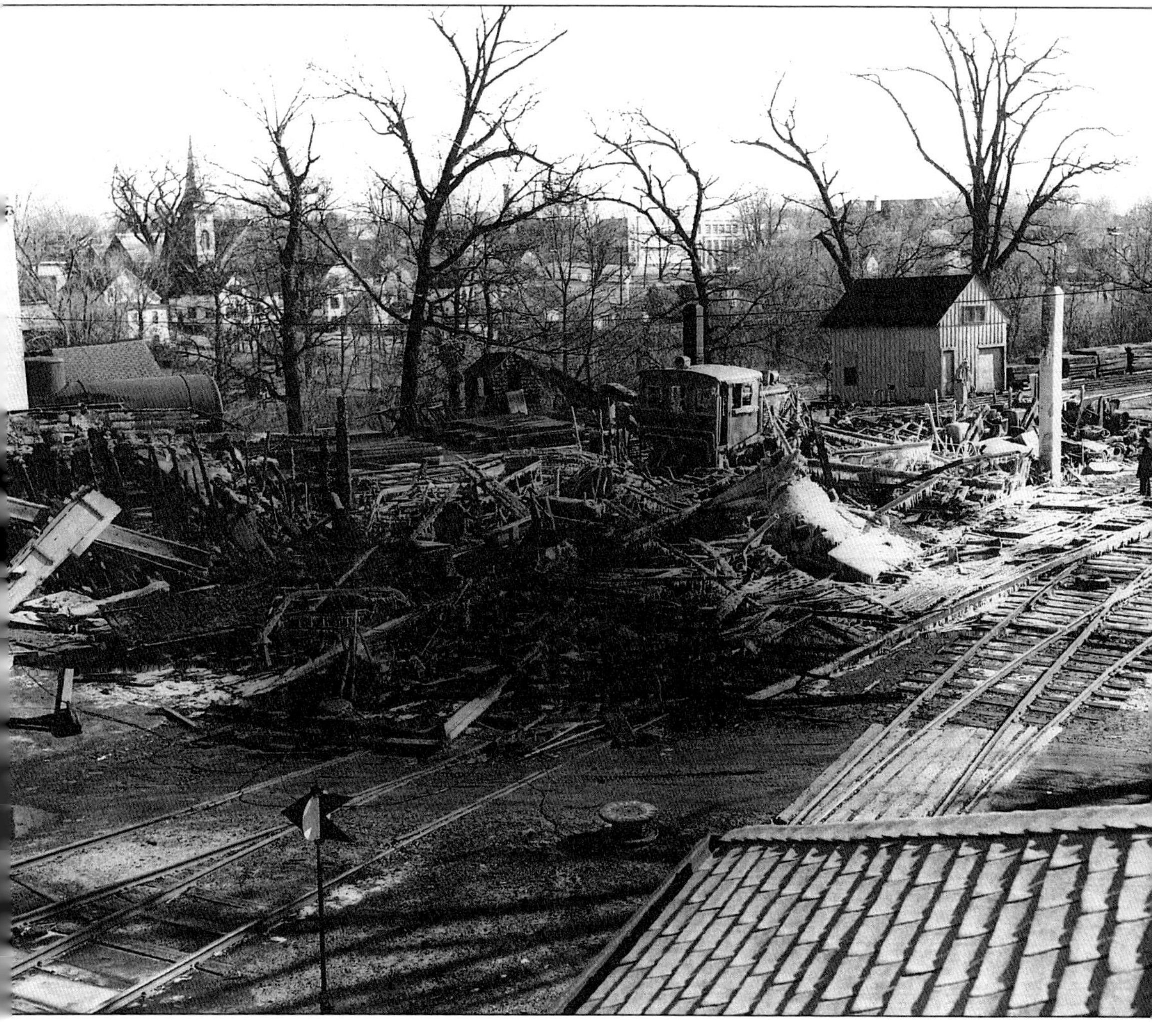

This is the aftermath of the Peace Dale Roundhouse after fire destroyed it. (Photo by Bob Wilkie, courtesy of Peace Dale Library.)

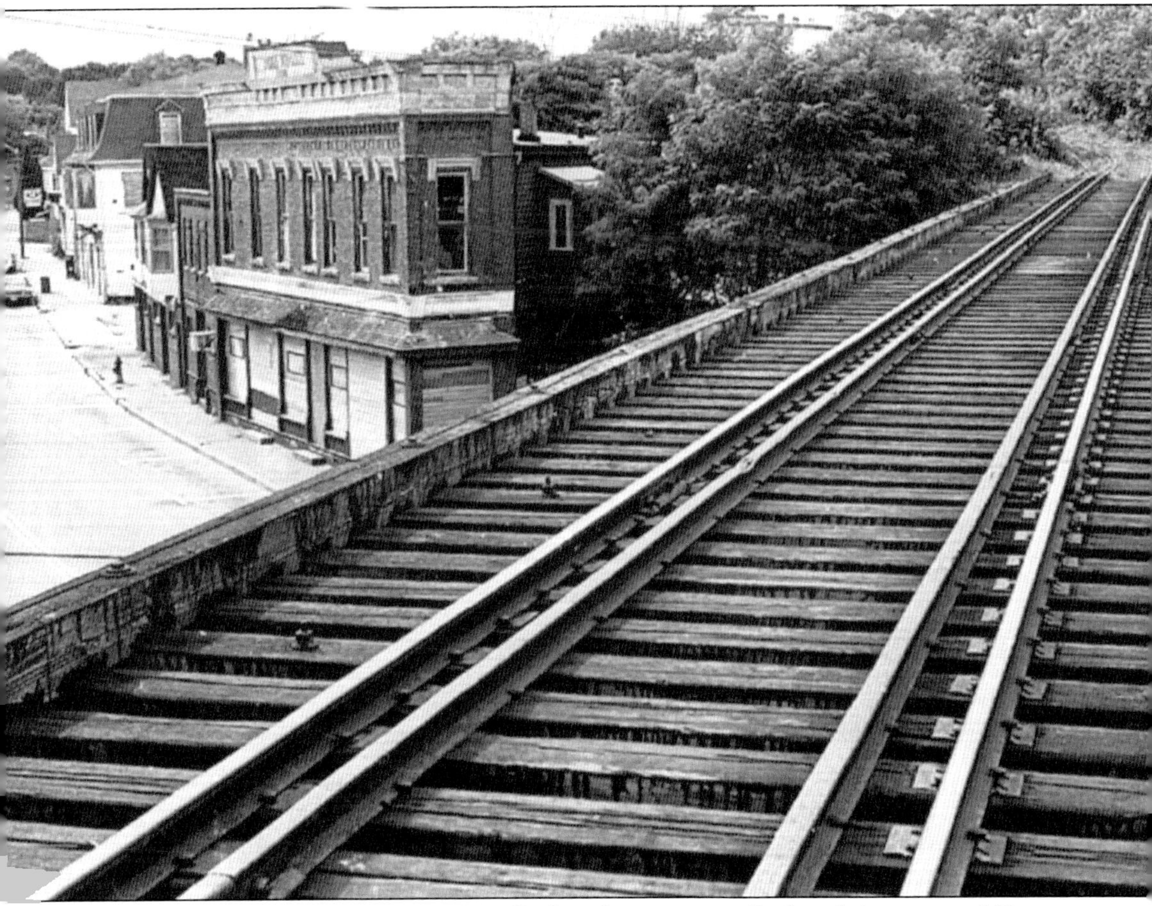

This photo from the Narragansett Pier Railroad overpass at Railroad Avenue and Route 108 shows the Flats in the late 1970s. The railroad had ceased to run in 1952, and the Flats was taking on a down-at-the-heels appearance. The tracks and overpasses were ripped out by Anthony Guarriello Jr. after he bought the railroad in the early 1980s. (Courtesy of Daniel G. Dunn.)

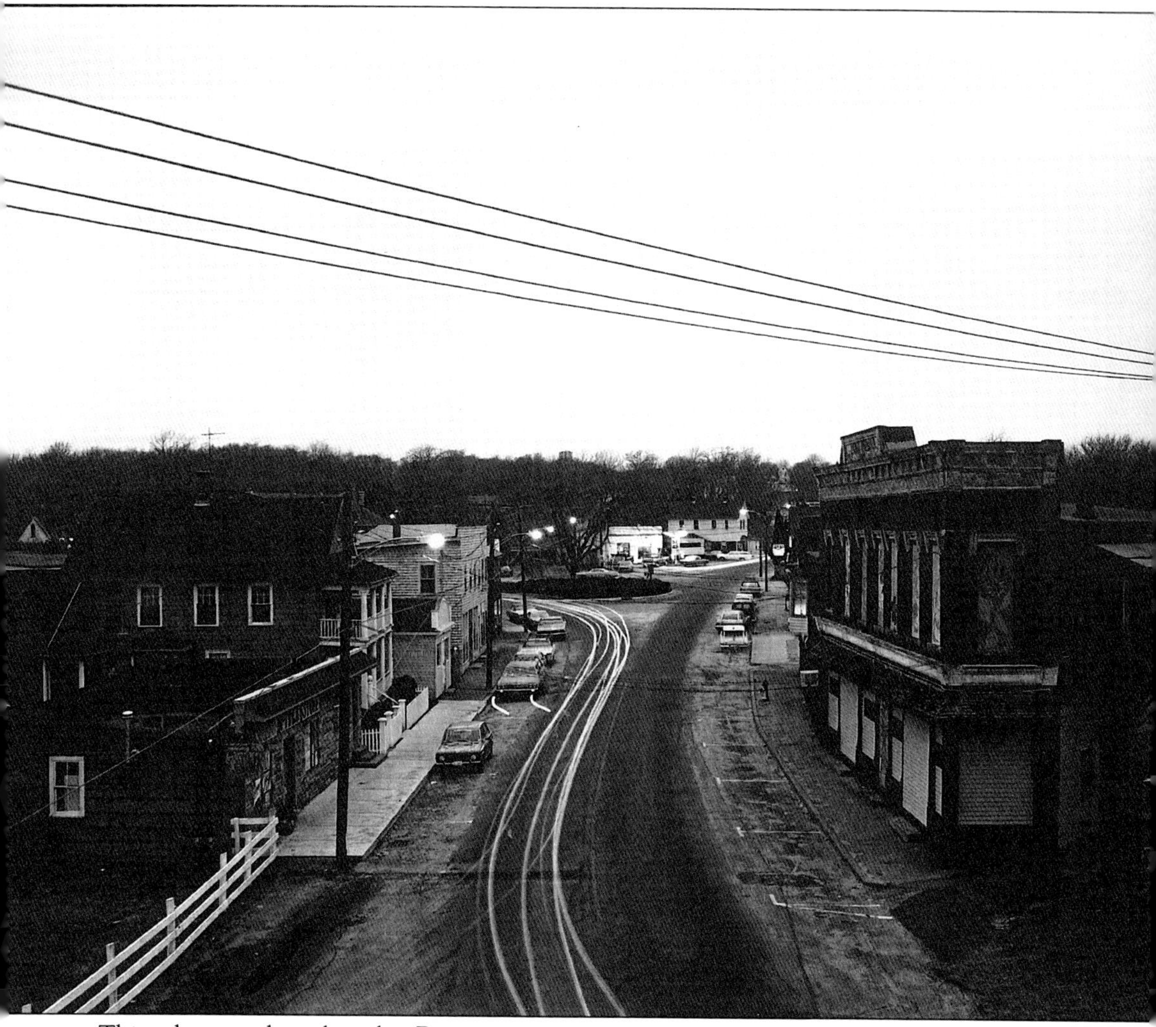

This photograph, taken by Dennis Haggerty in January 1976, shows Peace Dale Flats looking northwest from the railroad trestle. The automobile was now the dominant form of transportation, as evidenced by the neon glow of the gas station in the background. Gas was 57¢ a gallon. (Courtesy of Peace Dale Library.)

Eleven

Scenes from Long Ago

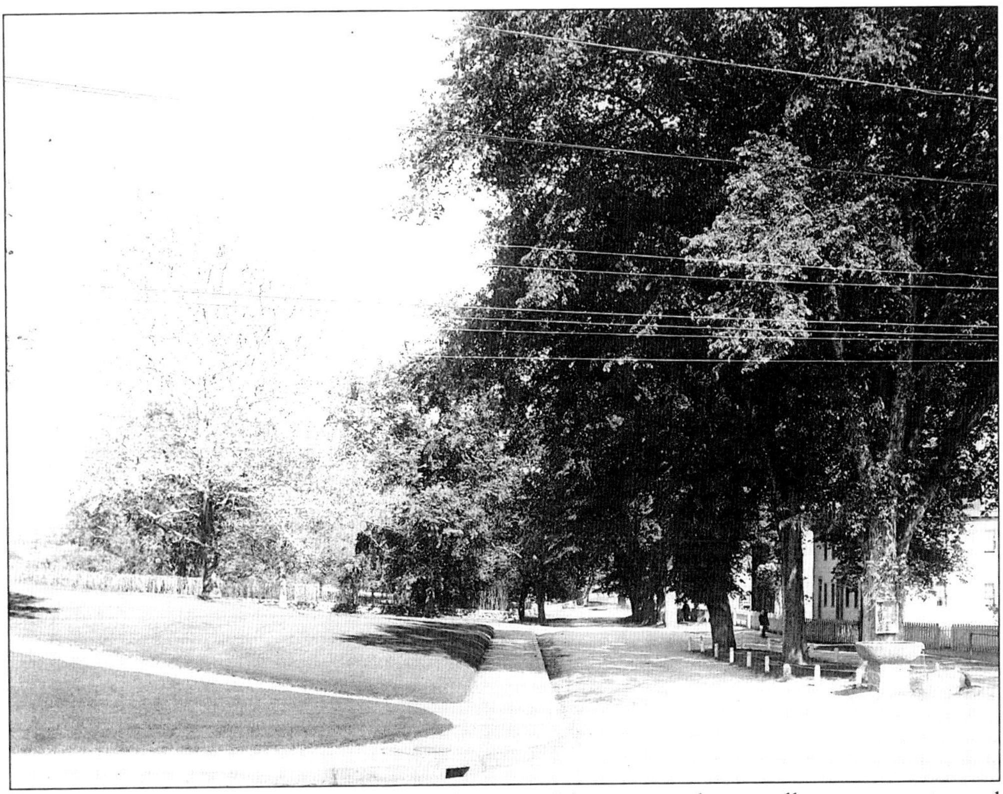

This peaceful view of Kingstown Road at the turn of the century shows mill tenements situated where the Village Green would later be developed. To the right in this photo can be seen a fountain with levels for horses, oxen, and dogs. Imagine the slower pace of life in Peace Dale when the main form of transportation was horse-drawn buggies, and entertainment was a play at the Hazard Memorial Hall. (Courtesy of Pettaquamscutt Historical Society.)

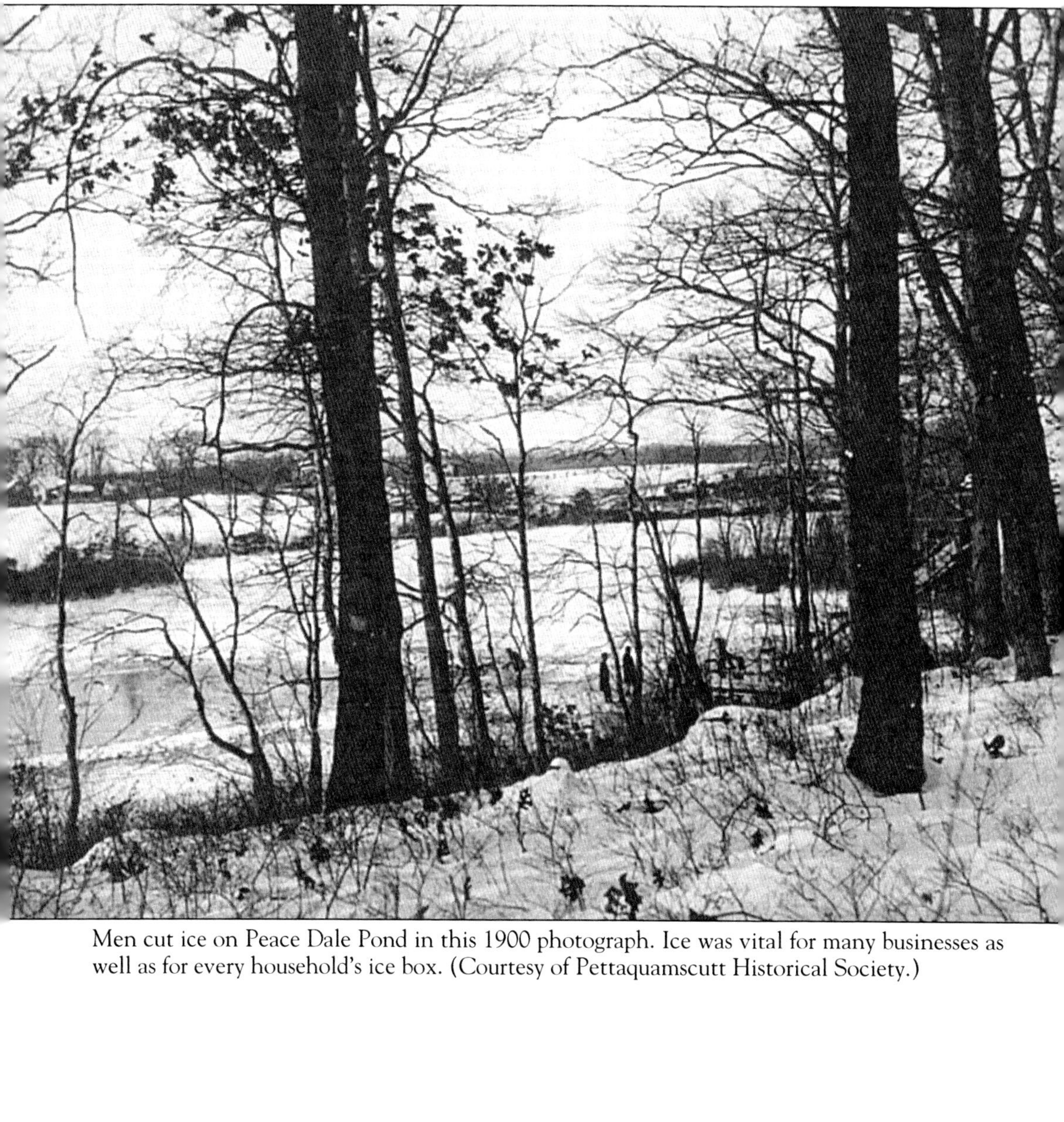

Men cut ice on Peace Dale Pond in this 1900 photograph. Ice was vital for many businesses as well as for every household's ice box. (Courtesy of Pettaquamscutt Historical Society.)

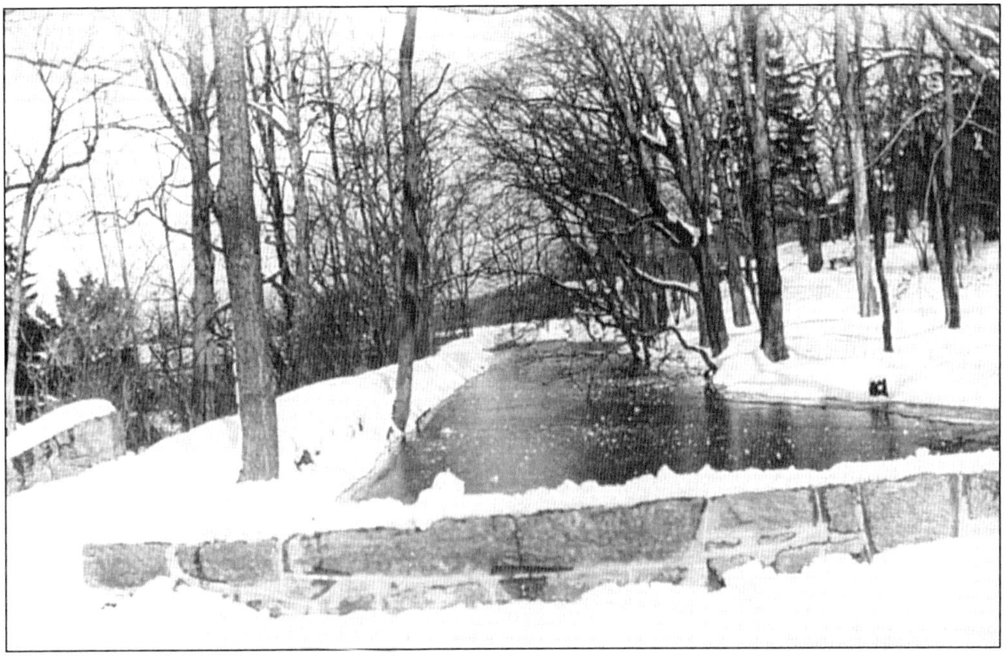

This is the Peace Dale Canal, developed to bring water to power the Peace Dale Manufacturing Co. The harnessing of the many streams running down toward the Saugatucket River made the mill possible, but it also changed the course of nature. It was not uncommon for some wetlands to be redirected and others to be filled in. In 1906, when the Hazards scrambled to erect new housing for workers brought in to replace strikers, a tenement was built "about where Fiske Pond was," the *Narragansett Times* reported. (Courtesy of Pettaquamscutt Historical Society.)

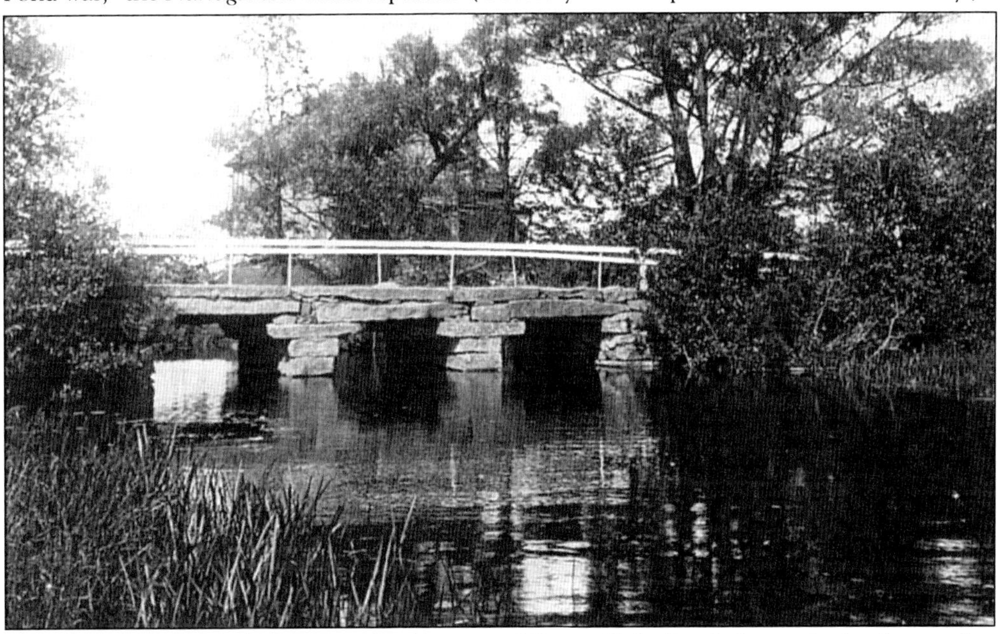

This bridge spanned the Saugatucket River and Peace Dale Pond. It was built of stone but not in the elaborate arched design that would become a village trademark. (Courtesy of Pettaquamscutt Historical Society.)

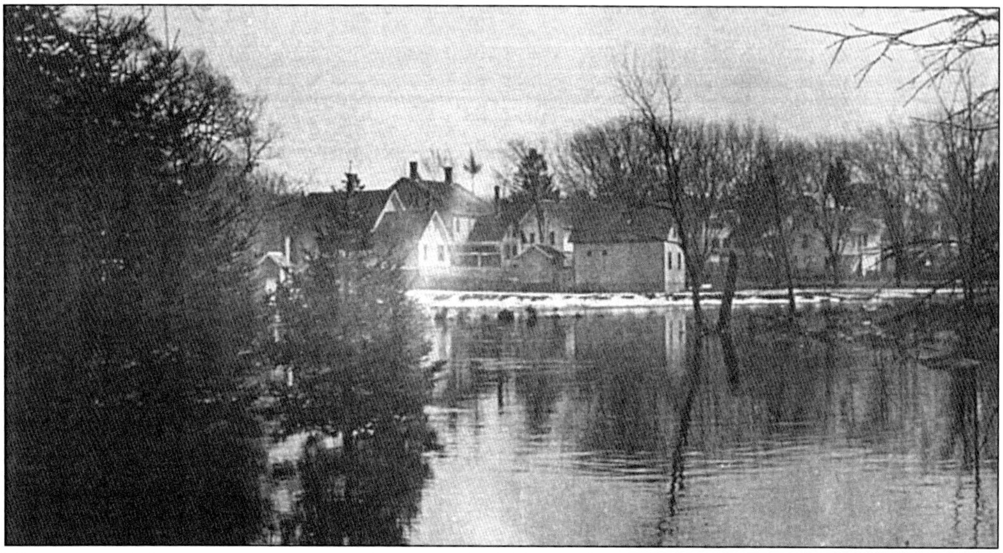

This turn-of-the-century photograph shows the Village Green flooded when Indian Run overran its banks. The streams that rush toward the Saugatucket River have a history of flooding, complicated by man's interference with their natural paths. (Courtesy of Pettaquamscutt Historical Society.)

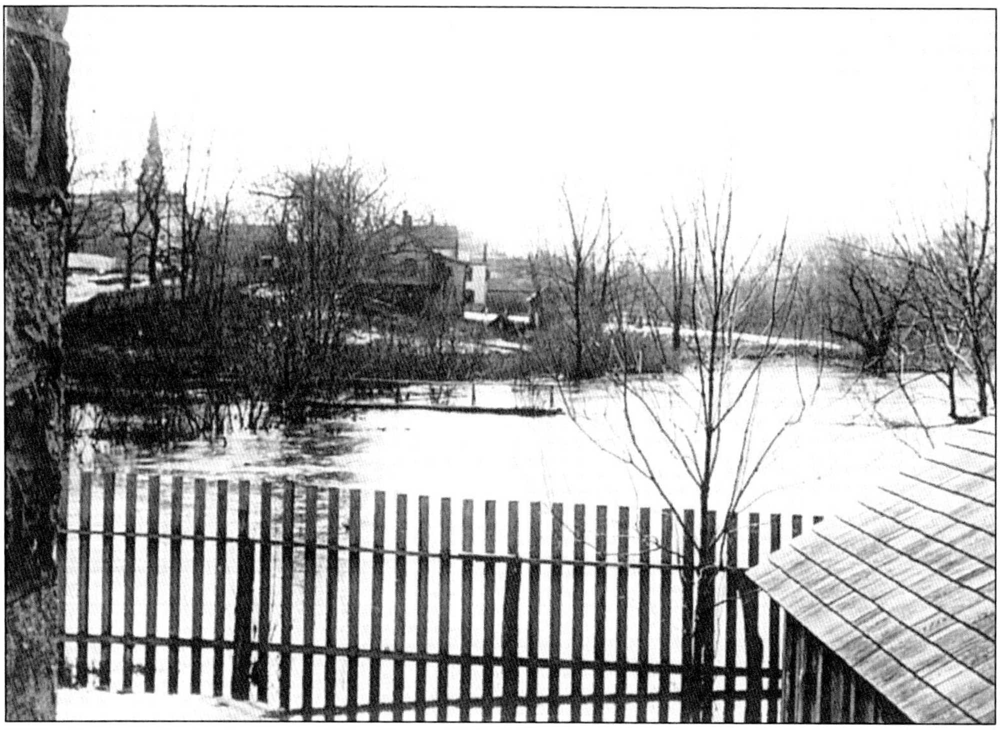

This photograph, in the area of the Peace Dale Manufacturing Co., is labeled "Flood of 1902." In February 1902, the *Narragansett Times* reported one flooding episode after a heavy snowfall and then rain. " . . . And Wednesday morning the streets were flooded, and one could not go dry shod with anything less than high rubber footwear. The road commissioners were busy with men making paths to guide the water off the streets." (Courtesy of Anthony Guarriello Jr.)

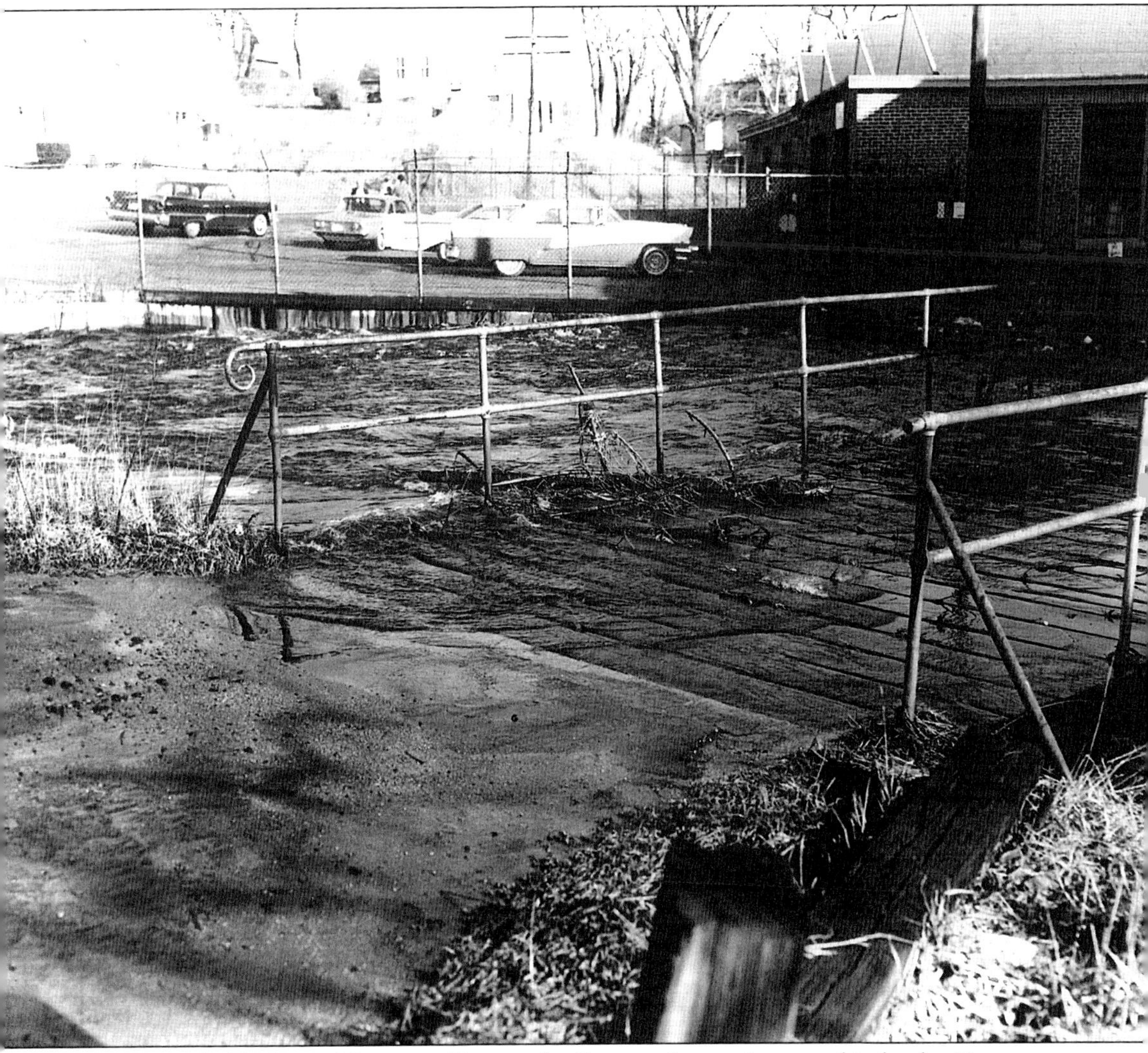

In 1960, probably during Hurricane Donna, the Saugatucket again crested its banks. Here water laps at a bridge near Warren Pumps, which occupied part of what had been the Peace Dale mill. The September hurricane felled trees and damaged boats elsewhere in town. (Photo by Robert Wilkie, courtesy of Anthony Guarriello Jr.)

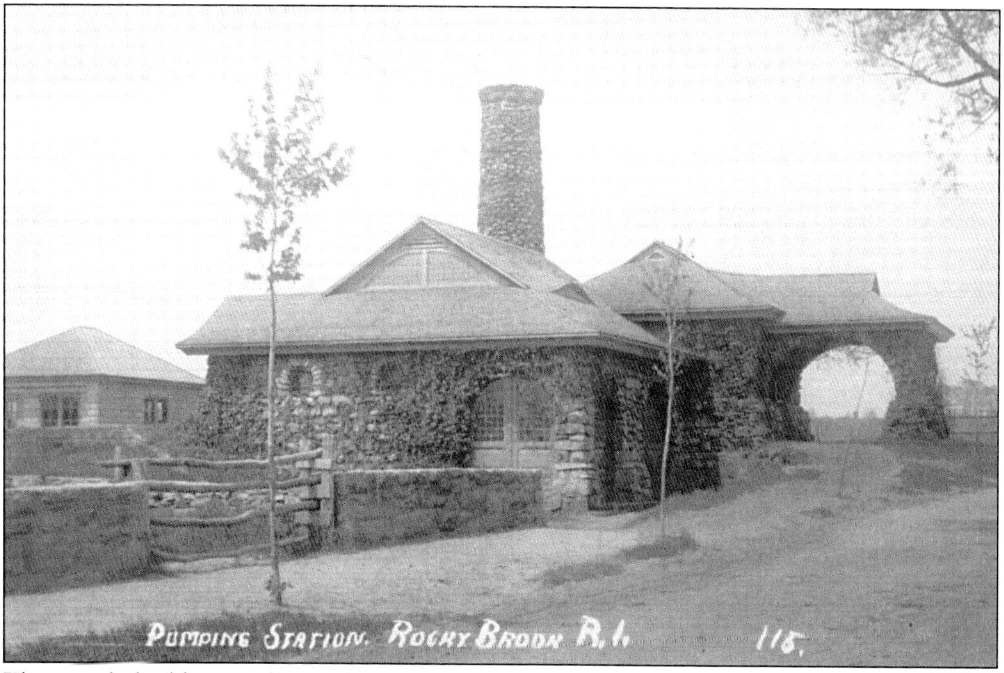

This stately building in the Rocky Brook section was the pumping station for the Wakefield Water Company, which took its water supply from the adjacent Rocky Brook reservoir. Today it is the Pump House Restaurant. (Courtesy of Pettaquamscutt Historical Society.)

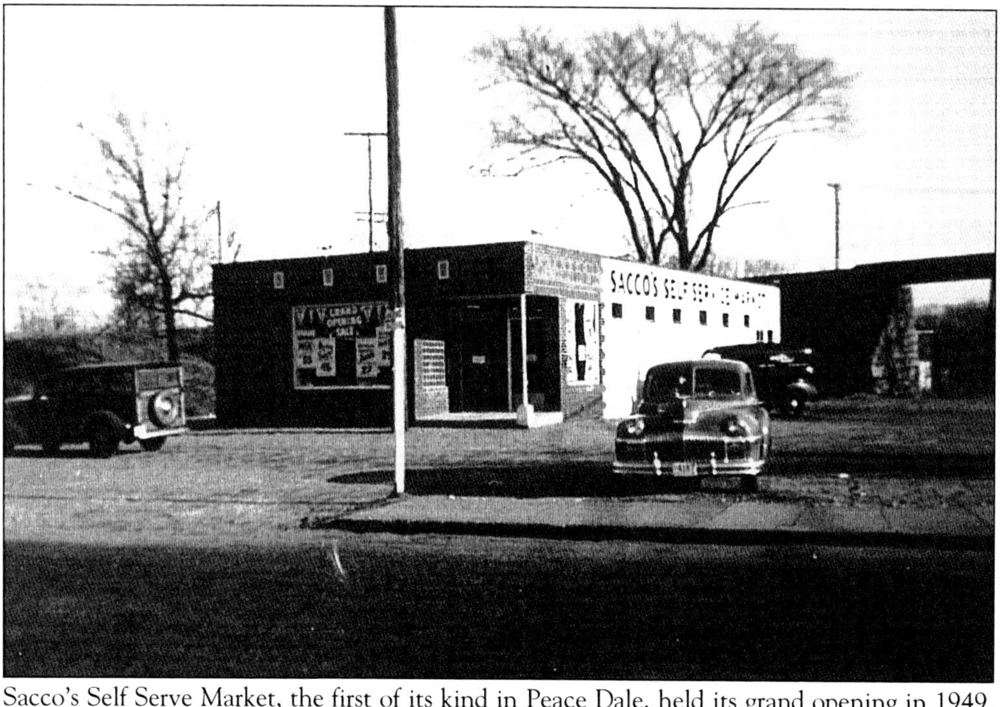

Sacco's Self Serve Market, the first of its kind in Peace Dale, held its grand opening in 1949. Located at the corner of Kersey Road and Route 108, the building is a rental business today. The railroad trestle can be seen in the background. (Courtesy of Everett Hopkins.)

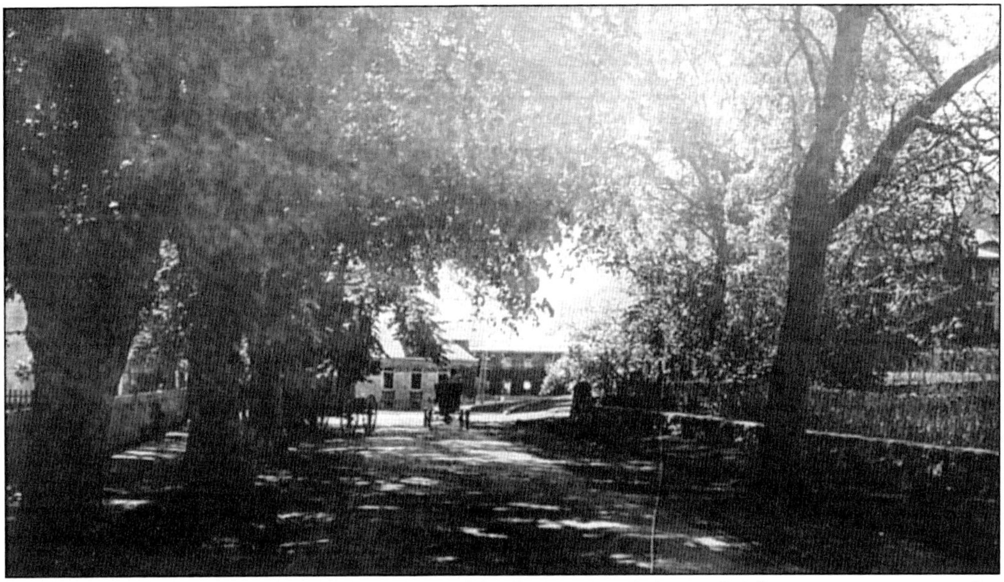

This is a bucolic glimpse of Kingstown Road looking toward the mill. The view is opposite the one at the beginning of this chapter. (Courtesy of Pettaquamscutt Historical Society.)

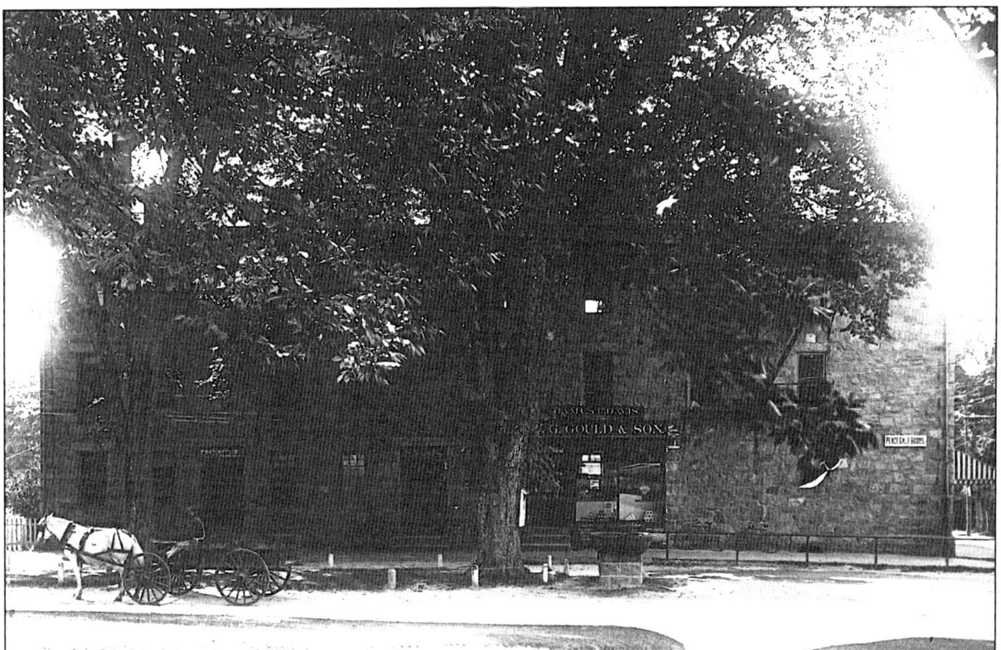

Known today as the Peace Dale Office Building, this granite structure at Columbia Street and Kingstown Road was built in 1856 by the Hazards. In its time, it housed the mill stores, the Peace Dale Post Office, mill workers' housing, the Narragansett Library Association, and the Narragansett Choral Society. Gradually, its occupants moved to other headquarters—the Guild to its own building in 1908–1909, and the library and choral society to Hazard Memorial Hall in 1891. Today, the structure is owned by the Town of South Kingstown and is home to several private businesses and the Museum of Primitive Art and Culture, which is a collection of artifacts established by Rowland G. Hazard. (Courtesy of Pettaquamscutt Historical Society.)

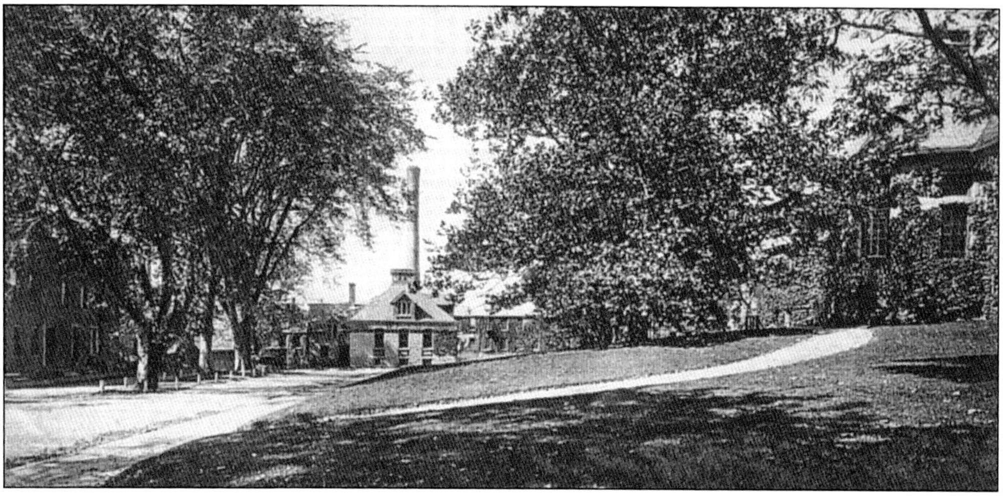

This Peace Dale street scene of 1906 looks peaceful, but the year was a trying one for the Peace Dale Manufacturing Co. A protracted strike by the weavers nearly shut down mill operations. Although the strike caused hardship on many sides, it could have been worse. "The employees have behaved themselves and it is not likely they will do anything violent," the *Narragansett Times* noted on March 9, 1906. (Courtesy of Pettaquamscutt Historical Society.)

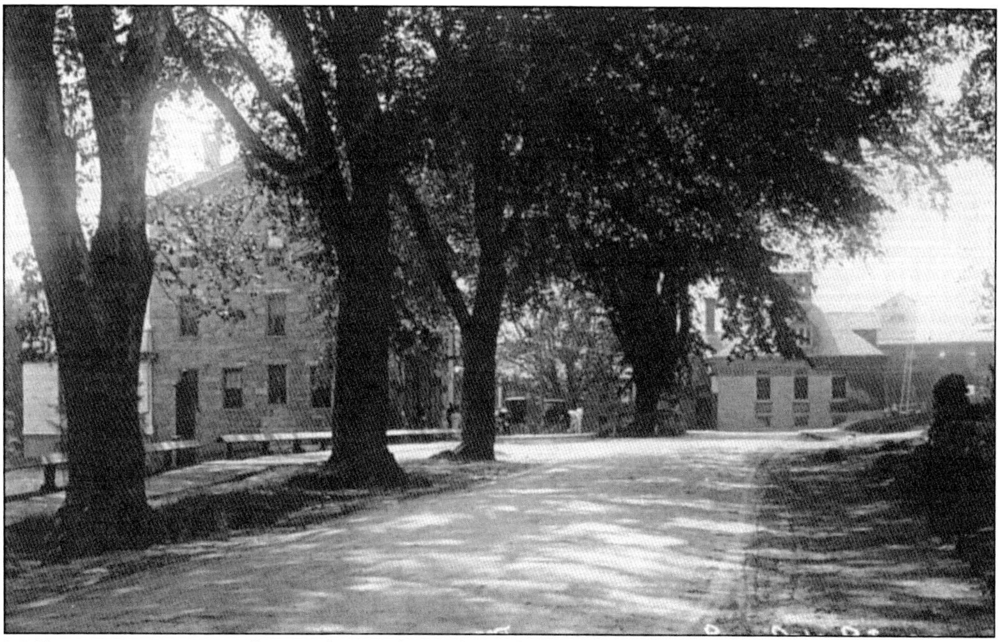

Mill expansion was taking place when this photograph was taken, as witnessed by the ladder up against a mill wall being erected in the far right corner. (Courtesy of Donald and Shirley Southwick.)

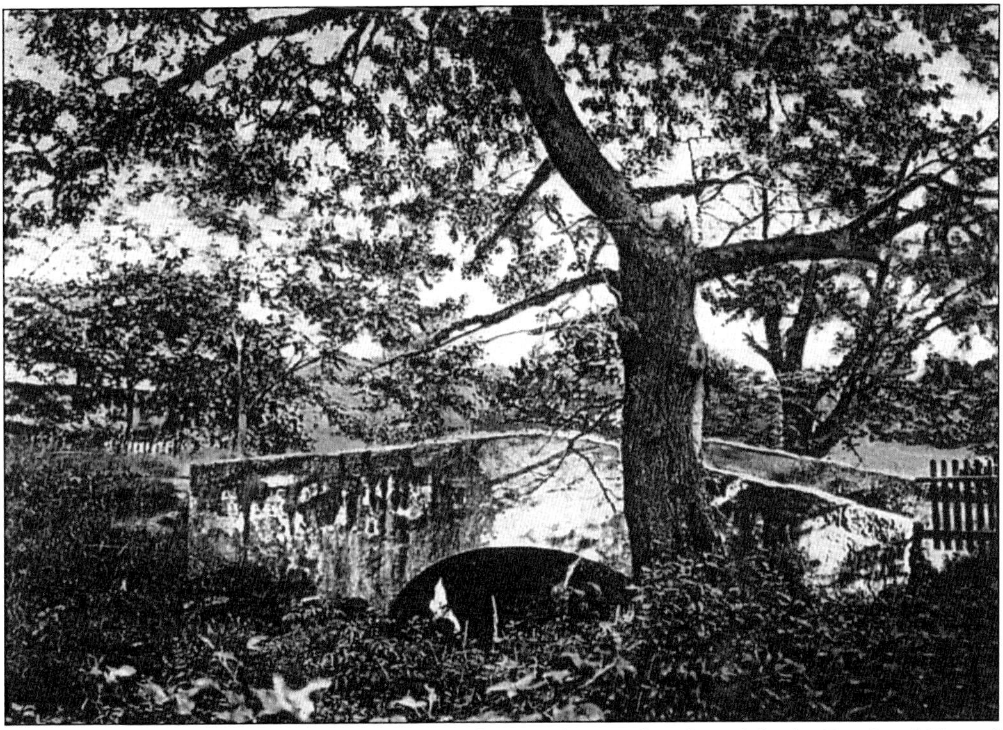

Indian Run Bridge in Peace Dale was one of seven designed and paid for by Rowland Hazard and built by masons working for Kneeland Partelow and George H. Bullock. Two are near the Guild, at Spring and Columbia Streets; two are on Church Street; one is on Railroad Avenue; and two are on Kingstown Road. (Courtesy of Donald and Shirley Southwick.)

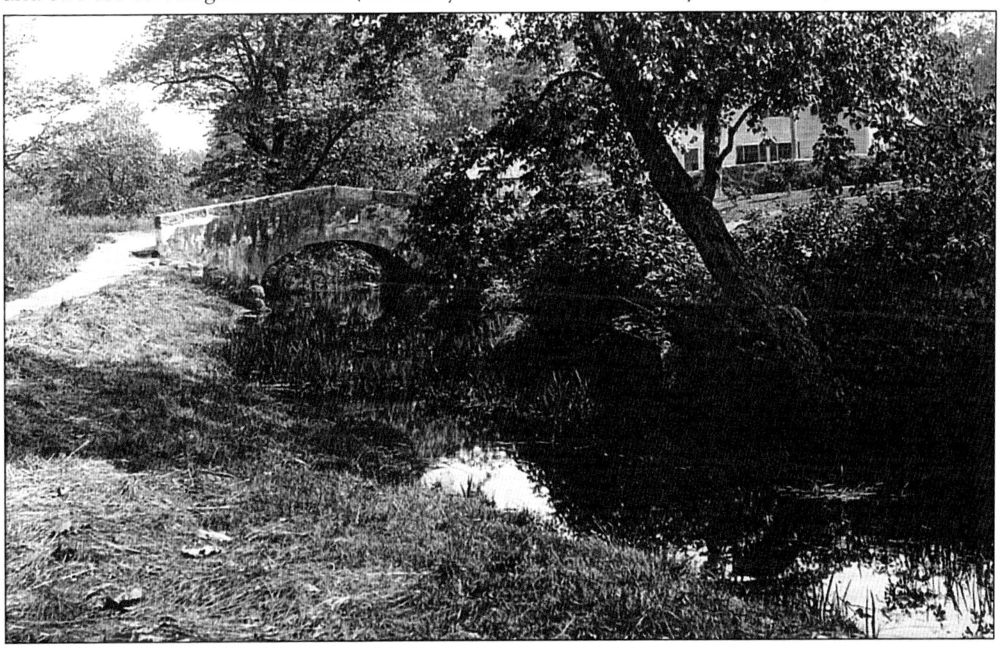

Another of the arched bridges is shown here, on what appears to be Church Street. (Courtesy of Donald and Shirley Southwick.)

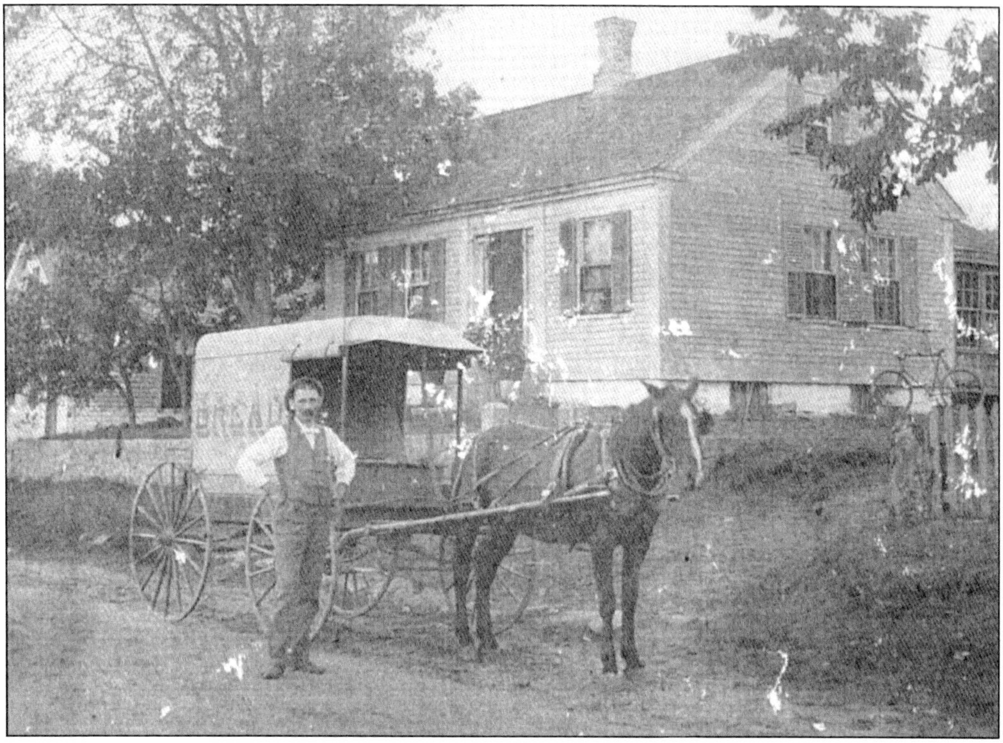

William A. Tennant, "the breadman," poses with his delivery vehicle at High and Austin Streets. He also worked at the Peace Dale mill. (Courtesy of Clara W. Smith.)

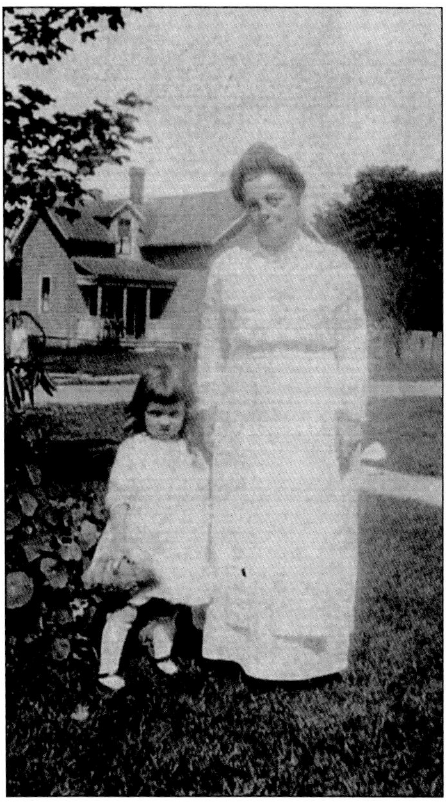

Clara Gould Tennant and her granddaughter, three-year-old Clara (Wilson) Smith, pose in this 1920s photograph near their home in Peace Dale. Circled in the background is Thelma Harvey. Although Peace Dale was a thriving village, many side streets had a distinctly rural character. (Courtesy of Clara W. Smith.)

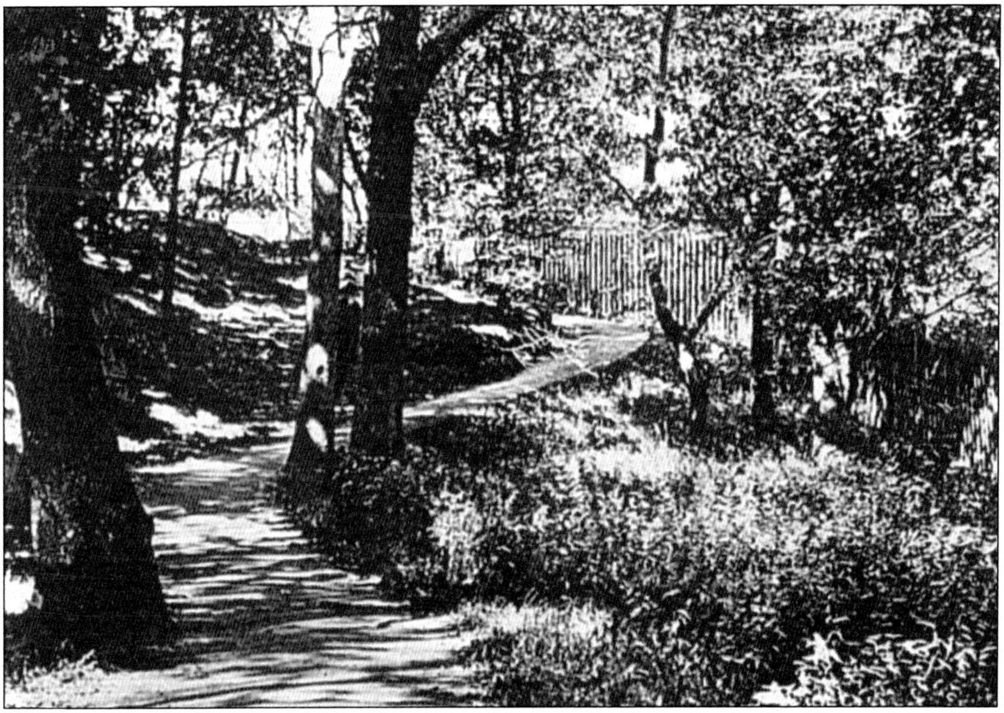

This path apparently led to the train depot. The postcard's message mentions the Kingston Fair, and passengers would crowd the platform of the Peace Dale Train Station to board a train for the fair. (Courtesy of Shirley and Donald Southwick.)

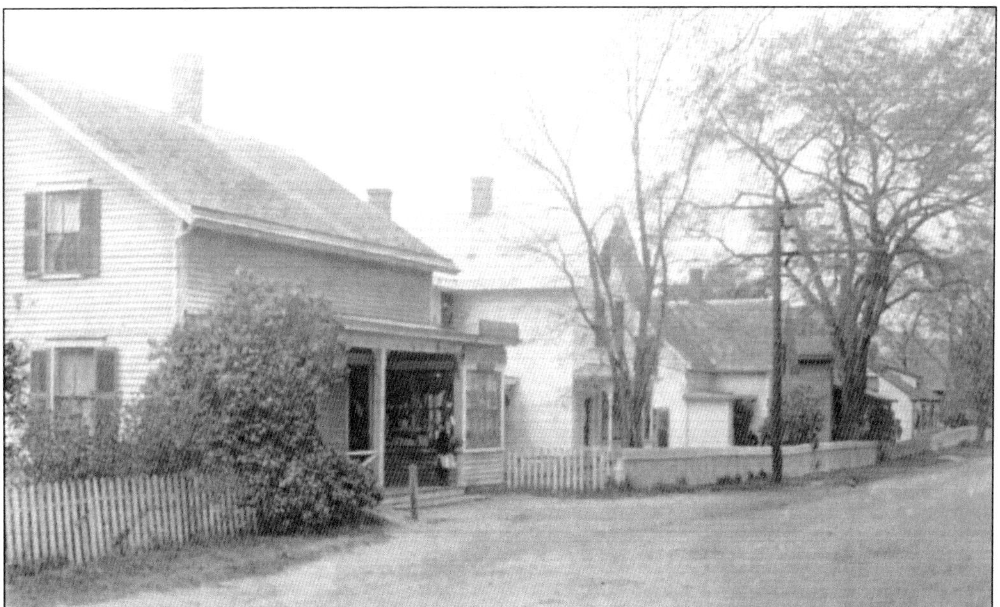

Philip Clemens ran a store from this building at the corner of Columbia and Church Streets, where in 1906 he advertised "glass, tin, iron and wooden ware, also a nice line of fancy goods selected from the latest styles." Julia Clemens lived across the street in a house where the Peace Dale Congregational Church's parking lot is now. (Courtesy of Peace Dale Library.)

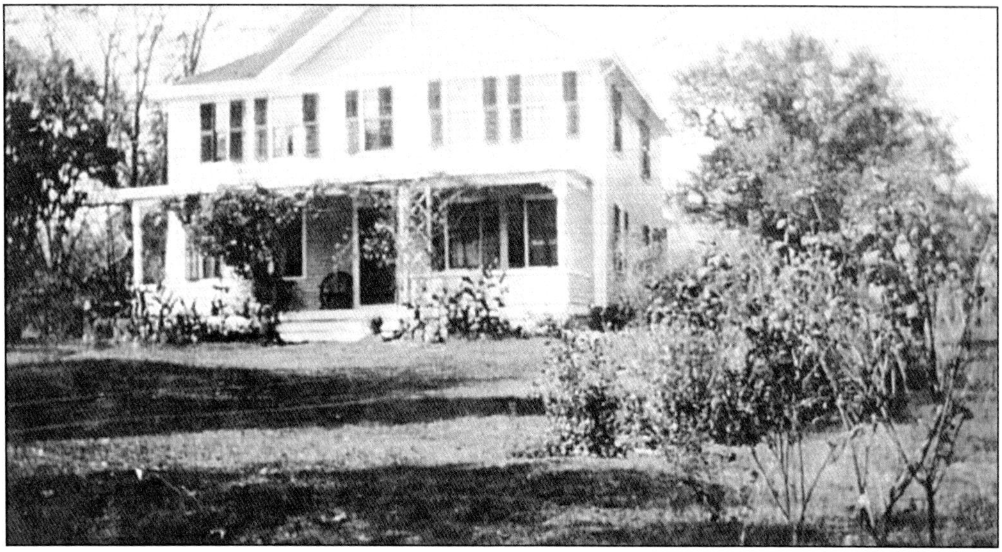

This was the home of George and Mary (Hunt) Helliwell on High Street in Peace Dale. George Helliwell first worked for William G. Gould at his store in the Peace Dale Office Building, taking over the store on Gould's retirement, and then selling clothing on his own at several locations. (Courtesy of Betty Tucker.)

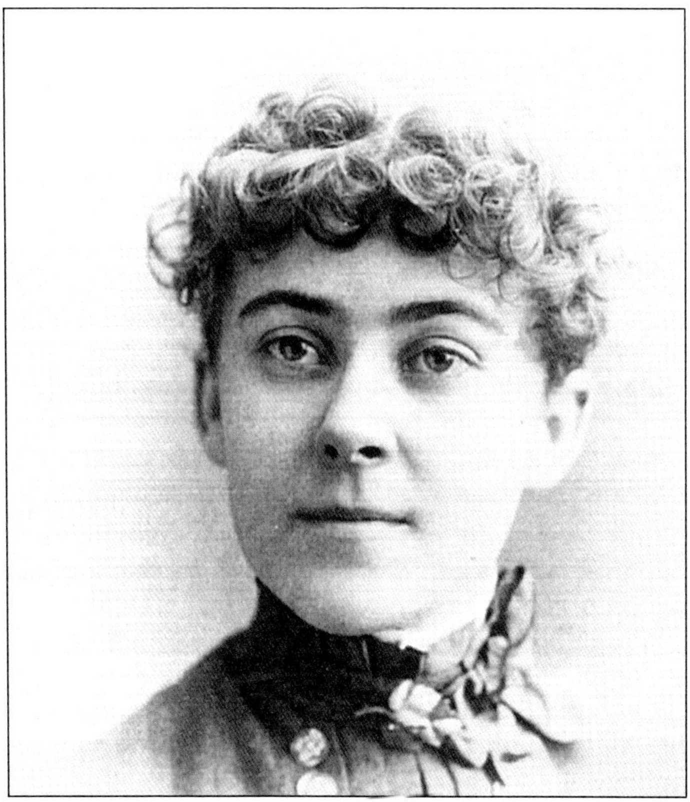

Mary Attmore Hunt (1867–1923) was the wife of George Helliwell, whom she married in 1893. They had three children and lived on High Street. (Courtesy of Betty Tucker.)

This is George E. Helliwell, probably at the time of his 1893 wedding. If he looks dashing, recall that he made his living outfitting men in suits and overcoats. (Courtesy of Betty Tucker.)

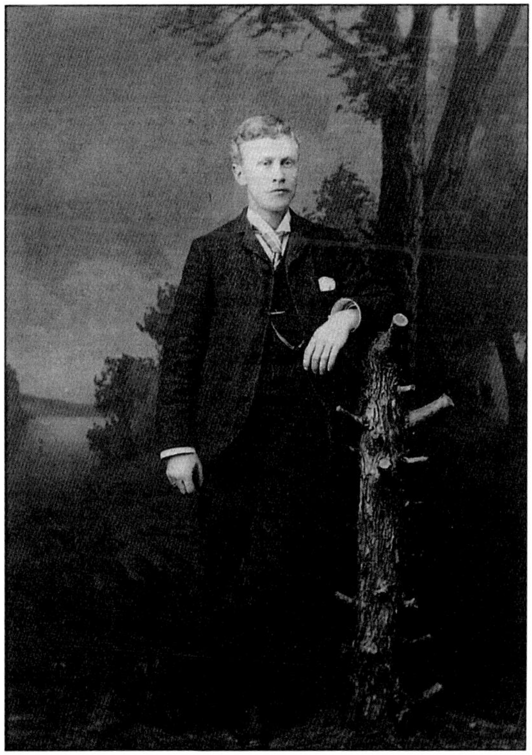

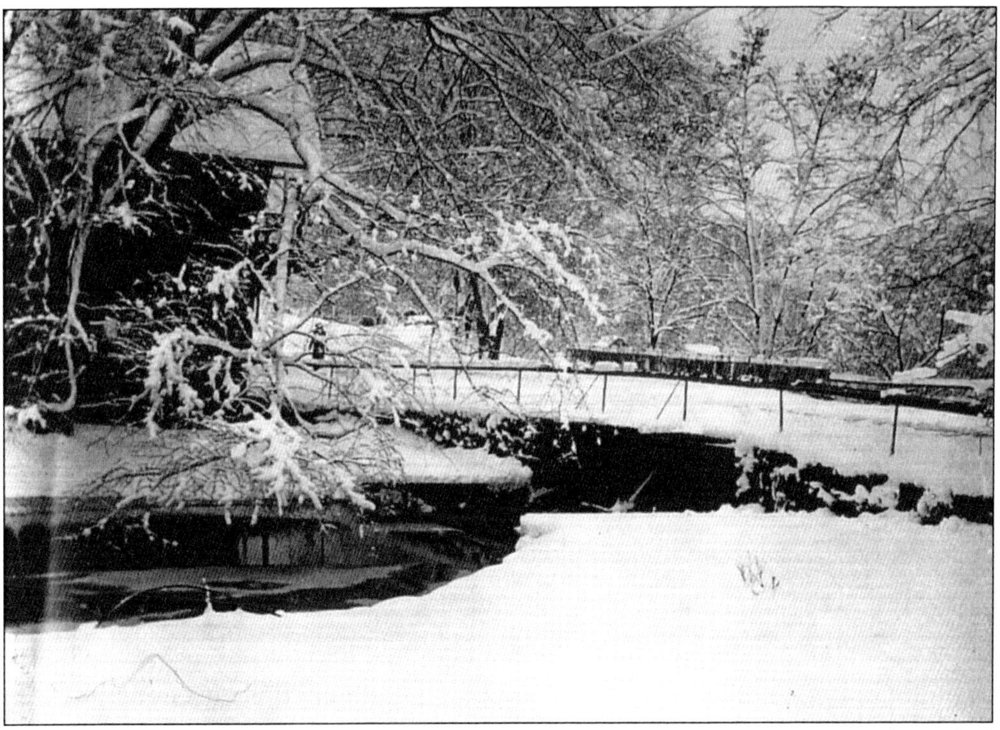

In 1905, Dexter Hoxie photographed the bridge at Columbia Street before an arched span had been built in the same place. (Courtesy of David Gates.)

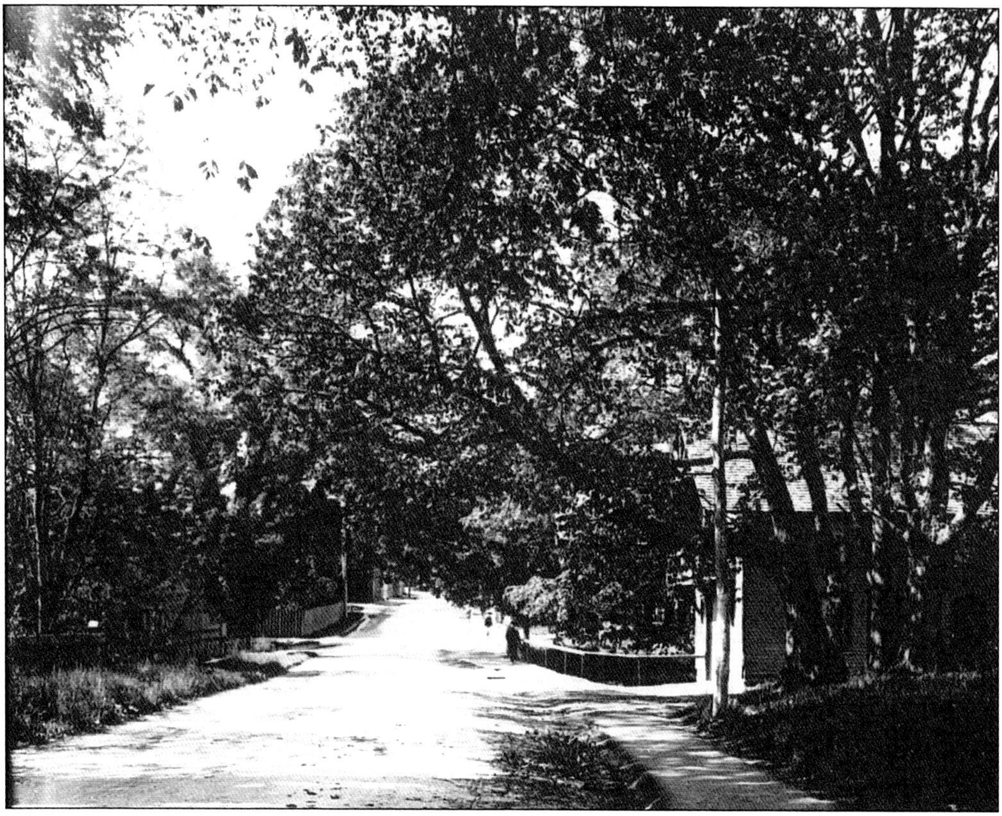

This view of Columbia Street facing north shows the Peace Dale Fire Station at the right. It would later be moved across the street. (Courtesy of David Gates.)

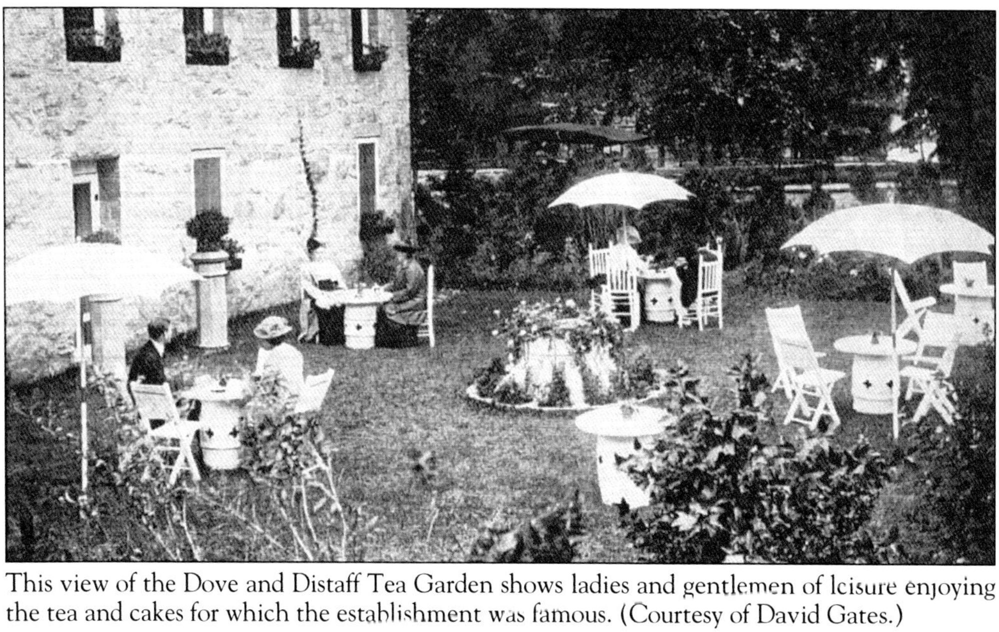

This view of the Dove and Distaff Tea Garden shows ladies and gentlemen of leisure enjoying the tea and cakes for which the establishment was famous. (Courtesy of David Gates.)

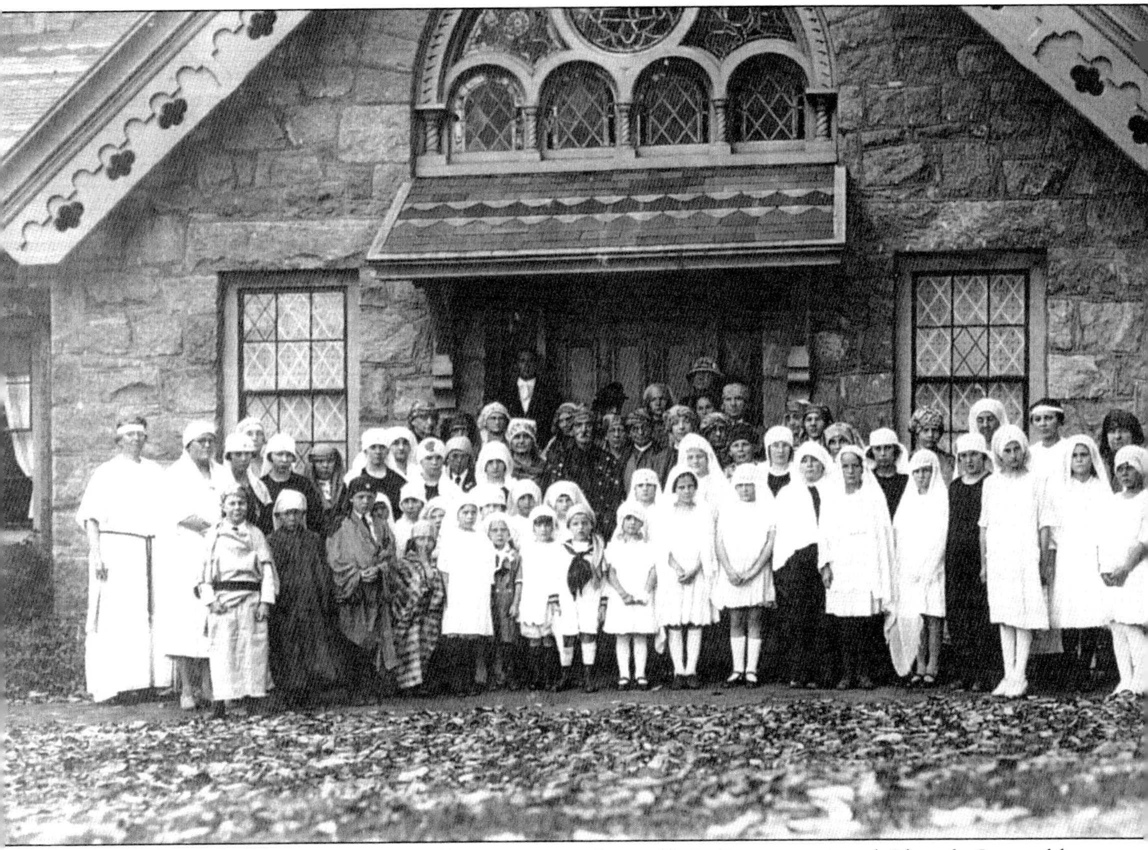

This photograph shows a pageant of some type at Peace Dale Congregational Church. It would appear to be from the early 1920s based on the woman's hat in the back row and the length of the young girls' dresses. (Courtesy of Marise Sykes.)

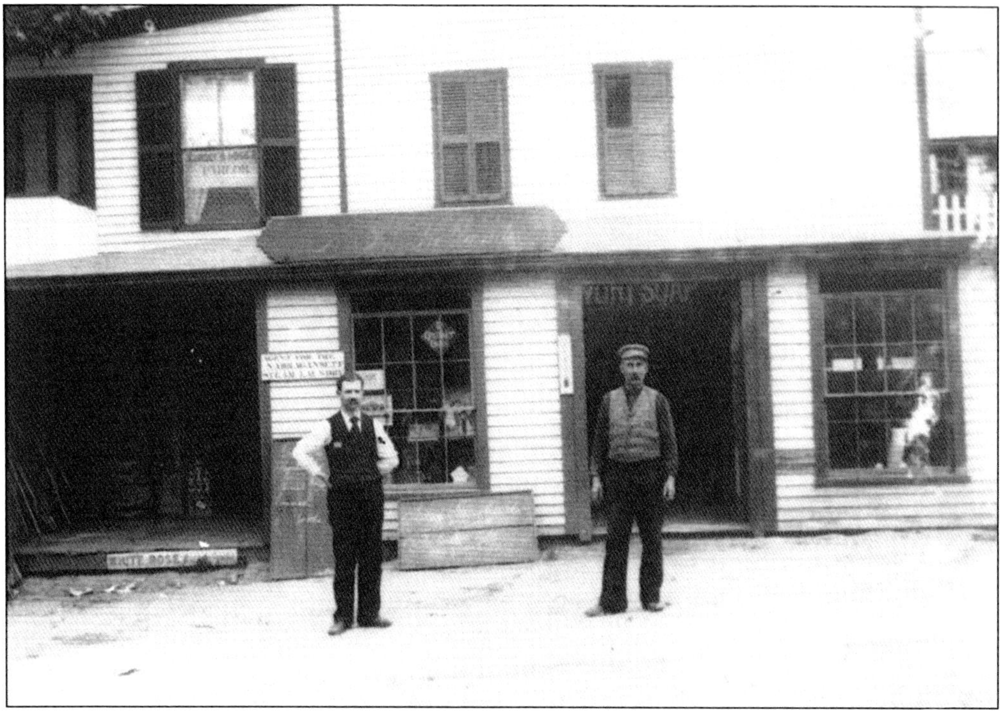

Workers of the Narragansett Steam Laundry pose outside the business. (Courtesy of David Gates.)

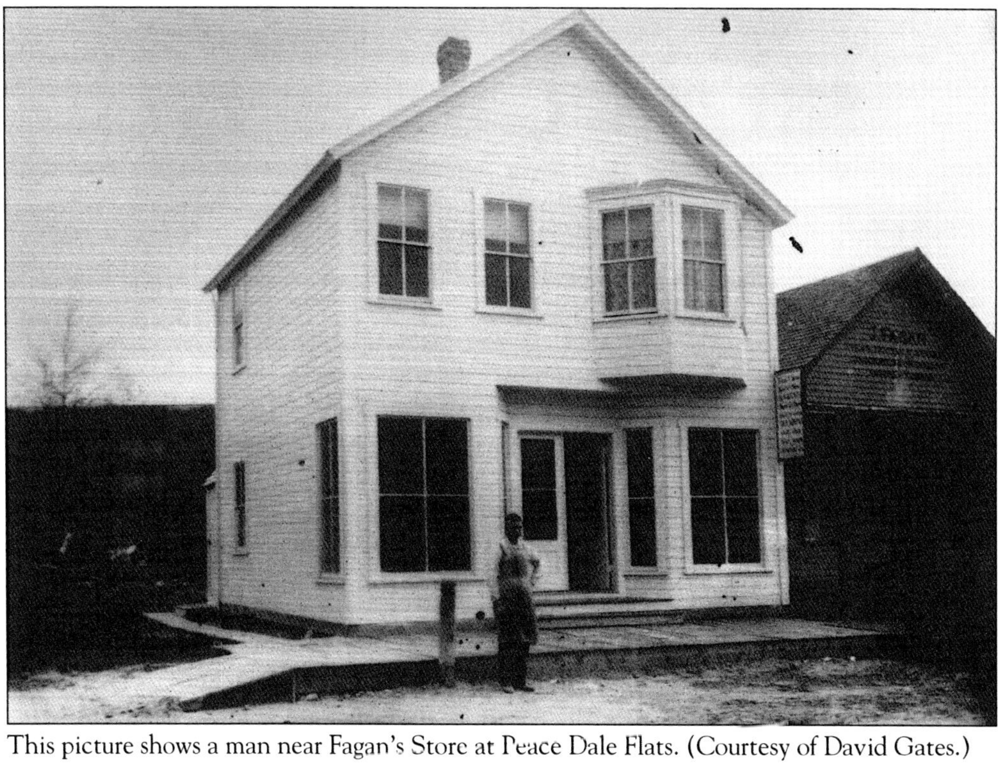

This picture shows a man near Fagan's Store at Peace Dale Flats. (Courtesy of David Gates.)

Twelve

The Peace Dale Fire Department

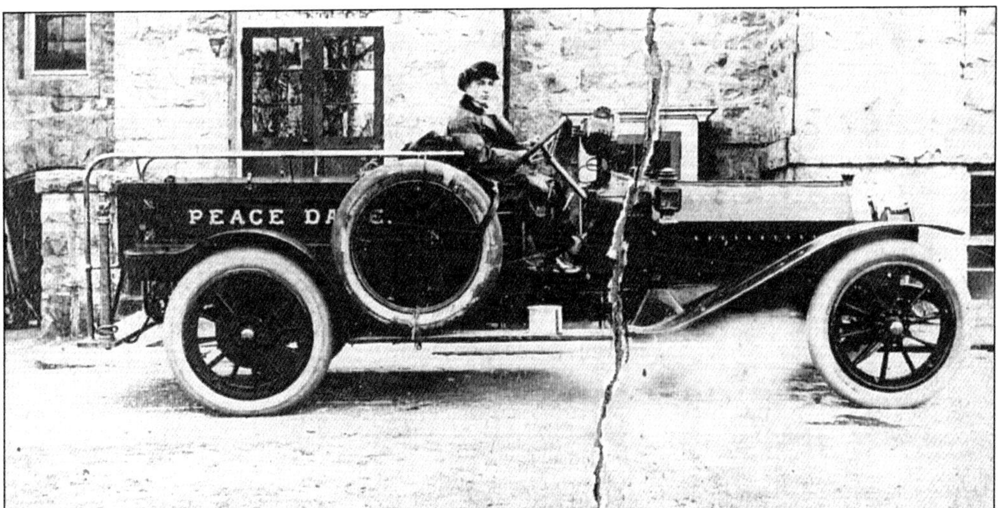

A firefighter from Peace Dale shows off a new truck outside the Neighborhood Guild. Chartered as the Narragansett Steam Fire Engine Co. No. 1 in 1867, the Peace Dale Fire Department is the oldest volunteer fire company still active in the state. Perhaps it best symbolizes the community and volunteer spirit of this mill town. (Courtesy of Peace Dale Fire Department.)

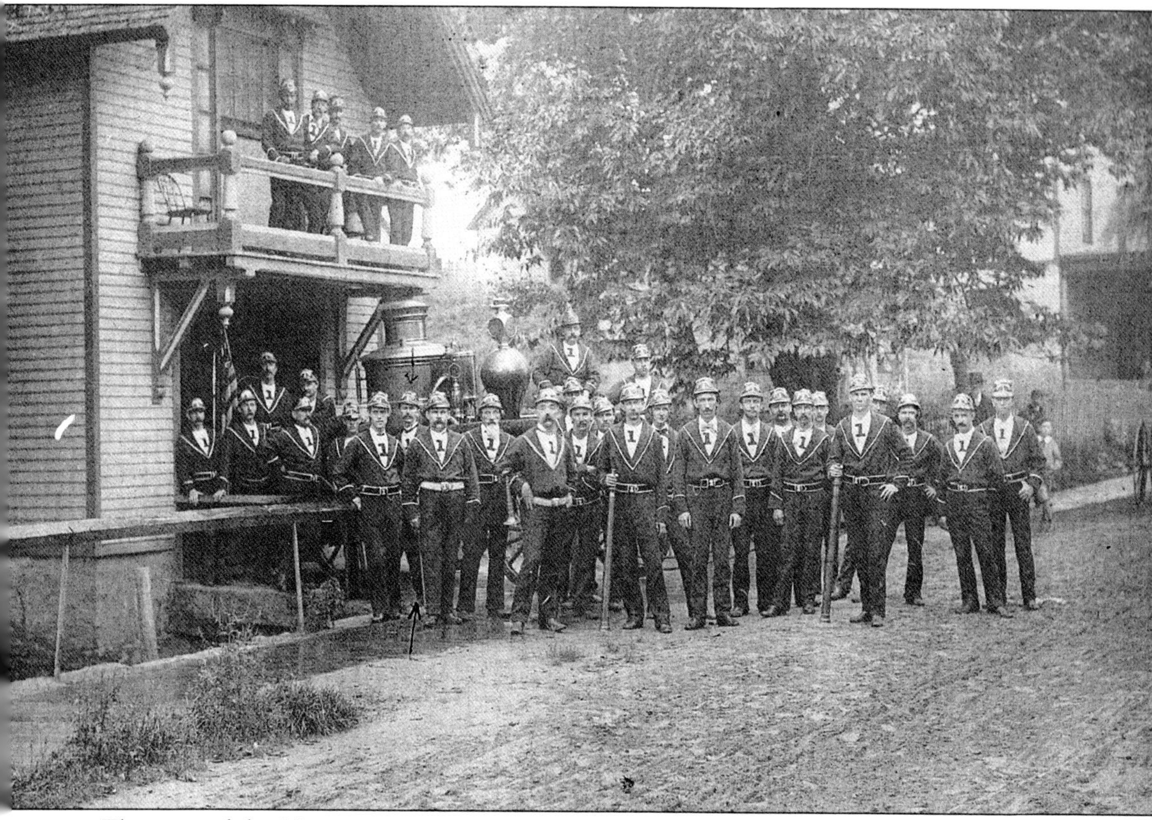

The men of the Narragansett Steam Fire Engine Co. No. 1 proudly show off their uniforms outside the station on Columbia Street. The first uniforms were of red flannel from the Peace Dale mill and had a blue number one on the center of the shirts; they also wore leather double-visor hats. The Hazards came to the aid of the company in a number of ways, by helping to obtain an engine for the company and by allowing it to be stored at first on the Hazard estate. The Hazards also paid to build the first fire station on Columbia Street. As mill owners, they had a keen interest in fire protection, both for their property and that of their tenants. (Courtesy of Pettaquamscutt Historical Society.)

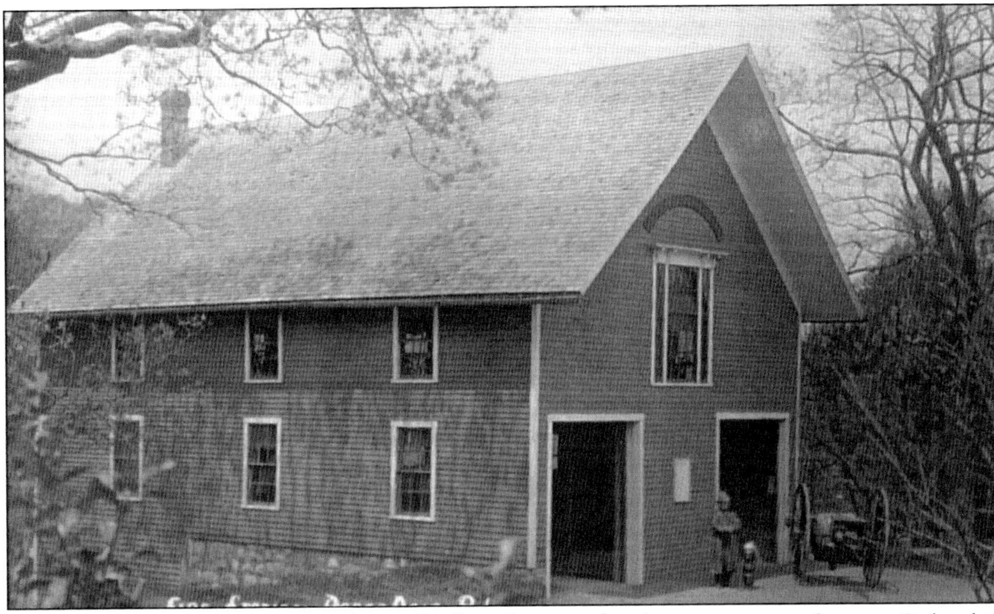

The Peace Dale Fire Station is shown in this photograph after it was moved across Columbia Street, where it now houses school maintenance equipment. The station was built to accommodate both the fire department and the local band, which practiced upstairs. (Courtesy of Everett Hopkins.)

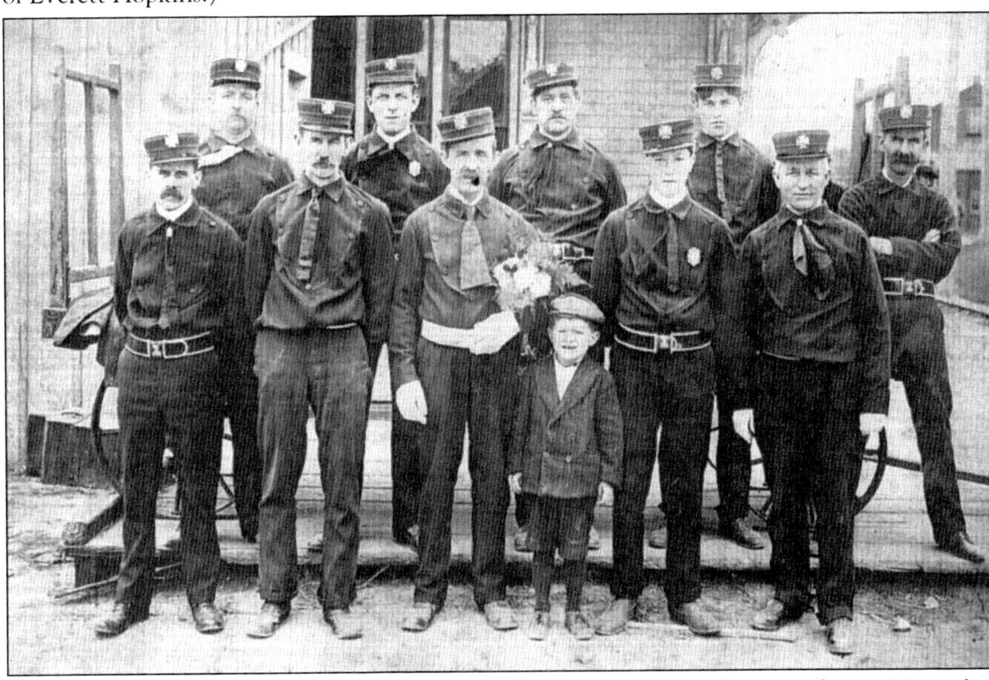

Some men of the Peace Dale Fire Department are seen here in later uniforms. Note that the "1" is now on the belt instead of the shirt. They are, from left to right, as follows: (front row) Hilgate ?, John Towers, Hilard Easterbrooks, George Smith, and John P. Molloy; (back row) Jim Firth, Ben Gardiner, unidentified, ? Potter, and J.E. Sykes Sr. (Courtesy of Peace Dale Fire Department.)

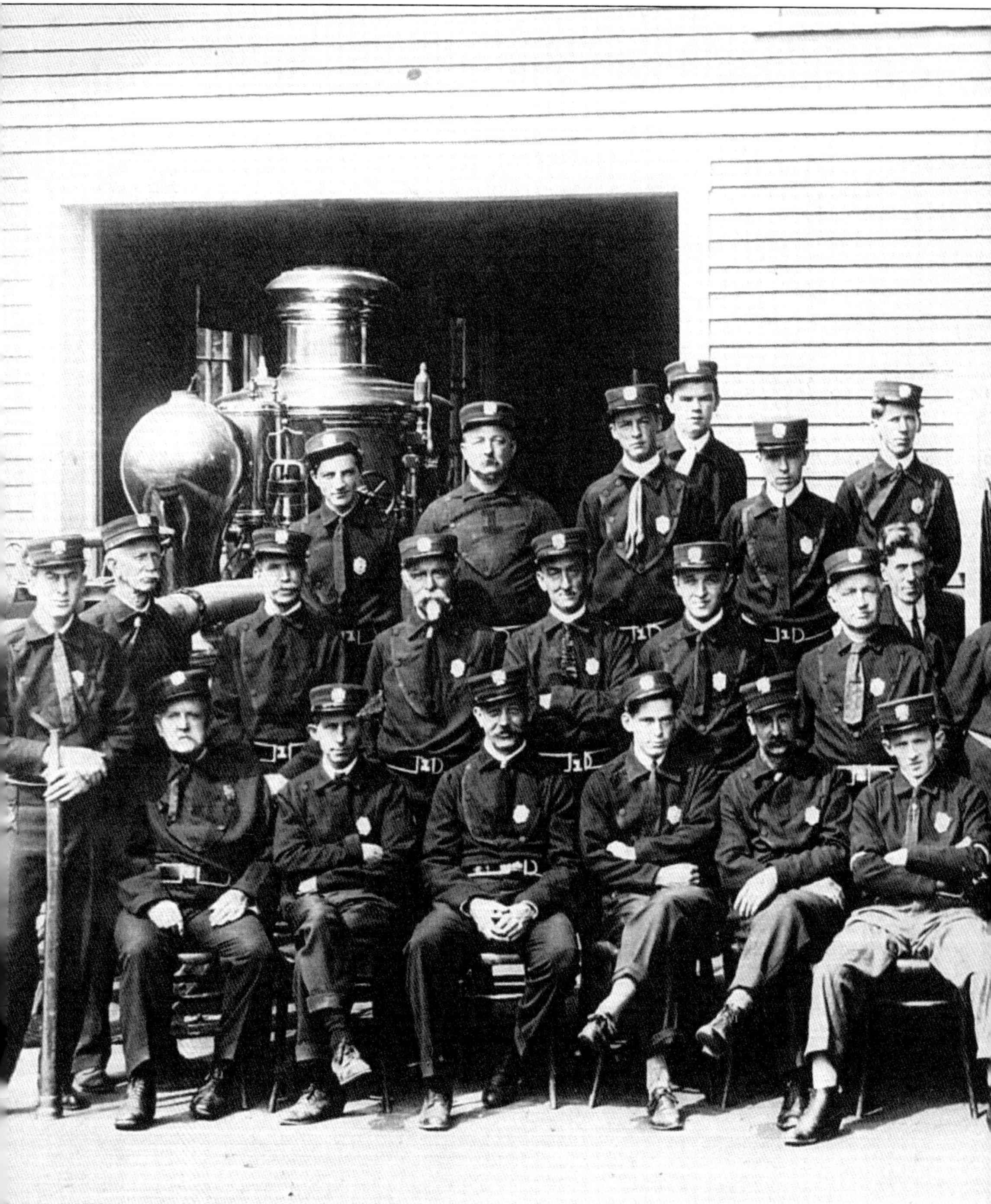

The men of the Peace Dale Fire Department pose in front of the station in this undated photograph. They are, from left to right, as follows: (first row) E. Moore, F. Molloy, E. Potter, I. Wilbur, A. Taylor, E. O'Rourke, William Brown, John Towers, E. Lyons, J. Sykes Sr., N. Potter, and George Potter; (second row) J. Sykes, H. Easterbrooks, John Casey, E. Gardiner,

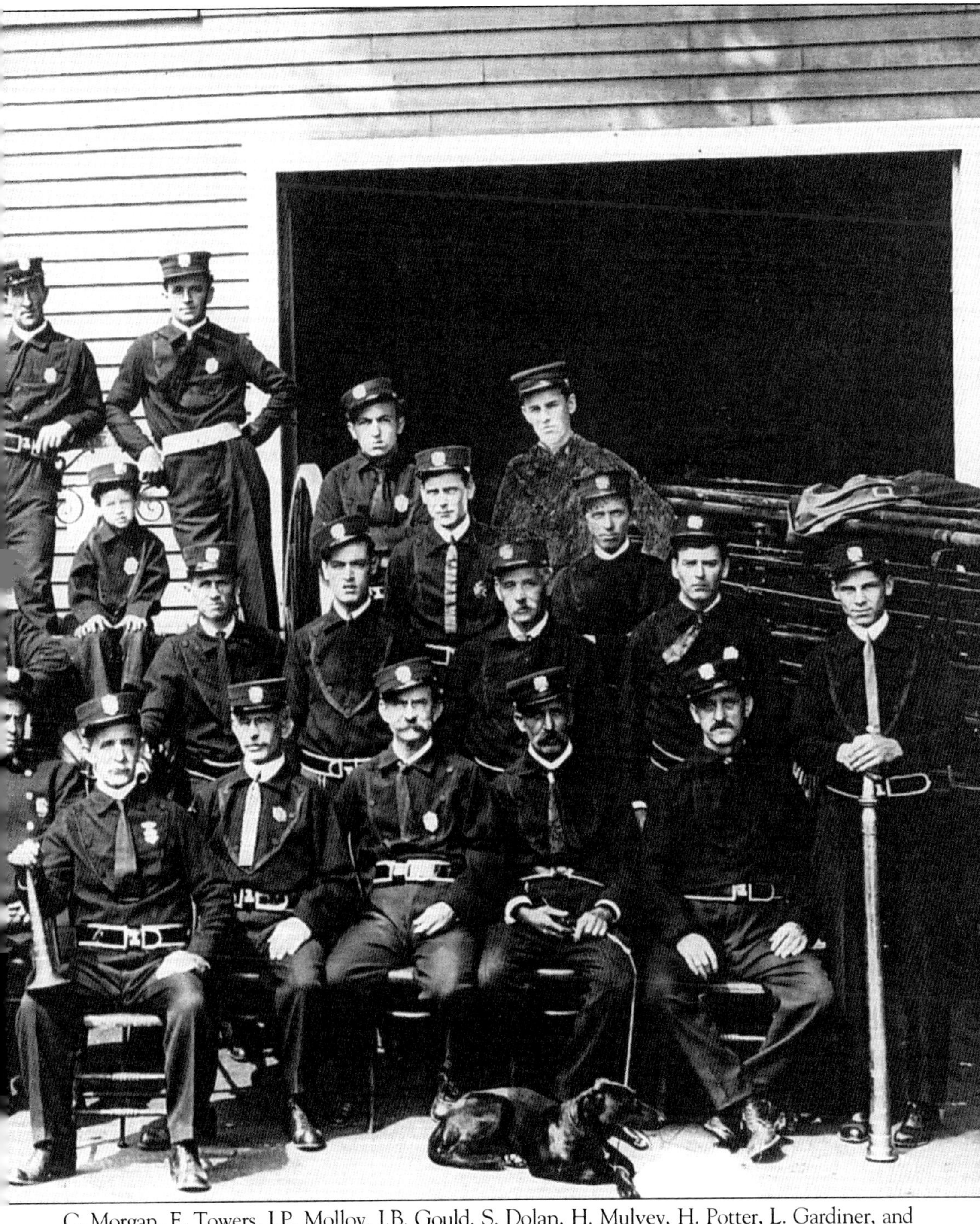

C. Morgan, E. Towers, J.P. Molloy, J.B. Gould, S. Dolan, H. Mulvey, H. Potter, L. Gardiner, and C. Wilbur; (third row) Tom Molloy, Jim Firth, L. Tourgee, James Tully, and mascot Tim Allen; (fourth row) J.E. Casey, A. Colston, Ed Northup, A. Manchester, Lyle Potter, and Mike Molloy. Standing at the top are Arthur Gould and William Towers. (Courtesy of Peace Dale Fire Department.)

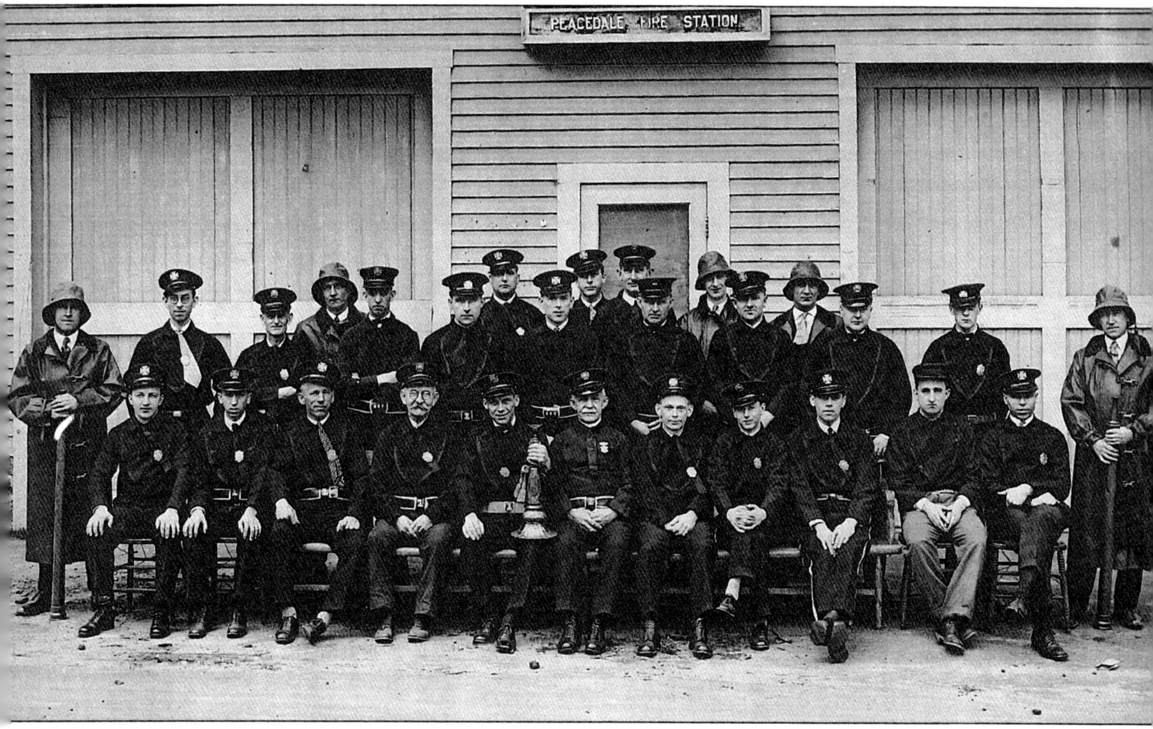

Another photo from the same era shows members of the Peace Dale Fire Department. They are, from left to right, as follows: (first row) Tom Molloy, P. Roy, A. Colston, J. Sykes Sr., C. Wilbur, J. Towers, I. Wilbur, S. Dolan, E. Sweet, H. Jacques, and A. Roy; (middle row) E. McCarthy, R. Barber, L. Matthews, W.E. Holland, B. Mullen, W. Ottinger, O. Boisvert, F. Gould, G. Smith, James Quinlan, and H. Thomas; (back row) T. Salzer Sr., O. Roy, J. Sykes, F. Sims, S. Hall, and Elmer Sweet. (Courtesy of Peace Dale Fire Department.)

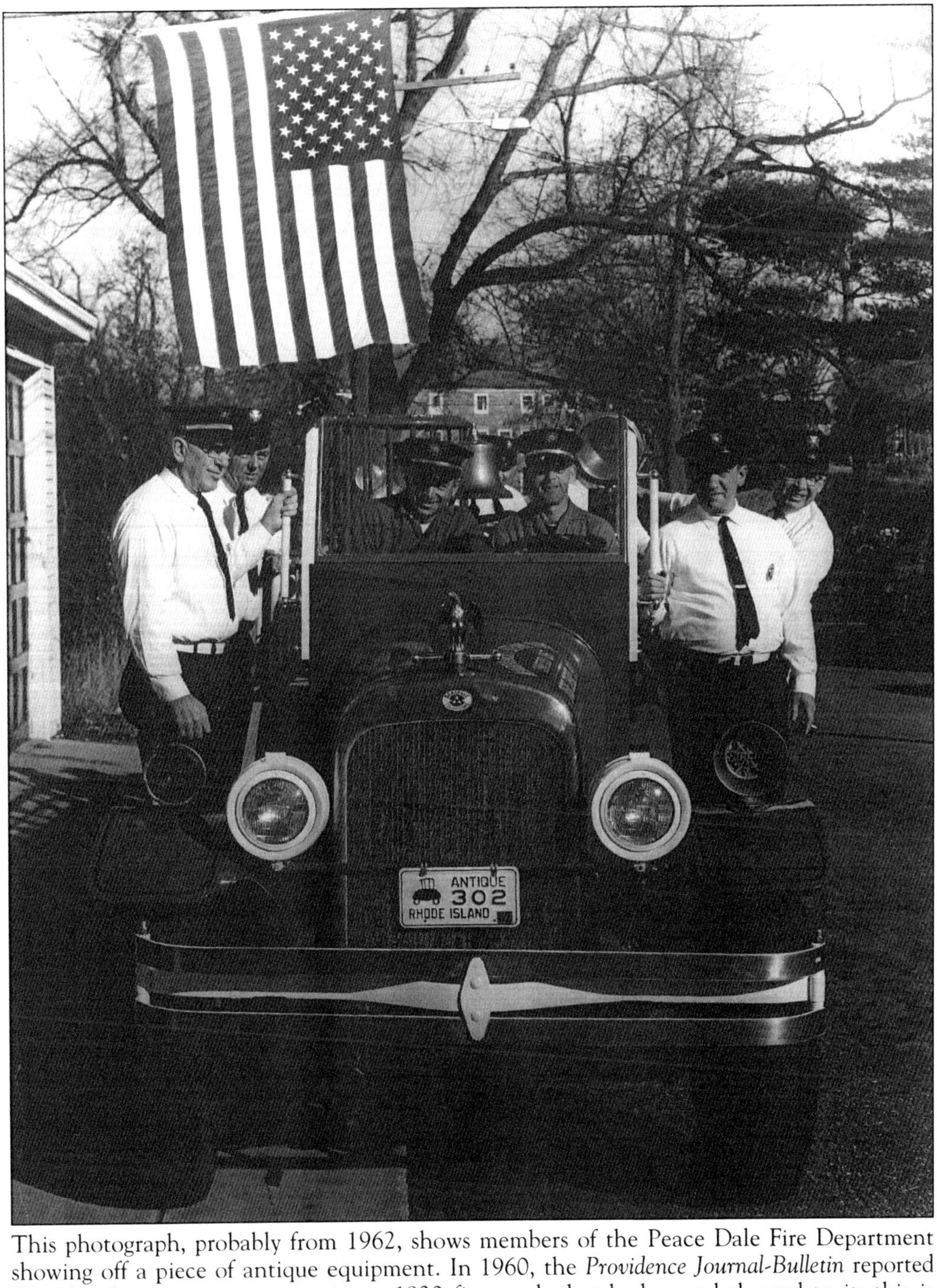

This photograph, probably from 1962, shows members of the Peace Dale Fire Department showing off a piece of antique equipment. In 1960, the *Providence Journal-Bulletin* reported that the department was restoring a 1930 fire truck that had once belonged to it; this is probably that vehicle. The department celebrated its centennial in 1967. (Courtesy of Peace Dale Fire Department.)

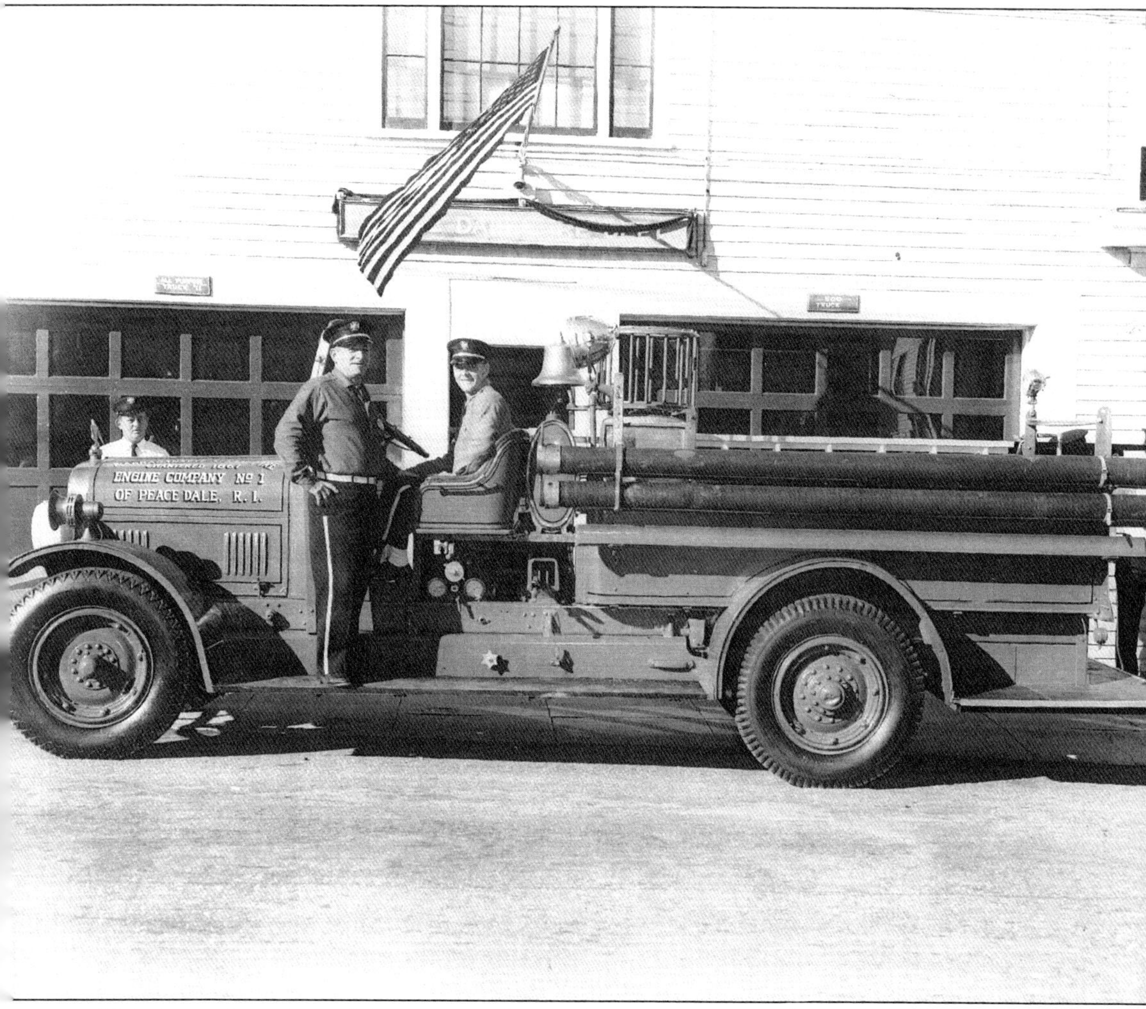

This is another view of the antique fire truck restored by members of the Peace Dale Fire Department after buying it back from the Kingston Fire Department in the early 1960s. The truck was proudly turned out during town parades. (Courtesy of Peace Dale Fire Department.)

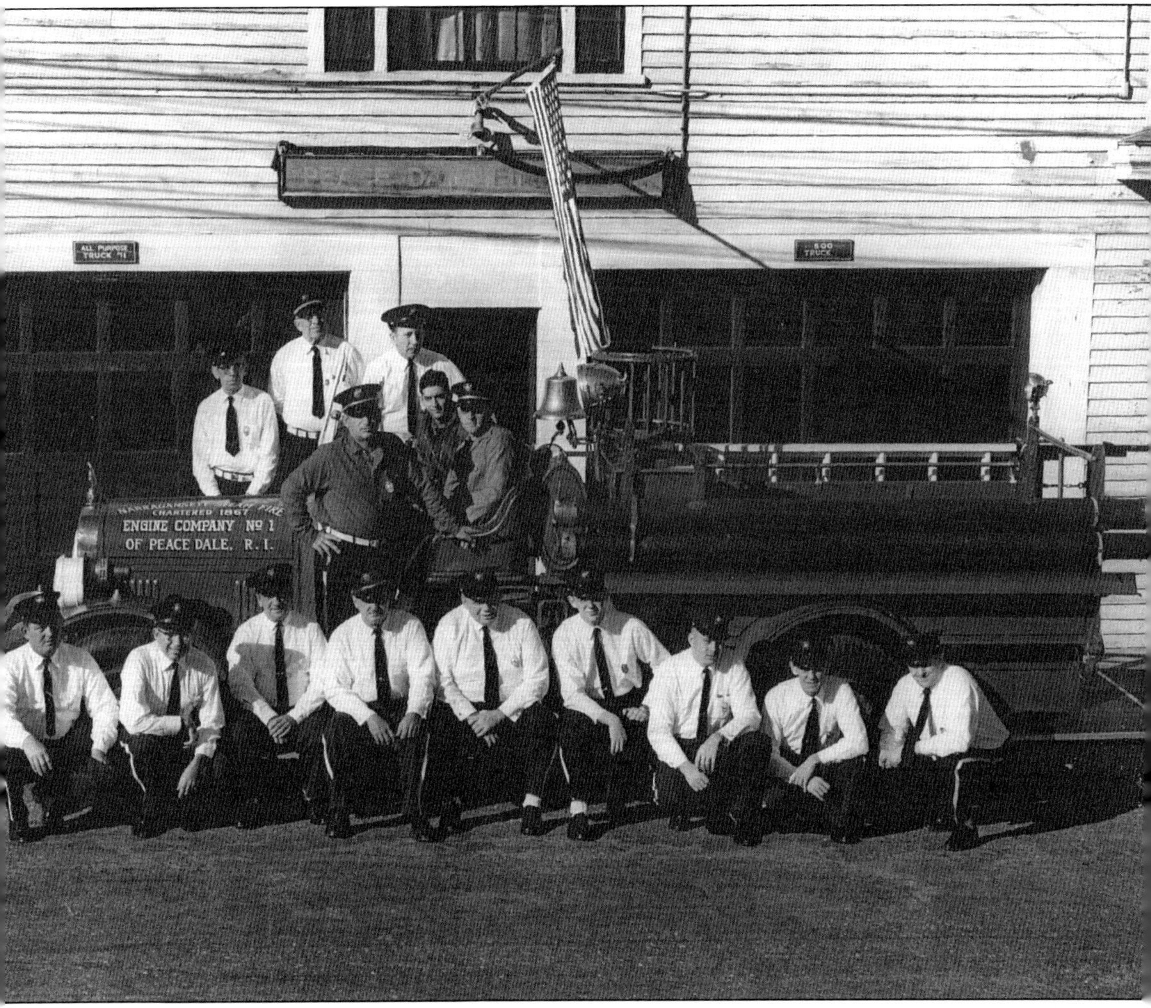

By this time in the early 1960s, the Peace Dale Fire Department's dress uniforms had changed considerably. Gone was the prominent number "1" that had been displayed on various parts of the uniform, although it was still an important part of the inscription on this antique fire truck. (Courtesy of Peace Dale Fire Department.)

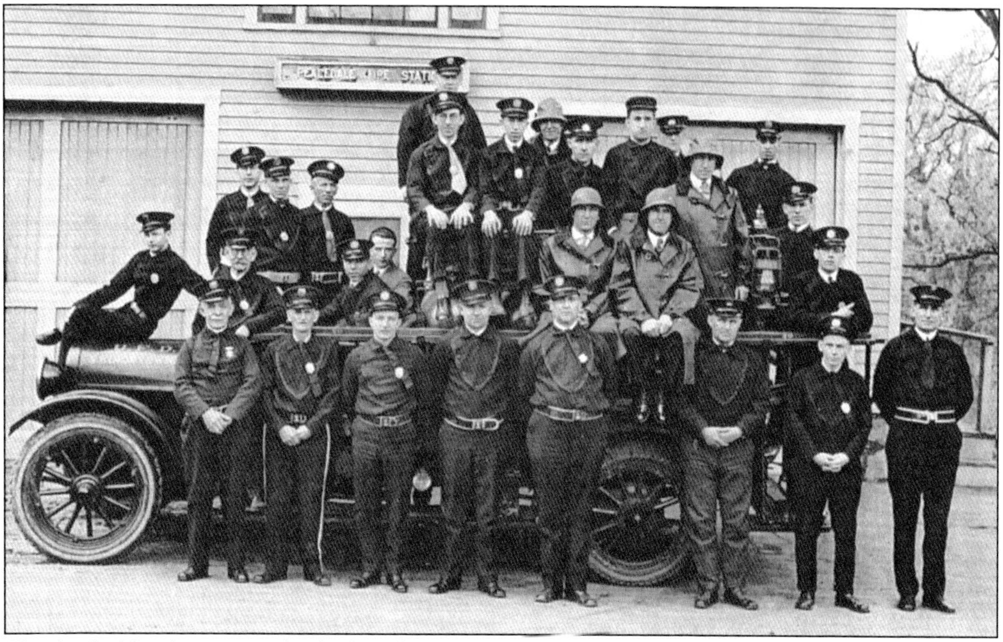

This looks like the same vehicle, but the photograph is from the 1930s, when the truck was still an active piece of equipment. In 1915, the department was the first to purchase motorized fire apparatus in South Kingstown, buying an old Premier touring car to tow the hose reel or hook and ladder truck to fires. (Courtesy of Peace Dale Fire Department.)

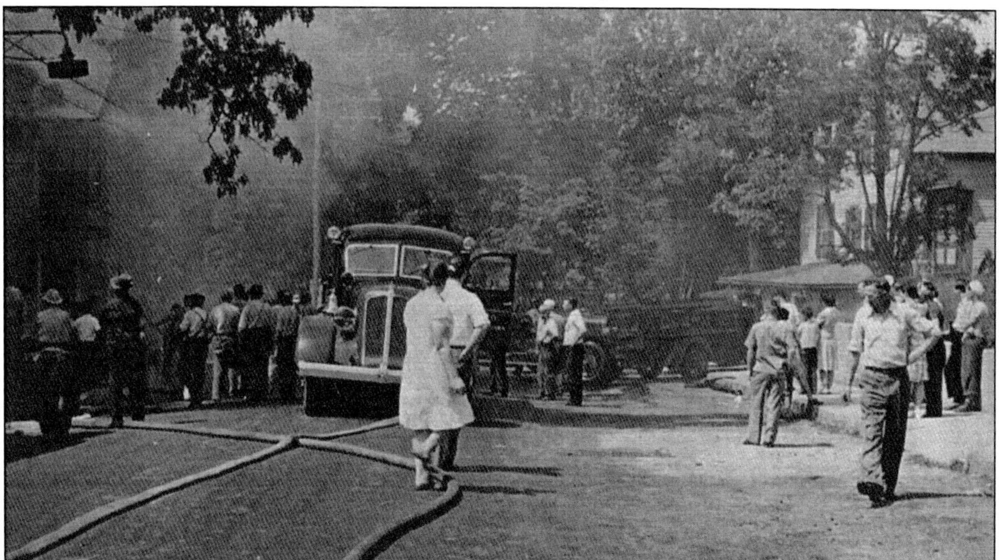

Over the years, the Peace Dale Fire Department had a role in extinguishing some spectacular fires, but perhaps none seared the memory more than the blaze on June 5, 1943, that nearly destroyed the department's own station on Columbia Street. Among the major fires the department fought are the Rocky Brook Mill fires of 1874 and 1877, the Wakefield Opera House fire in 1918, the Peace Dale School fire in 1902 (as well as several residences and barns torched by the same fire bug at that time), and the Wakefield Grammar School fire in 1963. (Courtesy of Peace Dale Fire Department.)

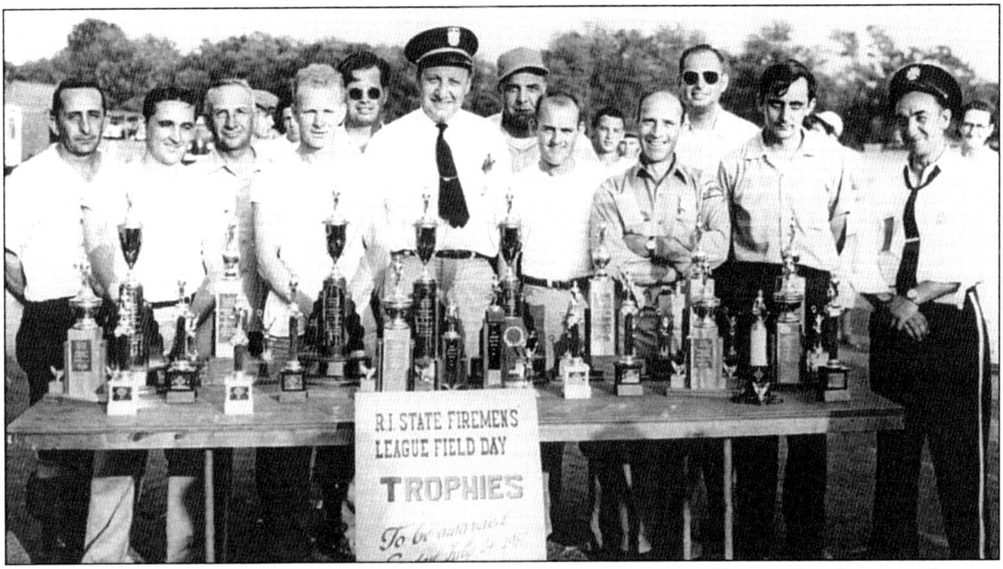

During the firemen's muster of July 13 and 14, 1957, winners proudly pose by their trophies at Old Mountain Field. The two-day event attracted Gov. Dennis Roberts and other dignitaries and included a parade. It was held to celebrate the department's 90th anniversary. (Courtesy of Peace Dale Fire Department.)

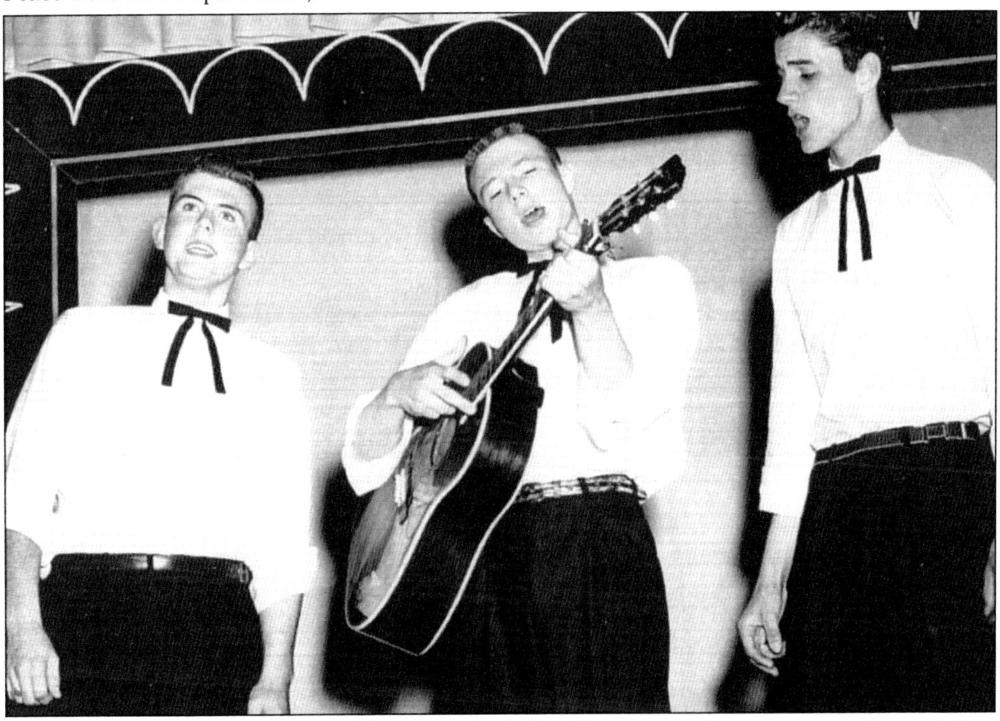

A variety show was a tradition of the Peace Dale Fire Department for many years. From left to right, David Pelton, Herbert Rice, and Bruce Slader do their own version of the "Kingstown Trio" in the 1959 show held at Patsy's Hall. Called the "Family Album," the show featured longtime member James Sykes narrating from an album of memories. (Courtesy of Peace Dale Fire Department.)

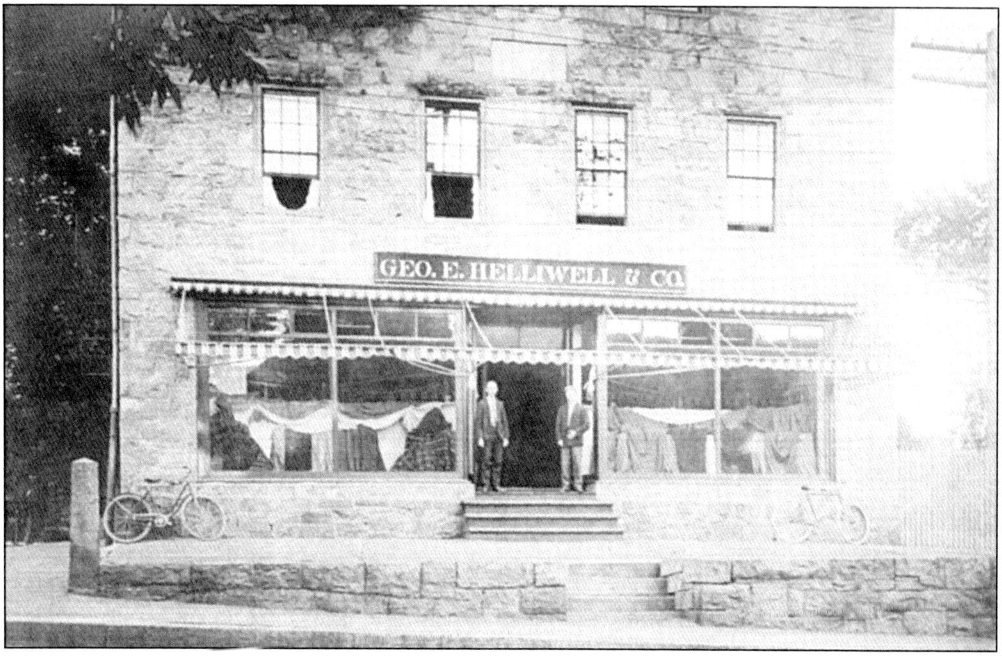

George Helliwell started this store in the Peace Dale Office Building after taking over a similar business from William G. Gould. (Courtesy of Pettaquamscutt Historical Society.)

BIBLIOGRAPHY

Cole, J.R. *A History of Washington and Kent Counties, Rhode Island.* New York: W.W. Preston & Co., 1889.

Hazard, Caroline. *A Precious Heritage.* D.B. Updike, The Merrymount Press, 1929.

Hoxie, Louise M. *The History of Peace Dale, Rhode Island.* Peace Dale, 1968.

The Narragansett Times, 1894–1927.

Nebiker, Walter. *State of Rhode Island and Providence Plantations Preliminary Survey Report, Town of South Kingstown.* Providence: Rhode Island Historical Preservation Commission, 1984.

Representative Men and Old Families of Rhode Island, Volume 2. Chicago: J.H. Beers & Co., 1908.

Rocky Brook Advent Christian Church. *Centennial: Rocky Brook Advent Christian Church, Peacedale, R.I.* 1952

South Kingstown and Narragansett Street Directory. Providence: White, Gordon Co., 1910.

South Kingstown and Narragansett Street Directory. Boston: Union Publishing Co., 1915.

South Kingstown School Committee. *Annual Report of the South Kingstown School Committee, South Kingston, Rhode Island.* 1903, 1910, and 1923.

Stedman, Oliver H. *A Stroll Through Memory Lane.* South Kingston: Kingston Press, Volumes I–V, 1978.

Stewart, Peter Crawford. *A History of the Peace Dale Manufacturing Company.* Master's thesis. Kingston: University of Rhode Island, 1962.

Sykes, James E. *History of the Narragansett Steam Fire Engine Co. No. 1.* Scrapbook.

IMAGES
of America

DeKalb County

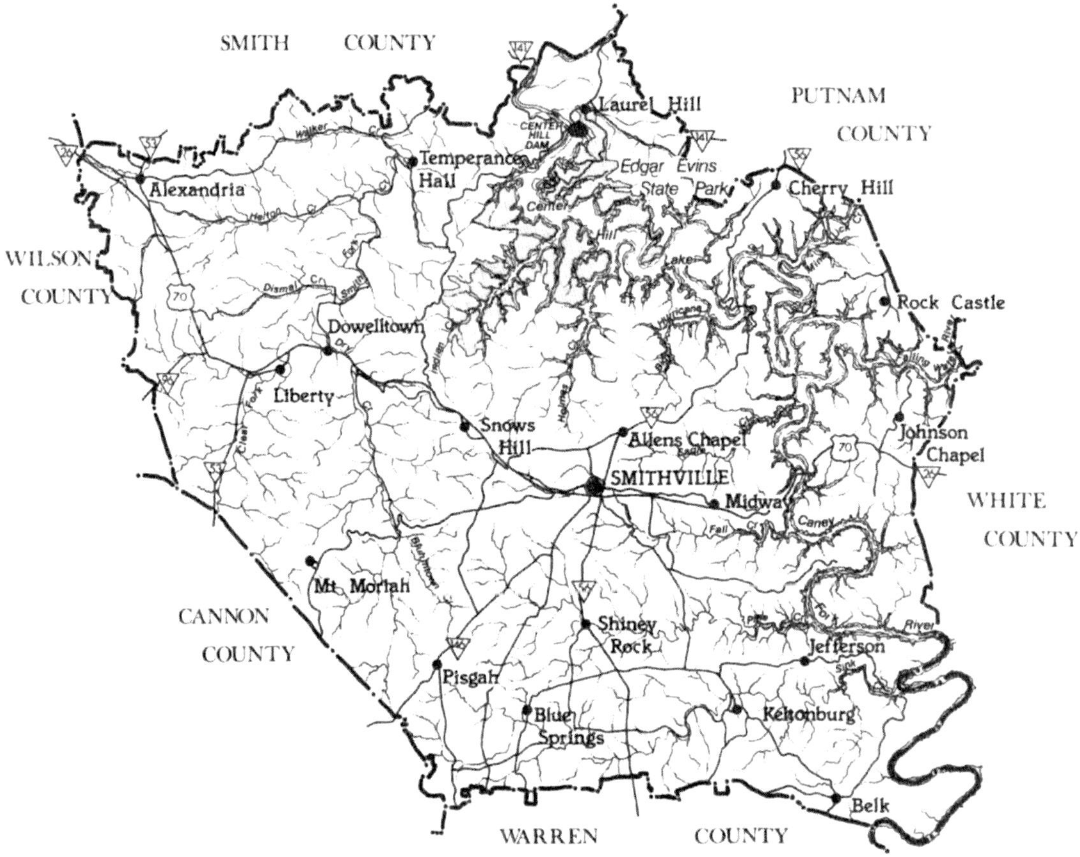

This map of DeKalb County shows the county's four incorporated towns—Alexandria, Liberty, Dowelltown, and Smithville, the county seat—and the surrounding counties around the edges. Several present-day communities are also noted, along with the main roads. The lake now takes up over 18,000 acres of the county. No interstate highways or railroads pass through this county. (Courtesy of Tommy Webb.)

ON THE COVER: Saturday afternoons found local farmers sitting in the shade swapping tales and deciding crops while their wives shopped. Seen here in Alexandria in the early 1960s are, from left to right, Andrew Foutch, Bob Oakley, Liv Malone, and Jeff Sandlin. They are sitting on the corner at the old Curtis Hardware Store where the Liberty State Bank is now. (Courtesy of Mac Willoughby.)